Pharmaceutical Marketing

Brent L. Rollins, PhD, RPh
Assistant Professor of Pharmacy Administration
Philadelphia College of Osteopathic Medicine–Georgia Campus
School of Pharmacy
Suwanee, Georgia

Matthew Perri, PhD, RPh
Professor
Clinical and Administrative Pharmacy
University of Georgia College of Pharmacy
Athens, Georgia

JONES & BARTLETT
LEARNING

World Headquarters
Jones & Bartlett Learning
5 Wall Street
Burlington, MA 01803
978-443-5000
info@jblearning.com
www.jblearning.com

Jones & Bartlett Learning books and products are available through most bookstores and online booksellers. To contact Jones & Bartlett Learning directly, call 800-832-0034, fax 978-443-8000, or visit our website, www.jblearning.com.

Substantial discounts on bulk quantities of Jones & Bartlett Learning publications are available to corporations, professional associations, and other qualified organizations. For details and specific discount information, contact the special sales department at Jones & Bartlett Learning via the above contact information or send an email to specialsales@jblearning.com.

Production Credits
Publisher: William Brottmiller
Senior Acquisitions Editor: Katey Birtcher
Associate Editor: Teresa Reilly
Production Manager: Julie Champagne Bolduc
Production Assistant: Stephanie Rineman
Marketing Manager: Grace Richards

Manufacturing and Inventory Control Supervisor: Amy Bacus
Composition: diacriTech
Cover Design: Scott Moden
Cover Image: © Phecsone/ShutterStock, Inc.
Printing and Binding: Edwards Brothers Malloy
Cover Printing: Edwards Brothers Malloy

To order this product, use ISBN: 978-1-4496-9799-0

Library of Congress Cataloging-in-Publication Data
Rollins, Brent L.
  Pharmaceutical marketing/by Brent L. Rollins and Matthew Perri.
      p. ; cm.
  Includes bibliographical references and index.
  ISBN 978-1-4496-2659-4 — ISBN 1-4496-2659-9
  I. Perri, Matthew. II. Title.
  [DNLM: 1. Drug Industry—economics—United States. 2. Marketing—United States. 3. Pharmaceutical Preparations—economics—United States. QV 736 AA1]
  338.4'76151—dc23
                                                                    2012036241

6048
Printed in the United States of America
17 16 15 14 13   10 9 8 7 6 5 4 3 2 1

To Deanna, Carson, Camron, and Breleigh.
Without your love and support,
this would not have been possible.
To Dr. Perri, a great mentor and friend.

—BLR

To Mickey C. Smith, distant mentor and the pioneer
of pharmaceutical marketing.

—MP

Contents

Preface

Over time, the mission of the U.S. pharmaceutical industry has remained greatly unchanged: Discover and then bring to market medications capable of saving lives and improving health and quality of life. However, as we have moved into the current information and technology age, the external environment in which the industry operates has greatly evolved and is drastically different. Not only have the number of blockbuster medications produced by pharmaceutical manufacturers decreased, but so has the presence of direct sales representatives in physician offices. Further, the past decade alone has seen significant company consolidation and legal/regulatory changes as well as the exponential rise in the importance of the Internet and social media. Thus, how the pharmaceutical industry markets its products has also adapted in the face of the ever-evolving external environment. Pharmaceutical and healthcare industry marketers must now work harder and smarter to maximize the potential of every product or service.

This text examines the current pharmaceutical marketing environment from both an academic and practical perspective. Given the internal and external changes throughout the pharmaceutical industry, this text is appropriate not only for those studying pharmacy practice or pharmaceutical marketing in an academic setting, but also for pharmaceutical industry professionals. Within each chapter, the reader will see clear learning objectives and key terms highlighted for their importance and the need for understanding. In addition, numerous "Case in Point" boxes are used to show practical, real-world examples of the various constructs and topics being discussed. Rarely do any of these marketing issues have one, clear-cut answer; thus, each chapter closes with discussion questions intended to provoke thought and bring about debate from an academic and practical perspective.

While specific medication and clinical knowledge and skills are at the core of the pharmacy profession, every new pharmacy school graduate theoretically enters the job market with these same capabilities and degree. Thus, while additional degrees, certifications, or residency training are beneficial, advanced knowledge of the healthcare system and pharmaceutical industry from a business and marketing perspective is needed in order to differentiate oneself in an increasingly crowded job market. For new industry professionals, particularly those with MBAs or other nonhealth professional degrees, the text provides the thorough overview necessary to allow you to hit the ground running from the first day of your new job at pharmaceutical manufacturer X or market research firm Y, further differentiating yourself in this highly competitive industry. In the end, *Pharmaceutical Marketing* should provide you, the reader, with a deep understanding of the current pharmaceutical industry, its marketing environment, and the challenges of the environment. In turn, this understanding can help you succeed in your career, regardless of the place in the healthcare system or pharmaceutical industry in which you work.

About the Authors

Brent L. Rollins, PhD, RPh
Assistant Professor of Pharmacy Administration
PCOM–GA Campus School of Pharmacy
Suwanee, Georgia

Brent Rollins is an assistant professor of pharmacy practice at the Philadelphia College of Osteopathic Medicine (PCOM)–Georgia Campus School of Pharmacy in Suwanee, GA. He earned his BS in Pharmacy at Ohio Northern University in 2004 and a PhD in Pharmacy Administration with an emphasis in Pharmaceutical Marketing at the University of Georgia in 2009. Since joining PCOM, Brent has presented and published on numerous subjects in pharmacy practice with a primary focus on pharmaceutical marketing, direct-to-consumer advertising, and healthcare consumer behavior. Further, he has coauthored one textbook, *Financial Analysis in Pharmacy Practice*, as well as book chapters on business and personal finance for pharmacists in the award-winning *Pharmacy Management, Leadership, Marketing, and Finance*. In addition to his academic endeavors, Brent has consulted with various market research firms, law firms, and the United States Department of Justice as a pharmacy practice and marketing expert witness. Brent also has more than 8 years of community pharmacy practice experience and still actively practices on a part-time basis.

Matthew Perri, RPh, PhD
Professor
Clinical and Administrative Pharmacy
University of Georgia College of Pharmacy
Athens, Georgia

Matthew Perri III is a professor in the Department of Clinical and Administrative Pharmacy at the University of Georgia College of Pharmacy. He earned his BS in Pharmacy at Temple University in Philadelphia in 1981 and a PhD in Pharmacy, with a major in Pharmaceutical Marketing, at the University of South Carolina in 1985. As a professor at the College of Pharmacy, in addition to involvement with the Terry College of Business, the College of Education, and the School of Public Health, he has taught courses and lectures in pharmacy and business, including the areas of pharmaceutical marketing, management, and research methods. Over his academic career, Dr. Perri has conducted extensive original research and received funding as principal investigator, co-investigator, or consultant for his research. He has also published and presented numerous articles and abstracts on various pharmacy practice and pharmaceutical marketing topics and serves as a journal referee for numerous peer-reviewed journals. Professionally, he has been involved with various paid and nonpaid consulting activities including the State of Georgia; Department of Community Health; Drug Utilization Review Board; consultant to the Georgia Senate Committee on Cost Controls in State Funded Health Plans; the U.S. Department of Justice; state and national pharmacy organizations; pharmaceutical companies; independent marketing research companies; chain and independent pharmacies; and long-term care facilities. Dr. Perri has been a registered pharmacist since 1981.

Contributors

Nilesh Bhutada, PhD
Assistant Professor of Clinical and Administrative Sciences
California Northstate University College of Pharmacy
Rancho Cordova, California

Nilesh S. Bhutada, PhD is an assistant professor of clinical and administrative sciences at the California Northstate University College of Pharmacy in Rancho Cordova, CA. His research interests include source effects, direct-to-consumer advertising (DTCA) of prescription drugs, consumer behavior, disease awareness advertising, patient medication adherence, and student learning assessment. In addition to presenting and publishing several papers and abstracts on DTCA topics, Dr. Bhutada has won best paper award for his research on coupon use in DTCA.

Julie Brideau, PharmD
Regulatory Affairs Consultant
Opus Regulatory, Inc.
Atlanta, Georgia

Julie is a registered pharmacist with more than 14 years of experience working in the pharmaceutical industry and pharmaceutical consulting fields. She has worked primarily in pharmaceutical regulatory affairs, with a focus on promotional and advertising material review and approval, policy and procedure, training, and compliance. Julie is currently employed by Opus Regulatory, Inc., providing consulting services to U.S. pharmaceutical companies in the area of regulatory affairs promotional review and compliance. Julie holds a BS in Applied Biology from Georgia Tech and a Doctor of Pharmacy from Mercer University College of Pharmacy and Health Sciences.

Kelly Dempski
Senior Executive
Accenture Technology Labs
Silicon Valley, California

Kelly is a senior executive with Accenture Technology Labs in Silicon Valley, where he is the head of Accenture's Enterprise Social Media Innovation Center. Kelly's work within the Center involves the creation of new social media technologies, working with leading vendors, and guiding social media strategies for clients. Kelly has personally designed Accenture's internal Facebook, and works with clients in pharmaceutical and other industries to craft social media strategies to help them implement the technologies that drive new forms of consumer engagement.

Dee Fanning, PharmD
Assistant Professor of Pharmacy Practice
PCOM–GA Campus School of Pharmacy
Suwanee, Georgia

Dee Fanning is an assistant professor of pharmacy practice and clinical coordinator of experiential education at the Philadelphia College of Osteopathic Medicine (PCOM)–Georgia Campus School of Pharmacy in Suwanee, GA. She received her Doctor of Pharmacy degree from Mercer University College of Pharmacy and Health Sciences and completed a post-graduate residency in drug information jointly sponsored by Mercer University and Solvay Pharmaceuticals, Inc. Prior to joining PCOM, she was a member of Solvay's medical affairs team, with approximately 2 years of service in medical communications and 8 years as a senior medical liaison. Over the course of her 10-year industry career, she was involved with every aspect of medical affairs, including, but not limited to, medical information requests; advertising and promotional review; publications planning; Thought Leader development; and compliance with state and federal regulations as the Medical Affairs delegate of the Compliance committee.

John Gardner, MBA
President and CEO
Integrative Logic, a division of Luckie
Suwanee, Georgia

John Gardner is President and CEO of Integrative Logic, a market research firm he launched in 2001. John is a strategic visionary with more than 17 years of experience in customer relationship management, database marketing, and business intelligence. A quick-thinking leader who knows how to steer progress, John inspires dedicated teams to blend The Science of Data with The Art of Marketing® and integrate technology and strategy into measurable, results-oriented programs. In 2010, John was named Small Businessman of the Year by the Gwinnett County Chamber of Commerce, and ranked #15 on the list of Atlanta's top entrepreneurs by *Business-to-Business* magazine. That same year his company, Integrative Logic, was named Small Business of the Year. Prior to launching Integrative Logic, John was vice president and chief technology officer at Braindance, director of business intelligence at imc2, and marketing manager at Southern Progress. John holds an MBA from the University of Alabama at Birmingham and an undergraduate degree from the University of Alabama.

Brian Mitchell, MBA, MPH
Associate Dean
Emory University Goizueta School of Business
Atlanta, Georgia

Brian Mitchell is an associate dean at Emory University's Goizueta Business School. Prior to joining Goizueta full-time, Brian spent more than 18 years in marketing and strategy roles in the pharmaceutical industry. After earning his MBA and MPH degrees, Brian joined Capgemini as a strategy consultant in its life science practice, working with clients including Eli Lilly, Pfizer, and Aventis. In 2002, Brian moved to Solvay Pharmaceuticals, where he held several leadership positions within U.S. and global commercial operations, including all levels of brand management, U.S. Head of Strategic and Business Analysis, and Director of Marketing for Specialized Products. As the leader of the specialized products business unit, Brian was responsible for delivering a P&L that grew from $250 million to over $600 million in 3 years. He also earned distinguished awards such as Brand of the Year, the Global Marketing Award, and the Solvay Summit Award—the company's highest individual honor. In 2010, Brian accepted an executive position with Accenture's strategy practice and led the strategic support team for brands at AstraZeneca.

Timothy Poole, PharmD
Chair and Associate Professor of Pharmacy Practice
PCOM–GA Campus School of Pharmacy
Suwanee, Georgia

Timothy Poole is the Chair of Pharmacy Practice and associate professor at the Philadelphia College of Osteopathic Medicine (PCOM)–Georgia Campus School of Pharmacy in Suwanee, GA. The foundation for his experience is grounded in more than 25 years in healthcare clinical practice, research, and the pharmaceutical industry. This experience includes strategic and operational leadership associated with a wide array of therapeutic categories for Pfizer Pharmaceuticals. With Pfizer, Tim contributed to the establishment and growth of a field-based corporate medical team. Through progressive levels of responsibility, Tim worked at the regional (Southeast) and national level in a director role. He hired, trained, and led large multi-functional teams while being responsible for multi-million dollar budgets and annual strategic planning. In all of his roles at Pfizer, he interfaced with numerous medical professionals, healthcare associations, and academic institutions.

Matthew Short
Accenture Technology Labs
Silicon Valley, California

Matthew graduated from the University of Washington where he studied informatics to understand the connection of people, information, and technology with a focus in social technologies. Within Accenture, he has worked on various social media and social collaboration strategies for the pharmaceutical industry as well as projects with the Digital Health research group.

Randall Tackett, PhD
Professor
University of Georgia College of Pharmacy
Athens, Georgia

Dr. Randall Tackett is a professor and graduate coordinator in the Department of Clinical and Administrative Pharmacy at the University of Georgia College of Pharmacy. He is also the director of the Clinical Trials Certificate Program in the Regulatory Affairs Program. Over the past 30 years, he has been involved in research and teaching of pharmacology and toxicology. He has interacted extensively with the pharmaceutical industry regarding drug development and testing. He has also been funded to develop educational modules on drug development, approval, and safety for prescribers.

Reviewers

Kim Broedel-Zaugg, PhD, MBA, RPh
Professor/Chair
School of Pharmacy
Marshall University
Huntington, West Virginia

Steven J. Crosby, MA, RPh, FASCP
Assistant Professor of Pharmacy Practice
Department of Pharmacy Practice
Massachusetts College of Pharmacy and Health Sciences
Boston, Massachusetts

Paul Gavaza, PhD
Assistant Professor of Pharmacy Practice
Appalachian College of Pharmacy
Oakwood, Virginia

Dennis W. Grauer, PhD
Associate Professor and Graduate Program Director
The University of Kansas, School of Pharmacy
Lawrence, Kansas

Debra A. Notturno-Strong, MS, RPh
Regional Dean–Abilene
Associate Professor of Pharmacy Practice
Texas Tech School of Pharmacy
Abilene, Texas

CHAPTER 1

Marketing Principles and Process

Brent L. Rollins, PhD, RPh

LEARNING OBJECTIVES

1. Define marketing and describe how it functions as a process.
2. Define and describe the general principles of marketing, including needs, wants, demand, and value, and apply these principles to the pharmaceutical industry.
3. Identify and describe the traditional marketing mix variables (product, price, place, and promotion) and how they uniquely function in the pharmaceutical industry.
4. Identify and describe how the principles of segmentation, targeting, and positioning uniquely function in the pharmaceutical industry.
5. Identify the determinants of marketing effectiveness and apply them to the evaluation of a pharmaceutical manufacturer.

CASE IN POINT 1-1
Marketing from Different Professionals' Perspectives

As a student, professor, or healthcare software company employee, more often than not at some point an individual attends a national association meeting or trade show event. In pharmacy, pharmacists, academics, and industry professionals can attend the national American Pharmacists Association (APhA) meeting held annually around the first of March. At this meeting, practicing pharmacists are updated on the latest medications and practice guidelines while they can also catch up on their continuing education or networking with various colleagues and employers. Academic pharmacists and researchers present their research, learn about others' work, network with colleagues, and, possibly, complete continuing education requirements. Industry professionals use this meeting to, among other things, introduce new product offerings or connect with potential future employees.

This meeting can be examined from three different perspectives. First, from the practicing pharmacist's perspective: BG decides to go the meeting based on a colleague's recommendation about its benefits. Her colleague states that, not only did he connect with his current employer, he was able to attend a special session to receive his immunization certification. Thus, based on this information, BG signs up to attend the meeting. While walking around the meeting's exhibit hall where a large variety of companies, from pharmaceutical manufacturers to chain pharmacies to pharmacy software companies, have set up information booths, BG happens to recognize a former classmate from pharmacy school working the booth for a competing chain pharmacy. After some casual conversation with her old classmate, who is now a district manager, BG explains that she is here to get her medication therapy management (MTM) certification and wants to start providing those services in her current position. Her classmate mentions opportunities at his company, which is actually getting ready to open a new store approximately 10 minutes from BG's home. Her classmate explains that the company is seeking a pharmacist who can bring MTM skills, specifically in the area of diabetes care and monitoring, into their pharmacy and train other pharmacists on the practice. After they exchange business cards and discuss a time for her to interview formally, BG takes a pamphlet that explains the benefits provided by her former classmate's company.

CJ, an academic pharmacist and researcher, attends the meeting to present his recent research project. While CJ stands by his poster, another academic pharmacist stops and asks a few questions about his research. After they discuss CJ's research project, the colleague mentions that she has just finished some preliminary data collection on a very similar topic and is intrigued by the methodology CJ used to test his hypotheses. She then suggests the possibility of combining their preliminary data and putting together a collaborative grant application. They exchange business cards and then set up a lunch meeting for the next day to discuss the potential project in more detail.

DL, a healthcare software industry professional, attends the meeting to demonstrate to pharmacists and pharmacies her company's new workflow management system. Given the large number of pharmacists, especially independent pharmacists and pharmacy owners, and national chain pharmacy representatives in attendance, DL surmises that this might be her best opportunity to gain a customer base. To fully demonstrate the system, DL and her coworkers set up a mini-pharmacy in the exhibit hall, allowing passersby (hopefully future customers) to view firsthand its capabilities.

INTRODUCTION

What does the multiperson example described in Case in Point 1-1 have to do with marketing? Marketing is a part of most every individual and business transaction. Most people link marketing traditionally to the area of consumer goods, where everything from sponsoring a NASCAR driver's car to television commercials to company logo stickers is a piece in the marketing process—all aimed at informing potential customers about a product or service offered by the company. However, as witnessed in the case, marketing can focus on monetary business transactions (such as the software company representative trying to sell the latest software) or nonmonetary transactions (BG marketing herself as a potential employee; CJ focusing on professional development in a collaborative research project).

Thus, what exactly is marketing and how can it be defined? The vital point is that marketing is not just a single TV commercial, email offer, or handshake introduction; it is a process. The singular events and items described in the case are just small pieces of a company's or individual's marketing efforts. Each piece, in addition to strategy, planning, and analysis, plays a role in the overall marketing strategy. According to Philip Kotler, academic and world-renowned marketing expert/author, **marketing** is

> the science and art of exploring, creating, and delivering value to satisfy the needs of a target market at a profit. Marketing identifies unfulfilled needs and desires. It defines, measures, and quantifies the size of the identified market and the profit potential. It pinpoints which segments the company is capable of serving best and it designs and promotes the appropriate products and services. (Kotler, 2012)

More concisely, marketing is the process of creating value for customers through exchange.

In this process, businesses examine their capabilities and the needs, wants, and demands of the marketplace to determine which customers they want to serve and how they want their products to be perceived by those customers. This involves market segmentation, targeting, and product positioning, where segmentation and targeting identify customers the business will try to serve, and product positioning creates the product's or service's desired image in customers' minds. Next, marketers design and implement marketing plans and programs to reach the target market and create the desired position in customers' minds. Marketing programs and the marketers' decisions revolve around the traditional marketing mix variables: product, price, place, and promotion. Marketing professionals manipulate these variables to create advantages for a firm's products and value for customers. Finally, businesses manage their marketing process by monitoring results obtained (e.g., sales or lack thereof) and adapting programs to stay on track as customer and market conditions change. The rest of this chapter develops the primary tenets and components of marketing overviewed here: customer needs, wants, demands, and value; product, price, place, and promotion; and segmentation, targeting, and positioning.

CUSTOMER NEEDS, WANTS, DEMANDS, AND VALUE

Although many variations of the definition of marketing exist, all include the primary determinant for marketing: Success is achieved by meeting customer needs. Though this might seem too simplistic, truly all the time, effort, and money put into the marketing process—the $3 million 30-second Super Bowl commercial ads, for instance—aim to meet customer needs.

The most basic **needs** are those inherent to human existence. For example, people have physiologic needs for food, water, and sleep in addition to safety, social, and personal needs. As individuals grow in their environment and into their own personality, these needs eventually become **wants**. For example, when a person is hungry for breakfast any food should satisfy that need, but perhaps the individual wants a Chik-fil-A Chicken Biscuit Combo with a large sweet tea because he just saw a commercial for it.

Further, one might ride mountain biking trails as a cross-training exercise of choice and need a new bike. Even though a reasonable and sufficient bike might cost $300–$500, an individual might *want* the Giant Reign X0 All-Mountain bike with an average retail price of $6,100. The next question is whether this person can actually afford to purchase a $6,100 mountain bike. If so, this then creates demand for the product. A want combined with the *ability to pay* creates **demand**.

However, Giant is not the only supplier of high-end mountain bicycles. Trek and Schwinn also provide high-tech and specialist mountain bikes. How does a consumer choose which bike to purchase? When multiple purchase options are available, a multitude of factors play into the consumer's decision, such as price and personal tastes and preferences. Ultimately, though, a consumer most likely chooses the option that provides the most value.

Value is typically viewed as the subjective relationship between the perceived benefits and perceived costs of a product or service. Mathematically, it can be expressed in the following manner:

$$\text{Value} = \text{Perceived benefit(s)} / \text{Perceived cost(s)}$$

Thus, if both benefits and costs are high or low, the product/service could be deemed to have little value. However, if the benefits greatly exceed the costs, then the product could be seen as having high value. With the mountain bike example, an individual might perceive the benefits (durability, speed, suspension, less maintenance, etc.) of the $6,100 bike to be far greater than the high price and associated maintenance costs. This individual might perceive this bike to be of great value. However, a different person might view the high monetary cost of the bike to be too great as compared to the bike's benefits and perceive the product as having little overall value. Although the value equation is shown as a mathematical expression that implies absolute objectivity, value, as illustrated in the bike discussion, is a highly subjective measure.

CASE IN POINT 1-2
Pharmaceuticals: Needs, Wants, Demand, and Value

CC, a 48-year-old male, visits his primary care physician for his annual checkup. During his visit, the physician informs CC that his total cholesterol has gotten too high and, in addition, his HDL, or "good cholesterol," levels are too low. The physician states that he *needs* to prescribe CC a medication to help get these numbers more in line with national guidelines. CC mentions that he saw an advertisement for a new cholesterol medication he *wants*, which increases the good cholesterol in addition to lowering the bad. The physician then explains to CC the high cost of the new brand-name medication, which CC then refutes because he has "great insurance and it shouldn't be too expensive—don't worry about the cost" (*demand*). After reviewing CC's other labs, the physician decides to prescribe an older, generically available medication because he thinks it provides the most *value* given CC's current labs, family history, and the medication's wealth of clinical effectiveness data and low cost.

In the quest to meet customer needs, wants, and demand while providing maximum value, companies employ a wide array of activities to make their marketing more effective. Through their own interactions with their customer base as well as the feedback through now mostly online media, companies can gauge the pulse of their customers on a day-to-day, real-time basis. Truly successful marketing organizations use this market intelligence and their own operational efficiency to adapt to any situation while continually focusing their energy and strategy on meeting customer needs.

MARKETING MIX: THE TRADITIONAL FOUR Ps

To develop effective marketing, companies must know, understand, and manipulate to the best of their abilities the marketing mix, a set of company-controlled variables, tools, and actions used to meet customer needs and wants while also trying to influence demand in favor of the company's goods and/or services.

Traditionally, a company examines four primary groups of variables to achieve its marketing and strategic goals: *product, price, place,* and *promotion.*

Product

Perhaps the most basic of the marketing mix variables, the **product** variable is typically associated with a tangible good provided or available for sale, such as a chicken sandwich or Apple's latest iPhone. As a company evolves, it must continually assess customer needs so as to know whether it is providing the right product or product features. In assessing which customers it wants to serve, a company gains direction in terms of the products or services it will offer. The company must determine whether meeting its targeted customers' needs requires a single product or multiple products and whether the targeted customers reside in a single market or in multiple markets (e.g., married males older than 25 years in metro Atlanta, Georgia, versus married individuals in the southeastern United States).

In the pharmaceutical industry, the primary product is the medication. Thus, from a pharmaceutical manufacturer's perspective, it should be straightforward to discover and manufacture a product that can improve health outcomes and quality of life. However, what if another company discovers a product that works twice as well with half the negative side effects? What would the first company do? In balancing the need for financial survival with improving health and quality of life, pharmaceutical manufacturers ask the strategic question of whether they should sell what they invent or invent what they can sell. One way to handle this issue is to have an efficient internal structure that includes marketing input

CASE IN POINT 1-3
Successful Product Offerings in Today's Marketplace

An amazing part of today's marketplace is the number of companies, especially dot-coms, that achieve great success and sales based on only a few product offerings. For example, Apple at its core offers only four products: the iPhone, iPad, iPod, and Mac computer. The proprietary Apple operating system is included in each. Apple sold its four products and managed its business so that it had more cash on hand, $76.2 billion, than did the United States Treasury based on its June 2011 quarterly earnings report (Griggs, 2011).

CASE IN POINT 1-4
Service as a Product: The Community Pharmacy

Some might wonder where in the traditional four Ps services fit. Services are also considered a product. Think about your most recent trip to the local community pharmacy. While picking up your monthly maintenance medication, you ask the pharmacist a question about some recent sinus issues you have experienced and whether there is an option available over-the-counter (OTC) to treat your symptoms. Not only does the pharmacist recommend a specific OTC product, she also explains its possible side effects and how it could interact with certain other medications if taken improperly. You do not specifically pay for the advice and counseling provided by the pharmacist. This value-added *service* is an intangible dimension of the product you did purchase.

in the company's research and development. As Kotler puts it, "Selling starts only when you have a product. Marketing starts before there is a product. Marketing is the homework the company does to figure out what people need and what the company should make" (Kotler, 2012).

Price

The recent economic issues in the United States have placed a great significance on one variable of the marketing mix, **price**. Now more than ever, consumers are price-conscious in most all their purchases. For companies trying to market their goods or services, understanding customers' needs and wants as they relate to the price variable is essential to survival. A great product priced too high will struggle, while a product priced too low might be devalued in the marketplace and hamper the company's profit and/or growth potential. Thus, it is important for companies to find the right price point that meets both customer and company needs.

A product's or service's price is not just a number; it defines other aspects of the product, service, or company. A premium or high price relative to a competitor's conveys the image of a premium product or service, especially in terms of quality. A much lower price compared to a competitor's conveys the opposite image and message. In pharmaceuticals, this dynamic plays a role in the consumer

CASE IN POINT 1-5
Pricing Variations in the Pharmaceutical Industry

Pricing in the pharmaceutical industry takes on many different forms depending on who pays. Because of manufacturers' large customer bases (e.g., wholesalers, retail pharmacies, pharmacy benefits managers [PBMs]), the key economic variables are **buying power** and **market share**. Those customers with the largest buying power and/or most potential to shift market share to a specific company's products receive the best pricing or actual acquisition cost, which is the bottom-line price after rebates or discounts are paid for the medication.

For example, manufacturers typically have a different pricing structure for various retail chain pharmacy customers. Large chain pharmacy customers, with their own warehouses and large numbers of physical stores, buy directly from the manufacturer and constitute a large portion of the manufacturer's business. Thus, the actual acquisition cost paid by large chain pharmacies is typically lower than the price paid by regional chain pharmacies, which typically do not have their own warehouses and work primarily through wholesalers.

In August 2000, the U.S. Department of Health and Human Services held a presidentially requested conference on pharmaceutical industry pricing, utilization, and costs. During the conference, participants debated the current and future pricing issues facing the pharmaceutical industry. Panelists from a wide variety of backgrounds, including industry and various areas of academia, pointed out concerns. Manufacturers charge different prices depending on the buyer. Also, the pharmaceutical market is inefficient by nature because decision makers, particularly physicians, do not know the ultimate price of a medication, let alone the hidden and "confidential" actual acquisition prices, discounts, and rebates provided by manufacturers (Kemp, n.d.). One panelist, Dr. Stephen Schondelmeyer, PharmD, PhD, of the University of Minnesota College of Pharmacy, advocated increased government regulation of pricing in the pharmaceutical industry to ensure transparency (Kemp, n.d.).

perception that generic medications are not as good as brand-name medications, even though scientific evidence suggests otherwise with certain medications.

In the pharmaceutical space overall, price has many different meanings, depending on the customer. Pharmaceutical manufacturers set a price on a medication for various suppliers, including wholesalers, retail pharmacies, and mail-order pharmacies. There are also the different prices for the end user, or patient, in the form of a flat copayment, coinsurance, or a non-insurance-based cash price. The price variable in the pharmaceutical industry has many forms and, depending on who pays, the number has many different possibilities.

Place

From a marketing perspective, **place** refers to any activity designed to create value and utility by making the product(s) available. Another term related to the place variable is *supply chain*. In any manufacturing industry, whether pharmaceuticals or pet food, products must be made, packaged, and then through some mechanism delivered to the point of sale. A company could make the best product, but if it cannot get that product into the hands of the customers, then the company's potential success is in jeopardy.

In the pharmaceutical industry, the supply chain traditionally is a path from the pharmaceutical manufacturer, who produces, sells, and ships products to a wholesaler, who stores the extreme volume of products and ships products sold to community and hospital pharmacies (**Figure 1-1**).

Over the years, competition has bred consolidation within the wholesale industry and left three primary wholesalers: AmerisourceBergen, Cardinal Health, and

FIGURE 1-1 General Pharmacy Supply Chain

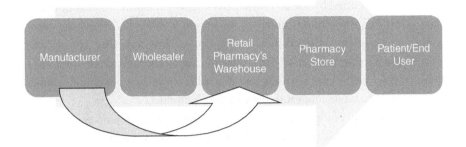

FIGURE 1-2 Large Retail Pharmacy Supply Chain Model

McKesson. Furthermore, many chain pharmacies, such as Walgreens, CVS, and Rite Aid, and grocery chain pharmacies, such as in Wal-Mart and Publix, now use their own warehouses and supply chains to store and deliver medication, making necessary purchases from a wholesaler only on an as-needed or secondary basis (**Figure 1-2**).

CASE IN POINT 1-6
Role of the Wholesaler for Small, Independent Pharmacies

In communities across the United States, small, independent pharmacist-owned pharmacies have been a hallmark of the profession. Many of the perceptions of the pharmacy profession, including, for example, trustworthiness and exceptional customer service, are rooted in independent pharmacy practice. For these small, and many times rural, pharmacies to serve their customers, they must have the inventory necessary to bring customers into their stores. Unlike many of the current large chain pharmacies that can buy in bulk directly from pharmaceutical manufacturers and then store and distribute through their own warehouses, the independent pharmacy relies exclusively on the wholesaler for its supply chain. Not only does the wholesaler deliver inventory, it typically provides other value-added services, such as computer and inventory management systems and increased buying power that enables the independent pharmacy to purchase medications at the best possible price.

Promotion

More often than not, the final P, **promotion**, is the marketing mix variable most commonly recognized by the consumer, given its visual nature, such as in television advertising. Promotion, however, is not just a 30-second television commercial or a massive billboard in Times Square in New York City. It functions as a company's communication arm, transmitting to consumers the other Ps—product, price, and place—in a manner that achieves the best possible consumer attitudes and purchase interest in the company's product.

In today's world of digital and mobile technology, promotion takes many new forms while still including traditional media. Companies use a variety of outlets to promote their products and/or services. The most common promotional methods used include the following:

- *Advertising.* Advertising consists of the promotion of a given product, service, or message through mass media channels, such as newspapers, billboards, magazines, radio, and television, and is used to both inform a given target market and persuade them in a manner leading to increased use or sale of the company's products or services. Within the pharmaceutical industry, advertising is most commonly associated with the direct-to-consumer (DTC) television advertising commercials for popular, high-selling products. For example, phrases and slogans such as the "Purple Pill" or "Viva Viagra" are now embedded in the minds of consumers as a result of the increasing use over the past 15 years of television as a prescription advertising media. In fact, the average television viewer sees as much as 30 hours of prescription advertising a year (Brownfield, 2004). Manufacturers have also begun to target healthcare providers, such as physicians and pharmacists, through the use of "product theaters" at various organizational meetings (e.g., American Pharmacists Association [APhA]) and educational conferences.
- *Sales promotions.* Sales promotions are found everywhere in society, such as 50% off, 0% financing, and the ever popular "buy one, get one . . .," or BOGO. Whereas mass media advertising is used to make the consumer aware of a product, its price, and place and entice consumers to purchase the product or service, sales promotions are used to entice consumers to buy the product or service at that specific moment in time, or while the sales promotion is going on. For example, every year in the weeks leading up to the National Football League's Super Bowl Sunday, retailers such as

Best Buy run sales promotions on their large, high-definition televisions, trying to entice purchasers to buy one just in time to watch the big game. For pharmaceutical companies, sales promotions have recently taken the form of coupons available in print and online media that reduce consumers' out-of-pocket cost or copay. Pharmaceutical manufacturers increasingly use promotions to penetrate crowded markets and maintain existing products sales. Large chain pharmacies also use this strategy to promote their specific generic program or, in some areas, offer gift cards for transferred prescriptions.

- *Personal selling.* Personal selling involves a one-on-one interaction between an individual salesperson and a prospective client. Generally speaking, a company's sales force is meant for personal selling. For years, companies have employed sales personnel to spread the word about their products or services and gain as many new customers as possible while developing solid relationships with the customers they serve. In the traditional consumer market, for example, Mary Kay Cosmetics uses independent sales consultants nationwide to sell its products personally through in-home parties and personal relationships with customers because its products are

CASE IN POINT 1-7
New Pharmaceutical Sales Promotion

In 2009, the Food and Drug Administration (FDA) approved Livalo (pitavastatin), a new Hmg-CoA reductase inhibitor, more commonly known as a statin, manufactured by the Kowa Company. This medication, which has been marketed in Japan and other Asian countries since 2003, was the seventh statin to be approved in the United States (DeNoon, 2009). To penetrate the already crowded market, which also includes generic versions of the brand-name medications, the Livalo campaign used multiple sales promotions to persuade consumers as well as physicians to purchase the new statin. Included in these sales promotions was, among others, a 30-day free trial offer for the medication (**Figure 1-3**; see also http://voucher .livalorx.com/coupon.cfm).

Begin LIVALO® (pitavastatin) with a FREE 30-TABLET TRIAL.

Give this card to your pharmacist, along with a valid prescription from your physician.

Ask your healthcare provider about LIVALO. This voucher for 30 FREE tablets is being provided to you by your prescriber and Kowa Pharmaceuticals America, Inc. and Lilly USA, LLC. This voucher should be taken, along with your new prescription, to your local pharmacy, where you will receive this product without charge.

(pitavastatin) tablets

1-mg, 2-mg, 4-mg

www.LivaloRx.com

To the Pharmacist:

- By accepting this offer, you certify that you understand and agree to comply with the offer terms set forth herein.
- Product dispensed as sample pursuant to the terms of this voucher shall not be submitted to any third-party payer, public or private (eg, Medicaid, Medicare, private insurance or any governmental program, any other federal or state program such as Champus, the VA, TRICARE, or a state pharmaceutical assistance program) for reimbursement.
- Submit claim online to RxSolutions. Processor requires Valid Prescriber ID #, Patient Name, DOB and PCN# for claim adjudication.
- This card must be accompanied by a new prescription.
- Valid for 30 free tablets of LIVALO® (pitavastatin) — All Strengths Covered.
- One voucher per patient per 12-month period.
- Refills will not be authorized with this card.
- Please remove this identification number from the patient profile after the claim.
- For assistance in filing this claim, contact the help desk at 1-800-510-4836.
- This offer may be terminated at any time.

RxBIN#	GROUP#	PCN#	IDENTIFICATION#	EXPIRATION DATE
610494	LIVALOWB	3333	LVWB9346612	11/19/2012

FIGURE 1-3 Livalo (Pitavastatin) 30-Day Free Trial Offer

not available in a retail setting. Pharmaceutical manufacturers, specifically branded-product manufacturers, also use this tactic to reach their primary customer through physician detailing. At the height of the blockbuster drug era, pharmaceutical companies employed more than 100,000 salespeople all with one goal in mind: build a sustainable relationship with prescribing physicians to increase the use of each company's specific products.

- *Direct marketing.* Whereas advertising is designed to reach a large market of customers through various media channels, direct marketing is much more focused and targeted promotion. Traditionally, direct marketing is associated with mail, catalog, or telephone marketing. Customer databases are created based on consumer/buyer demographics, and then direct marketing approaches focus on the *individual*. However, in the current market, direct marketing has greatly expanded its reach as a result of the Internet and mobile technology. These always-expanding channels enable message customization and personalized marketing messages to be directed at a specific person, place, and time. The pharmaceutical industry has begun to harness the power of the Internet with customized messaging and promotional offers based on an individual's Web-based behavior.

- *Public relations (PR).* As its name implies, PR involves relating with the public, or those considered to be company stakeholders. PR efforts, including communications such as press releases, sponsorships, and corporate literature, are used to generate positive attitudes and feelings, or goodwill, toward the company and its products and services. In addition, any negative press or public information can be addressed quickly and nullified by a responsive PR department or director. In the pharmaceutical industry, public relations can take many forms. With a press release about a newly approved indication for a drug or an informational flyer on the upcoming release of a new drug, pharmaceutical manufacturers use a wealth of PR promotions to inform key stakeholders about their products. The primary form is disease awareness campaigns. These campaigns aim to raise awareness and educate stakeholders, including potential consumers, of a particular disease or condition. For example, Boehringer Ingelheim's "Drive 4 COPD" campaign uses NASCAR driver Danica Patrick to raise awareness about chronic obstructive pulmonary disease (COPD). The company provides general information and a screening survey on its website (www.drive4copd.com) in addition to sponsoring various events and discussions.

CASE IN POINT 1-8
Pharmaceutical Manufacturer Promotional Budgets

Over the years, pharmaceutical manufacturers have spent billions of dollars promoting their products to physicians and consumers. Based on the most recent accessible data from IMS Health, a healthcare information and analytics company, total promotional spending by pharmaceutical manufacturers, including physician detailing, medication samples, meetings and events, journal advertisements, and direct-to-consumer (DTC) advertisements, peaked in 2007 at approximately $27 billion and decreased to approximately $24 billion in 2010 (DTC Perspectives, 2011a). DTC advertising has followed a similar trend, with spending peaking in 2006 around $5.2 billion and steadily declining to around $4.4 billion in 2011 (DTC Perspectives, 2011b). However, pharmaceutical manufacturers' commitment to online advertising has been growing and is expected to continue double-digit growth to slightly less than $2 billion annually by 2015 (Iskowitz, 2011). Although these totals have greatly increased since the early 1990s, the amount spent has held relatively steady at approximately 10–12% of sales (Congressional Budget Office, 2009).

While the four traditional marketing mix variables—product, price, place, and promotion—can be examined from the company's, or seller's, point of view, they can also be examined from the end user's or customer's perspective. Regardless of whether it is a tangible product or intangible service, the customer seeks an answer or solution to a problem. For example, a customer who goes to the pharmacy to pick up blood pressure medication is there to retrieve a medication as well as improve his or her health and reduce risk of future cardiovascular problems. The customer might only slightly consider the pricing strategy of the company, but greatly considers eventual out-of-pocket costs and how to find the greatest value. For place, whereas the company concentrates on how best to set up its supply chain and distribution channels, the customer is primarily concerned with access to the product or service and the convenience of that access. Last, as a company considers a multitude of factors in deciding how to promote its products and services, a customer focuses on the clarity, quality, and integrity of the communication. Given that the traditional marketing mix variables can be examined from both the seller's and customer's perspectives, the company that best balances these perspectives provides itself a distinct advantage in the marketplace.

SEGMENTATION, TARGETING, AND POSITIONING

How does a company decide which customers it should target? Wouldn't a company want everyone to purchase its product or service? Are the needs of a 32-year-old mother of three different from those of a 70-year-old retired grandfather? How should the young mother view the company and its product or service? The next set of marketing variables answers these questions: segmentation, targeting, and positioning. Marketing professionals continuously monitor and analyze these variables to be sure companies are serving the needs of the target customers.

Segmentation is breaking down a mass market that includes all individuals into a variety of segments, or fragments, of the population who have similar characteristics. Typically, in a defined market segment, the customer group has a relatively homogenous profile of personal characteristics, common needs and wants, and, theoretically, similar responses to specific marketing messages.

A specific customer group could be segmented using numerous characteristics. The two most common characteristics are the following (Kotler & Keller, 2011):

- *Demographic.* These segments are based on personal characteristics such as age, gender, race, religion, occupation, and income level. Although all companies, including pharmaceutical manufacturers, pay attention to demographic variables, the key is not to use these variables as the sole basis for analysis. For example, a pharmaceutical product class such as oral contraceptives is primarily designed for women of childbearing age, but the products have alternative approved uses, such as acne treatment, and marketers would be unwise not to consider these possibilities and only market the product based on its primary indication.

- *Geographic.* Given the geographic variability in the United States, companies can easily segment and then analyze a market based on its geographic location. For example, customers located in urban versus suburban versus rural settings have unique needs, as do those living in "Ski Town, USA" (Steamboat Springs, Colorado) compared to customers living in Miami, Florida. The various needs and wants of customers in China, the fastest growing and now third largest pharmaceutical market worldwide, are greatly different from those of customers in the United States, where growth has slowed down and begun to plateau (Gatyas, 2010).

Numerous other ways to segment a market exist, including basing segmentation on customer lifestyle, motives, personality, price sensitivity, and level of brand loyalty.

Once marketers have sufficiently segmented the market into groups most likely to respond positively to the company's marketing messages and eventually purchase its product or service, they must then decide which of those groups they want to focus on or target. **Targeting** is picking which segment of the population to market the company's products or services to. The decision revolves around the company, its specific products or services, and the company's ultimate strategic goal. Does the company want to focus its efforts on the most potentially profitable, largest, or most easily reachable segment? For example, physicians who prescribe medications can be segmented by specialty. A pharmaceutical manufacturer might then identify a segment of cardiologists in the major metropolitan areas of the southeastern United States to target its communications to. Further, the manufacturer might specifically focus on cardiologists in that segment who are classified by marketing research as "early adopters," or those who traditionally respond to marketing messages and are early prescribers of new medications.

Based on their segmentation and targeting data and analysis, companies then decide where they want to position their product. Essentially, a company must decide what it wants the customer to think of its product or service or what position the product occupies with respect to the competition. For example, in its very popular and successful "Mac vs. PC" advertising campaign, Apple famously positioned itself as the much more user-friendly and problem-free computing solution compared to a personal computer running Microsoft Windows. In the pharmaceutical industry, **product positioning** is also very important in marketing over-the-counter (OTC) medications. For OTC medications, consumers can

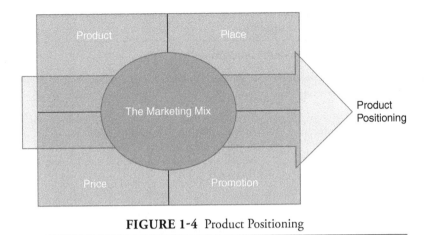

FIGURE 1-4 Product Positioning

easily recognize competing products. Thus, marketers for Claritin (loratadine) work strategically to place it in consumers' minds as the most effective, nonsedating antihistamine (**Figure 1-4**).

THE MARKETING PLAN

All of the strategies, including the four Ps and segmentation, targeting, and positioning, come together in the **marketing plan**. The marketing plan is the single document that holds all the research, strategy, and forecasts for a company and its products/services. The document itself could focus specifically on one product or service or be the company's overall marketing strategy document. For example, with only four product offerings, Apple could put together marketing plans for each individual product (iPod, iPad, iPhone, and Mac computers) or combine plans into one overall marketing planning document.

Pharmaceutical manufacturing companies typically employ product managers to be responsible for the details of a particular medication. The product manager and his or her team usually assemble marketing plans for the specific products they oversee. Although reprinting a real company's pharmaceutical marketing plan would be the best way to demonstrate marketing plans, the information contained in such a document is highly confidential. Instead, **Table 1-1** provides a comprehensive template based on firsthand experience with pharmaceutical manufacturer marketing plans and their development.

Table 1-1 The Marketing Plan

Phase	Areas of Review	Description
Executive Summary	Overview of the marketing plan	Highlights key areas, decisions, and expected outcomes.
Situation Analysis	External environment	What regulatory, political, economic, or social issues can affect the product? Will the product be marketed globally? Is new technology being implemented? How rapidly is the technology changing?
	Internal environment	What are the mission, corporate vision, and strategic intent associated with this product? How does this product fit with other products/brands within the corporation? What are corporate plans, long-term goals, and objectives (profits, return on investment, share price)? How will the product be managed within the organization (e.g., organizational chart)?
	Product and category review	What is the product category, its background, development, technology, stage in adoption and diffusion, and product life cycle, and where are these variables heading? What are the nature and characteristics of consumer demand for the product? What are the sales trends associated with the product category (e.g., total sales, regional sales, year-over-year growth, seasonality, and competitive market share)? What are current pricing trends, and how will these affect brand development and profit potential?
	Competitive analysis	What is the overall view of and degree of competition in the product category? Describe the major competition, its strengths, and weaknesses from a marketing perspective, such as the product itself (benefits), its pricing, and distribution. Where is the competition positioned in the minds of purchasers? What are the trends in advertising (e.g., media spending, sales promotions, targets)? Are there new developments expected from the competition, such as product improvements, changes in distribution, pricing, or advertising?
	Consumer analysis	Who are the customers or buyers? What influences purchase decisions? What are the demographic, epidemiological, or psychological characteristics that affect purchase decisions? Is there loyalty for existing brands?

Phase	Areas of Review	Description
	Brand review	For existing products, what are the current positioning, sales trends, and pricing history? Where is the product in the product life cycle? Are there new areas of business that have been identified?
Problems and Opportunities	Strengths, weaknesses, opportunities, and threats (SWOT)	Evaluation of the internal strengths and weaknesses of the corporation, brand team, or product. Similar evaluation of the external opportunities and threats posed by competition. Assessment of the problems and opportunities created by this analysis. What does this SWOT analysis mean to the company, the product, and even the competition? What are the competitive advantages and disadvantages?
Strategic Planning	Marketing objectives and strategies	Define high-level marketing objectives such as sales, market share, or formulary status. What strategies will be employed to achieve the marketing objectives of the firm?
	Targeting and segmenting	Who are the customers? What are the characteristics of the market segments? Do customers have similar needs? Are they accessible?
	Identification of competitive advantage	Based on the SWOT analysis, what competitive advantages exist?
	Positioning	Define the desired position for the product in customers' minds.
Marketing Mix Objectives, Strategies, and Tactics	Product	How will the product be managed? How will product data and information from production, research, and development shape marketing mix decisions?
	Place	What are the objectives with regard to market penetration, where the product will be sold, value-added services associated with the product? How will the product be distributed?
	Price	What are the pricing objectives, strategy, and tactics?
	Promotion	What forms of promotion will be employed? Personal selling? Advertising? DTC advertising? Will sales promotions be used? What role will packaging have on promotional issues?

(continues)

Table 1-1 The Marketing Plan (*continued*)

Phase	Areas of Review	Description
Control, Evaluation, and Feedback	Forecasting and benchmarking	What are the expectations for the product? Are there competitors or other products that can be used to set success metrics?
	Budgeting	Assessment of marketing budgets and achievement of goals and objectives.
	Scheduling and timing	Setting time frames for evaluation of success.
	Evaluation and feedback	What results are being achieved? How does success or failure affect current plans, strategies, tactics? What needs to change or remain the same?

MARKETING EFFECTIVENESS

One way to assess whether a company successfully practices marketing is to assess its overall level of marketing effectiveness. Marketing effectiveness is a measure of how well a firm understands and practices marketing and is assessed on a continuum, from no marketing effectiveness to superior marketing effectiveness. Marketing effectiveness is based on five dimensions, including a firm's degree of holding to a customer-oriented philosophy, strategic marketing orientation, ability to gather relevant and timely market intelligence, level of integration of the marketing organization, and operational efficiency (Kotler, 1977).

Customer and Strategic Orientation

Successful marketing in any industry, including the pharmaceutical industry, is based on being able to meet customer needs. Marketing, and the effectiveness of the marketing campaign/program, is highly dependent on knowing, analyzing, and meeting customer needs as opposed to a singular focus on the product or general sales. The key evaluative criteria look at the company from its mission statement all the way to its day-to-day customer interactions. Is the mission statement customer centered? Does the company respond quickly to customer issues or distress?

From a strategic point of view, the marketing professionals in a company must function with the long-term strategy and success in mind. This typically takes the form of formal marketing planning and a culture of strategic, long-term thinking. Further, does the company have a strategic contingency plan in case the product or service is not adopted in the marketplace?

CASE IN POINT 1-9
Product Failure: Pfizer's Exubera

In 2006, Pfizer introduced a product it thought would transform the diabetes market and better the health of patients. The new product, an inhalable insulin called Exubera, enabled patients to get insulin without having to inject themselves. However, the product, originally invented by Nektar Therapeutics, was large, inconvenient, and hard to dose and, thus, never gained any momentum in the marketplace. In October 2007, after only achieving $12 million in sales during the previous 9 months, Pfizer voluntarily removed Exubera from the market. Pfizer had invested $2.8 billion into marketing Exubera (Weintraub, 2007).

Market Intelligence

To serve customer needs, a company and its marketing professionals should have as much objective information regarding its status in the marketplace as possible. In addition to having the necessary information for planning and resource allocation from their own internal data and sources, key decision makers should also have at their disposal up-to-date information about the external market. Information regarding customer perceptions, buying habits, and attitudes is vital, but one of the most important pieces of market intelligence is data and analyses of the competitive environment (i.e., the competition). Within the extremely competitive marketplace of the pharmaceutical industry, and specifically the generic pharmaceutical industry, where price, consistency of supply, and the ability to offer a "full line" of products are the primary components affecting purchasing decisions, gathering competitive market intelligence is a daily task.

Organizational Integration and Operational Efficiency

The last two marketing effectiveness constructs go hand in hand in execution and level of importance. Based on the competitive intelligence the company gains, a company must react in an integrated and efficient manner to maintain its level of customer service and, if necessary, adjust its strategy. Integration focuses on how well marketing and other departments in an organization communicate and work together. For example, if broken machinery in the production assembly line is going to delay product delivery for a week, the organization must be integrated well enough so that manufacturing notifies all departments involved to ensure customers are notified and forecasts and strategy are adjusted on the fly.

Operational efficiency speaks to how effective the organization is at its business. How well are the decisions made at the higher levels of marketing filtered throughout the organization? How responsive is the marketing department to problems and issues? Most important, how responsive is the organization, and marketing in particular, to customer requests for any type of information or product?

Evaluating an organization's marketing effectiveness gives insight into a company's day-to-day operations and how well the company functions. If a company is found to have a good to superior level of marketing effectiveness, from a sales perspective this should logically translate into a highly successful organization. However, a company could be run in a nearly perfect manner and be vastly superior to its competitors with its level of marketing but achieve little sales success. Numerous internal and external factors affect how well a company performs in the marketplace, and although a high overall level of marketing effectiveness is a positive for a company, it does not guarantee sales success.

SUMMARY

This chapter shows that marketing is not just a single advertisement or public relations campaign; it is a continual process of creating value for customers and meeting their needs. Through managing and manipulating the four primary marketing mix variables (product, price, place, and promotion), identifying appropriate customers (segmentation and targeting), and placing the desired product or service image in the minds of those customers (positioning), pharmaceutical marketing professionals put their companies in a position to succeed.

DISCUSSION QUESTIONS

1. Who are the different customers of pharmaceutical manufacturers? How are needs, wants, demand, and value different for each?
2. How do pharmaceutical products differ from other consumer goods in terms of product benefits and product selection?

3. Does a lower price always attract customers to a pharmaceutical product? What other factors might a consumer weigh when deciding whether to purchase (and eventually take) an OTC medication? Prescription medication? Community pharmacy buying medications from a pharmaceutical manufacturer?

4. Explain why having prescription pharmaceutical products available in both traditional, community-based pharmacies and mail-order outlets can be a good strategy from a target marketing perspective.

5. In regard to the use of direct-to-consumer (DTC) prescription advertising, assume it is widely accepted that patients (consumers) simply do not have sufficient knowledge to understand DTC ads. Should this assumption be enough to discourage pharmaceutical companies from using this form of advertising? Why or why not?

6. With physicians as the customer base of choice, how might pharmaceutical manufacturers segment physicians into groups?

7. Based on the information presented, does a high level of marketing effectiveness equal sales success? Explain.

8. If pharmaceutical pricing was transparent for all customers at all times (in particular the price actually paid for the product by the pharmacy), how might the market, specifically consumers, respond?

9. Given the various promotional strategies discussed, how might a pharmaceutical manufacturer choose to market a new brand product within a market of few competitors? Numerous competitors?

10. In the generic pharmaceutical marketplace, where products are viewed as commodities (interchangeable), how might a generic company choose to promote its products?

REFERENCES

Brownfield, E. D., Bernhardt, J. M., Phan, J. L., Williams, M. V., & Parker, R. M. (2004). Direct-to-consumer drug advertisements on network television: An exploration of quantity, frequency, and placement. *Journal of Health Communication, 9*(6), 491–497.

Congressional Budget Office. (2009, December 2). Promotional spending for prescription drugs. Retrieved from https://www.cbo.gov/sites/default/files/cbofiles/ftpdocs/105xx /doc10522/12-02-drugpromo_brief.pdf

DeNoon, D. J. (2009, August 3). Livalo, a new statin, gets FDA nod. WebMD Cholesterol Management Health Center. Retrieved from http://www.webmd.com /cholesterol-management/news/20090803/livalo-a-new-statin-gets-fda-nod

DTC Perspectives (2011a, June). IMS Health: overall DTC declines, but top 25 brands buck the trend. Retrieved from http://www.dtcperspectives.com/wp-content /uploads/2011/02/DTCP_0611_web.pdf

DTC Perspective (2011b, Spring). Top 20 promoting brands post significant increase in 2011. Retrieved from http://www.dtcperspectives.com/images/email/DTCPM -Spring2012.pdf

Gatyas, G. (2010, October 6). Biopharma forecasts and trends. IMS. Retrieved from http://www.imshealth.com/portal/site/ims/menuitem.d248e29c86589c9c30e81c03 3208c22a/?vgnextoid=119717f27128b210VgnVCM100000ed152ca2RCRD

Griggs, B. (2011, July 29). Apple now has more cash than the U.S. government. CNN Tech. Retrieved from http://articles.cnn.com/2011-07-29/tech/apple.cash .government_1_ceo-jobs-apple-cash-balance?_s=PM:TECH

Iskowitz, M. (2011, April 27). Pharma poised to up online ad spend: eMarketer. MM&M. Retrieved from http://www.mmm-online.com/pharma-poised-to-up -online-ad-spend-emarketer/article/201584/

Kemp, K. (n.d.). II. Pricing practices in the pharmaceutical market. In conference summary— pharmaceutical pricing practices, utilization, and costs. Retrieved from http://aspe.hhs .gov/health/reports/drug-papers/Kemp2.htm

Kotler, P., & Keller, K. (2011). *Marketing Management* (13th ed.). Upper Saddle River, NJ; Prentice Hall.

Kotler, P. (1977). From sales obsession to marketing effectiveness. *Harvard Business Review*, (Nov–Dec), 1–9.

Kotler, P. (2012). Dr. Philip Kotler answers your questions on marketing. Retrieved from http://kotlermarketing.com/phil_questions.shtml

Weintraub, A. (2007, October 18). Pfizer's Exubera flop. BloombergBusinessweek Technology. Retrieved from http://www.businessweek.com/stories/2007-10-18/pfizers -exubera-flopbusinessweek-business-news-stock-market-and-financial-advice

CHAPTER 2

Pharmaceutical Marketing and the Industry Environment

Brent L. Rollins, PhD, RPh

LEARNING OBJECTIVES

1. Describe how the advent of the prescription altered the dynamics of the pharmaceutical industry.
2. Identify pharmaceutical manufacturers' customers, describe their needs, and assess how those needs are met.
3. Describe the social, ethical, political, and legal issues unique to the pharmaceutical market and how these issues affect the marketing and choice of pharmaceuticals.
4. Describe the issues unique to pharmaceutical marketing, including differentiating the marketing focuses between prescription and over-the-counter medications and brand and generic medications.
5. Assess the pharmaceutical industry's future and evaluate the role of marketing and possible changes necessary.

While watching television one Saturday afternoon, a 58-year-old seemingly healthy man sees an advertisement for Livalo (pitavastatin). The advertisement depicts the diet and lifestyle choices that lead to high cholesterol and the subsequent cardiovascular and heart problems that can result. After seeing the ad, the man realizes his cholesterol is probably too high and that he should check into getting Livalo or something similar. In a different scenario, an 8-year-old child has been having difficulties with bedwetting. His parents have tried limiting his fluid intake late in the evenings and are sure to take him to the bathroom right before bed, without success. In both of these scenarios, the consumer has a problem that can likely be solved through the use of a pharmaceutical. Why can't they go to a community pharmacy and simply purchase the medication that would help them solve their problem, as people routinely do for most other consumer goods?

In health care, the issues and solutions for supply and demand are different from those of other consumer goods and vary depending on cultural norms, societal values, and even government regulation. In other cultures, the solution to a health issue might be a visit to a medicine man or ingesting an herb or natural substance. In the United States, the primary answer to most health problems is a trip to the physician. Physicians then use their education, training, and experience and data they collect from the patient (e.g., physical exam or blood analysis) to determine the cause of symptoms (i.e., they make a diagnosis). More often than not, a physician visit usually concludes with the physician prescribing some type of medication for the patient to purchase to help alleviate symptoms or prevent future negative health outcomes.

THE PRESCRIPTION

Sickness can take many forms, including bacterial infection, elevated blood pressure, pain, erectile dysfunction, depression, and even extreme cognitive issues, such as schizophrenia or Alzheimer's disease. Thus, in the mind of the consumer, the factor sparking the need for help can be physical or cognitive. To ensure proper diagnosis and treatment of health issues, laws and regulations have been passed to ensure the safety and well-being of consumers in the healthcare environment. For example, the authority of the Food and Drug Administration (FDA) has been augmented over time, requiring pharmaceutical manufacturers to conduct rigorous research and work through an extensive application process to have a medication approved for use in patients and available for sale in pharmacies.

Of the many laws and regulations related to pharmaceuticals, none has altered the pharmaceutical industry like the advent of the prescription. In 1951, when the Durham-Humphrey Amendment to the original Food, Drug, and Cosmetic Act of 1938 was passed, the requirement for a written prescription from an authorized prescriber was legislated, creating a distinction between prescription medications and all other types, such as nonprescription or over-the-counter (OTC) medications. Whereas the prescription requirement is rigid, the generation of a prescription is quite flexible. Currently, a prescription can be written by an authorized prescriber, phoned in to a dispensing pharmacy by an agent of the prescriber, faxed in, or, increasingly popular, submitted electronically with an e-prescribing software system (Surescripts, 2011). The requirement for a prescription to purchase certain medications has created a distinct environment in which pharmaceutical manufacturers market and sell their products, one much different from the market for traditional consumer goods.

From the pharmaceutical manufacturers' and marketers' perspectives, the Durham-Humphrey Amendment created opportunities for healthcare businesses. Although most people cannot recall a time when they did not have to obtain a physician's written prescription, a world did exist prior to the prescription requirement, a virtual "wild, wild west of health care." The use of prescriptions creates barriers to entry that help manufacturers remain competitive. It prevents "snake oil" salesmen from putting together a concoction, claiming it has therapeutic benefits, and selling it. Second, the amendment creates a unique business environment that operates on the idea of directed demand. **Directed demand** in the pharmaceutical industry means the prescriber, the learned intermediary, usually a physician, determines which medication(s) or treatment the consumer needs.

Continuing the situations posed at the beginning of the chapter, the man with high cholesterol and the boy who wets his bed must confirm they indeed have a medical condition and determine the best corrective action or treatment. The man who saw the Livalo advertisement might, for example, do extensive research on the subject of cholesterol, purchase a home cholesterol test, and determine that his cholesterol level is well outside the normal limits and should be treated. He might then research the literature and decide, based on his cholesterol numbers and personal medical history, that Lipitor (atorvastatin) is his best treatment option. However, to purchase Lipitor, he must see his primary physician, obtain a written prescription for that medication, take the prescription to a pharmacy, and purchase the medication when the prescription is filled by the pharmacy. The caveat with directed demand is that, although the patient might request a specific drug, the prescriber might deem another medication the best choice based on the patient's clinical case.

This situation presents a unique challenge for the pharmaceutical industry and its marketers. Whereas marketing is a process that creates value for customers through exchange, in pharmaceutical marketing the value medicines bring to patients and society are actualized. Given the nature of the pharmaceutical market and the fact that medicines might be necessary to sustain life, pharmaceutical marketers play a vital role in health care. In being responsive to this role, pharmaceutical marketers recognize the unique nature of their operating environment (e.g., legal, social, political, technologic, regulatory, or economic issues), especially the fact that often the customer is not the patient but rather a third party, such as a physician or pharmacy, that is, in turn, reimbursed by insurance companies or government payers. From a societal marketing perspective, the challenge for the pharmaceutical marketer is to meet customer needs across each potential target market, while keeping patient welfare in mind.

CUSTOMERS OF PHARMACEUTICAL MANUFACTURERS

From a marketing perspective, the key to success and long-term survival in any industry is continually understanding the organization's customers and working to meet their needs in the most efficient manner possible. In the pharmaceutical industry, the customer takes many forms, depending on the perspective taken. This is especially true when examining a pharmaceutical manufacturer's customer base. Given the desired end result of continual new prescriptions filled and purchased, the product ultimately dispensed is primarily a function of three entities: the prescriber, consumer/patient, and third-party payer. **Figure 2-1** graphically depicts this interaction in which the dispensed product is represented by the point of intersection among the three and shows the point at which each customer's needs have been met. Physicians desire the best product to treat the patient therapeutically, while consumers and third-party payers want the best value, or the highest therapeutic benefit at the lowest cost.

The use of the term *dispensed* as opposed to *prescribed* is significant. Whereas the physician can prescribe a medication based on available knowledge and patient characteristics, the consumer must take the prescription to the pharmacy and determine whether it is covered by his or her prescription insurance at a desired co-payment or coinsurance and, if not, whether it is a reasonable cost. Third-party prescription insurance has grown from only a small percentage (5–10%) in the 1970s to 80% or more of the typical pharmacy's prescription business (Kaiser Family Foundation, 2010).

Even though prescribers, patients, and payers do not all work together, each contributes to the decision about which product

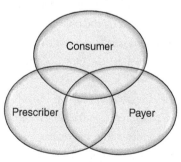

FIGURE 2-1 The Ultimately Dispensed Product

FIGURE 2-2 The Ultimately Dispensed
Product—Expanded

is dispensed, especially for generic medications. Each of these three entities is a customer of the pharmaceutical manufacturer. If Figure 2-1 is expanded to include those logistically involved, the pharmacy and wholesaler are included in the model as well (see **Figure 2-2**).

The following subsections examine the various customers of pharmaceutical manufacturers, discuss the needs of those customers, and illustrate how manufacturers work to meet those needs.

Physicians

In the United States, when someone gets sick, he or she typically goes to the doctor. The doctor, using specialized knowledge and experience and through the use of prescriptions, has long been pharmaceutical manufacturers' primary customer.

For physicians as customers of the pharmaceutical industry, the primary "need" or solution to a problem is information. Physicians must constantly stay up-to-date on the drugs they prescribe and the associated medical information on diseases and treatments. By staying abreast of the most current medical and drug information, usually through published research, physicians can make the most appropriate (in terms of cost and quality) treatment decisions. Additionally, pharmaceutical manufacturers that want physicians to prescribe their products must work to provide as much information about the products as possible so this information can lead to prescription trials and adoption.

CASE IN POINT 2-1
Are There Enough Physicians?

One debate in U.S. health care is whether there are enough physicians to meet the nation's healthcare needs (Sataline & Wang, 2012). Currently, those arguing there are enough physicians cite comparisons to global health indicators, where the United States falls in about the middle of the range of physicians per capita when compared to other industrialized countries (CodeBlueNow!, 2008). However, those on the other side of the issue cite the large numbers of specialist physicians compared to primary care physicians (only about 35% of all physicians) as evidence that the U.S. per capita ratio is overestimated (AAMC, 2011).

An argument also exists as to the adequacy of the future physician supply. Those who believe enough physicians are being trained point to the increase in the amount of nursing and home care in addition to the increasing role of other providers, such as physician assistants, nurse practitioners, and pharmacists, which all serve to extend the supply of physicians. Those who argue the nation will not have enough physicians in the coming years point to the increasing age of the population and the increase in the number of insured lives resulting from the Patient Protection and Affordable Care Act of 2010.

The sheer number of practicing physicians makes them important pharmaceutical industry customers. According to the Association of American Medical Colleges (AAMC), there are currently about 680,000 actively practicing physicians (AAMC, 2011). Further, there are approximately 97,000 enrolled medical school (MD) and osteopathic medical college (DO) students. Finally, each of the 680,000 physicians sees multiple patients daily, with many visits resulting in a prescription. According to the Centers for Disease Control and Prevention (CDC) national health statistics, there were nearly 1 billion physician office visits in 2010 (Schiller, Lucas, Ward, & Peregoy, 2012), which generated approximately 4 billion prescriptions. This number includes both new prescription orders by physicians as well as refill prescriptions. Generally, new prescriptions are about 40% of the prescriptions filled (Kaiser Family Foundation, 2010).

How pharmaceutical manufacturers provide the necessary drug and medical information needed by physicians has evolved over the last 50 years as physicians' time and pharmaceutical industry access to physicians have decreased. Even though pharmaceutical manufacturers are still the primary providers and sponsors of continuing medical education (CME), gone are the days when pharmaceutical manufacturers could shower physicians with gifts and trips that provided information while trying to entice written prescriptions. Further, based on the voluntary yet universally followed Pharmaceutical Research and Manufacturers of America (PhRMA) Code on Interactions with Healthcare Professionals (PhRMA, n.d.), the popular "reminder items" such as pens and coffee mugs with a product's name on it have disappeared. The code describes guidelines that manufacturers should follow in their interactions with healthcare providers, including rules on educational items, consultant arrangements, meals, and support of educational events, such as CME, speaker programs and speaker training meetings, scholarships and educational funds, interactions with healthcare providers on formulary committees or developers of clinical practice guidelines, and use of prescriber data. This code is meant to help member companies comply with the Office of Inspector General (OIG) guidelines and relevant laws and regulations. Even given these restrictions, pharmaceutical manufacturers spend approximately $12 billion to $16 billion annually on marketing to physicians (Blumenthal, 2004; Deloitte, n.d.).

The staple and still primary route of information delivery is through pharmaceutical manufacturer sales representatives and medical science liaisons (MSLs). The roles of these two professionals differ with respect to compliance with industry regulations and the topics they are allowed to discuss: The sales representative focuses on product promotion, while the MSL cannot promote product sales and functions instead as the drug and medical information expert. MSLs, in particular, work to identify and develop various experts, or key opinion leaders (KOLs), within their field or disease specialty. KOLs often serve as speakers or information experts who perform a variety of functions depending on need, such as consulting for clinical trial design or presenting clinical trial data at a national conference. KOLs, usually leading physicians, expand the pharmaceutical manufacturer's reach and information delivery network.

Pharmaceutical manufacturers have also begun to harness the power of the Internet for information delivery. Product-specific websites now exist for most all branded medications and include a separate section for prescribers and other healthcare professionals. In addition, many manufacturers now operate disease-specific educational websites and online communities. Perhaps most important in today's society, manufacturers are now communicating through mobile technologies, including tablet and smartphone messaging and applications. Pharmaceutical marketers can deliver product messages to physicians' personal devices without incurring the expense of a sales representative. The messages can be changed as needed in real time, are customized according to the recipient, and even provide the ability to receive physician feedback. Obviously, as technology evolves, pharmaceutical manufacturers must continue to adapt their information delivery methods to ensure that they meet the information needs of their physician customers in the most cost-effective and efficient manner.

Pharmacies

One of the pharmaceutical manufacturers' largest direct customers is the community pharmacy. Pharmacies across the country that dispense medications have to keep in stock the manufacturers' products in order to provide these medications to consumers. As mentioned earlier, prescription volume has continued to grow over the past few decades, with almost 4 billion prescriptions (including both new and refill prescriptions) filled in the community pharmacy setting in 2010, approximately 40% more than a decade earlier (Kaiser Family Foundation, n.d.).

The primary business needs of pharmacies are the best possible pricing and consistency of supply. Even though community pharmacies offer a variety of services to patients, much of the community pharmacy business model is tied to dispensing prescription products. Inability to stock their shelves with adequate inventory to meet consumers' needs hurts the bottom line and can also drastically reduce patient care and customer service levels. In addition to a consistent supply of medications, pharmacy buyers need manufacturers to ensure their medications can be reimbursed by third-party payers (e.g., insurance companies, pharmacy benefits managers, and the government through Medicare or Medicaid). Typically, the first question a practicing community pharmacist asks a pharmaceutical manufacturer's sales representative is whether the medication is included and preferred on the Medicaid formulary. The answer to this question has a significant impact on the numbers of prescriptions generated for that product.

To meet the needs of their community pharmacy customers, pharmaceutical manufacturers work diligently to provide the best possible pricing and maintain supply chain links. Firms that are successful in these functions typically have the marketing department working closely with both the pricing department (if it exists; at some companies the marketing department decides pricing issues) and the manufacturing division. In these cases, sudden changes in pricing or supply in the marketplace can be quickly communicated through marketing to the rest of the company. The company can then efficiently act to solve any customer problems as well as reconduct its own analyses for forecasting and planning purposes.

CASE IN POINT 2-2
Various Pharmacy Customer Types

Pharmaceutical manufacturers primarily meet pharmacy customer needs associated with price on a customer-by-customer basis. By negotiating with a national chain pharmacy differently from how they negotiate with smaller, regionally located independent pharmacy buying groups, manufacturers base the price variable on customer buying power and how much market share the customer can drive.

One primary categorization for manufacturers as a starting point in pricing negotiations is whether the chain pharmacy has its own warehouse for medications. If so, the pharmacy is classified as a **warehousing chain** that buys medications directly from the manufacturer, has the product shipped to its own warehouse, and then subsequently distributes the medications to its individual stores when necessary. Pharmacy chain customers that do not have warehouses, **nonwarehousing chains**, typically negotiate directly with the manufacturer and then work through a wholesaler for day-to-day shipments of medication. Independently owned pharmacies often negotiate through a **buying group**, or multiple pharmacies banding together as a single unit to buy medications directly from pharmaceutical manufacturers, so as to increase their buying power (i.e., lower prices) and, ultimately, improve their bottom-line profits.

Most manufacturers set prices based on customer type, for example, categorizing the different types of chain customers, wholesalers, mail-order pharmacies, hospital buying groups, and others into different pricing levels. Then, as with any item bought in bulk or at large-dollar volumes, the pricing level is only that—a starting point for negotiation.

Wholesalers

How do drugs reach the pharmacy? Do manufacturers deliver their medications to individual pharmacies? Logistically, that would be next to impossible given the thousands upon thousands of community pharmacies throughout the United States. Thus, the role of the wholesaler is created, and the need for supply chain management. For medications made in manufacturing facilities around the world to end up in a local community pharmacy, wholesalers serve as the warehousing and distribution arm and are vital to the success and survival of the pharmaceutical industry.

Over time, the pharmaceutical wholesale industry evolved in a very similar fashion to pharmaceutical manufacturers. In the 1960s and 1970s, without the aid of today's technologies, pharmaceutical wholesaling was primarily a retail business driven by sales representatives who made daily or weekly sales visits to pharmacies and called in medication orders to the warehouse. Once the order was placed, the product was then delivered within a few days. The core business of wholesalers revolved around the **pick, pack, and ship model**. As technology advanced and enabled ordering and delivery to become more efficient, wholesalers began to expand their service offerings into, for example, reimbursement, packaging, and consulting, otherwise known as **value-added services**.

As buyers of medications and customers of pharmaceutical manufacturers, wholesalers need the best available pricing and a consistent supply of medications. Given the continual pricing pressure applied by manufacturers and the competition, the years have brought constant profit erosion, and it has become generally accepted knowledge that the pick, pack, and ship component of the wholesale industry works off very small margins (profit), typically in the 2–4% range. Further, wholesalers traditionally bought, held, and then sold medications as their main revenue model. Recently, the model has evolved into a **fee-for-service (FFS) model** in which manufacturers pay wholesalers a fee based on the

CASE IN POINT 2-3
AmerisourceBergen

In keeping with the evolution of the industry, AmerisourceBergen Corporation (ABC)—created in 2001 with the merger of Amerisource Health and Bergen Brunswig—has expanded its reach outside of the core pick, pack, and ship model for pharmaceutical products. ABC also has a specialty group that handles various biologic medications and their distribution, consulting services companies that work with manufacturers and healthcare providers to maximize efficiency in all areas, and World Courier, which specializes in logistics for global clinical trial administration and distribution.

services (e.g., ordering technology, emergency shipments, contract administration, returns processing) provided (Baumer, 2005).

In addition to price erosion, the wholesale industry was marked by increasing competition in the marketplace, leading to the same fate as befell the pharmaceutical manufacturer industry: increased consolidation through mergers. Currently, the wholesale industry is dominated by three large, multi-billion-dollar firms that have eliminated or bought up a majority of the competition: AmerisourceBergen, Cardinal Health, and McKesson. At this point, the "Big 3" wholesalers control approximately 85% of the market share in the United States (Fein, 2011).

General Consumers/Patients

In 1997, in response to a growing use by manufacturers of direct-to-consumer (DTC) advertising for medications, the FDA released a "Draft Guidance for Industry" document addressing the DTC issue and, in particular, television-based medication advertisements (final version released in August 1999) (Food and Drug Administration, 1999). These new regulations (broadcast advertising had been greatly restricted prior to this) allowed manufacturers to advertise their specific medications in television commercials and led to an extreme growth period in pharmaceutical advertising directed at general consumers. In fact, the average American television viewer is exposed to as much as 30 hours of prescription drug advertisements annually (Brownfield et al., 2004), and television ad spending accounts for the majority of DTC spending (Arnold, 2006).

This expansion of television advertising coupled with the evolution of communication, information availability, and the Internet has led to a new age model of healthcare dynamics and **shared decision making**. No longer are information, knowledge, and choice of drugs driven by the physician/prescriber, but typically the consumer/patient actively participates and works with the physician/prescriber to determine the best treatment choice based on the individual's unique wants and desires. Given this change, the general consumer/patient has become a primary customer of pharmaceutical manufacturers, with both healthcare and information needs.

Pharmaceutical manufacturers' products are intended to meet the most basic needs of consumers with healthcare issues: improved health outcomes, increased quality of life, and prevention (or cure) of long-term complications and disease. Although the types of products researched and eventually produced vary by manufacturer and market conditions, each product aims to affect one of the areas described. (Here, *products* refers to branded and innovator products rather than generic products, for which the primary focus is making sure the quality of the drug is equivalent to the branded/innovator product.) Even medications viewed primarily as lifestyle choices (e.g., Viagra [sildenafil]) can work to enhance quality of life and well-being of the individuals taking them. Pharmaceutical manufacturers spend billions annually on product research and development to discover new entities to meet consumer/patient needs and improve the efficacy and effectiveness of existing therapies. In fact, in 2011, PhRMA members spent approximately $49.5 billion on product research and development (PhRMA, 2012). With this investment over time, manufacturers have made great advancements in all treatment areas, particularly in the areas of cancer, HIV, rheumatoid arthritis, and multiple sclerosis. Further, as the industry moves forward, pharmacogenomics and the ability to tailor a medication to an individual's (or group of individuals') DNA offers endless possibilities.

A driving force behind consumer information needs has been the expansion of consumerism and general consumer involvement (referred to as shared decision making) in healthcare decisions. With consumers playing a greater role in healthcare decisions, including the choice of a drug product, pharmaceutical manufacturers have learned they must provide much more nontechnical medical information to the general consumer. One way manufacturers have accomplished this has been the proliferation of DTC ads since the late 1990s. The use of DTC ads has created a far more consumer-driven pharmaceutical manufacturer than ever before. In addition to the information provided to consumers, pharmaceutical manufacturers continue to expand the channels of communication with consumers, including use of personal electronic technology and social media.

Third-Party Payers

One dynamic unique to health care (and the insurance business in general) is when insurance is involved in the payment for services; often patients are not responsible for the greatest majority of payment. Thus, a patient can use physician services at little or no cost. In general, well exams might be covered 100% or be zero cost to the patient. This means a patient can go to the physician for an annual checkup and leave the office without paying a penny, with the health insurance company, or third-party payer, paying the physician fees. To clarify the terminology, the *first party* is the patient/consumer, the *second party* is the physician, and the *third party* is the insurance company that pays for the services rendered. The same low/no-cost possibilities exist for obtaining a prescription. Just as the insurance company pays the physician, the prescription health insurance payer, typically called a **pharmacy benefits manager**, or **PBM**, pays the pharmacy a contracted amount for the prescription dispensed. In their current form, third-party payers are not "direct" customers of pharmaceutical manufacturers because they do not actually buy, stock, dispense, and sell medications (except for PBM-owned **mail-order pharmacies**, which do buy, stock, and dispense medication). They are, however, manufacturer customers given their ultimate responsibility for prescription claim payment and the dynamics of the U.S. reimbursement system.

Third-party payers reimburse pharmacies based on a variety of mechanisms, including reimbursement formulas, usual and customary prices, reimbursement based on the "lower of" a series of potential reimbursement rates, a maximum allowable cost (MAC), or an upper limit on product cost (also called a federal upper limit, or FUL). Third-party reimbursement to pharmacies is based on benchmark prices created, controlled, and published by pharmaceutical manufacturers for third-party payers to use in reimbursement formulas. These benchmark prices include the following:

- *Average wholesale price (AWP):* Typical reimbursement formula of AWP minus a discount plus a fee paid to the pharmacy for dispensing the prescription, calculated as follows:

Reimbursement = AWP – % Discount + Dispensing fee

- *Wholesale acquisition cost (WAC):* Typical reimbursement formula of WAC plus a percentage plus the dispensing fee, calculated as follows:

Reimbursement = WAC + % + Dispensing fee

Pharmacy profit margin then depends on the difference between the negotiated acquisition cost with the manufacturer or wholesaler and the reimbursement amount.

Pharmaceutical marketers operating in the industry need to be aware of the various aspects of third-party reimbursement. For products to be reimbursed by third-party payers, manufacturers must report benchmark prices to the pricing compendia, such as First DataBank and Redbook. Failure to publish benchmark prices (either AWP or WAC) effectively excludes manufacturers' products from coverage by third-party insurers and, in turn, decreases their market share dramatically.

The primary third-party payer is the federal government. Through the Medicare (for older adults and persons with disabilities) and Medicaid (for individuals below a specific income level) programs, the federal government pays for approximately

40% of all prescription drug expenditures (Kaiser Family Foundation, n.d.). Other entities functioning as third-party payers are private insurers/insurance companies, such as BlueCross BlueShield, Aetna, and United Healthcare, and pharmacy benefits managers (PBMs), such as CVS Caremark and Express Scripts.

CASE IN POINT 2-4
AWP Litigation

When manufacturers do not follow the OIG guidelines for price reporting of benchmark prices, a situation could exist in which the actual price paid by the customer (e.g., chain pharmacy) greatly differs from the amount reimbursed by the government as payer. The difference between the price paid for the product and the amount reimbursed for the product is referred to as the **reimbursement spread**.

Prudent pharmaceutical marketers know the dynamics of the marketplace, including what customers want, price levels, costs, and other barriers to entry (patents and other regulatory barriers such as exclusivity, production and supply issues), before the manufacturer enters the market, and they monitor these variables continually. When market conditions deteriorate to the point where a manufacturer can no longer profitably meet the competition and win sales, the manufacturer must decide whether to continue production and remain in the market. This kind of decision is common in industry and must be continually evaluated. Creating a differential product advantage by reporting inflated benchmark prices to enhance reimbursement spread disrupts marketplace dynamics and shifts the burden of financing a product's benefit from the manufacturer to Medicaid and other third-party payers.

Over the past decade, whistleblowers have filed lawsuits based on a provision of the federal False Claims Act. Through these lawsuits, the federal government and various state Medicaid programs have recovered billions of dollars from pharmaceutical manufacturers that reported inflated AWPs in comparison to actual acquisition costs (Harris, 2008; Voreacos, 2012; Voreacos & Fisk, 2012).

Given their role as payers in the healthcare and pharmaceutical industries, these customers focus on price as their primary need. Associated with price are the reimbursement benchmark prices. In accordance with the Office of Inspector General compliance guidance of May 2003, manufacturers must set and publish reimbursement benchmarks that reflect prices generally and currently paid in the marketplace (OIG, 2003). Therefore, third-party payers, in particular the federal government, need pharmaceutical manufacturers to comply with the OIG guidance and report accurate prices.

ISSUES UNIQUE TO THE PHARMACEUTICAL MARKET

Just as in any other industry, external factors and pressures apply to the pharmaceutical industry on a daily basis. Whether it is the latest round of negative press on the rise of prescription drug costs or the passing of new healthcare reform laws, the external environment in which the pharmaceutical industry operates changes on a daily and weekly basis. This section discusses the specific positive and controversial issues unique to the pharmaceutical industry and market, focusing on the industry's various social, ethical, legal, and political environments.

Social Environment

"Do more, feel better, live longer" and "to serve patients." These simple statements are the mission statements of global pharmaceutical manufacturer GlaxoSmithKline and global biotechnology/pharmaceutical company Amgen, respectively. While countless space and time could be used to discuss the advances and innovations of the pharmaceutical industry in areas such as cancer, HIV/AIDS, and cardiovascular disease, from the societal perspective, the pharmaceutical industry and its discoveries have not only saved countless lives, but improved health outcomes (which provides a positive economic impact) and quality of life for millions of people.

In addition to its impact on patient health and welfare, the pharmaceutical industry is a massive economic engine. The most recent published data show the industry is directly responsible for more than 670,000 jobs and indirectly responsible for another 3.4 million, bringing the total to more than 4 million jobs produced (Battelle Technology Partnership Practice, 2011). Further, with the average annual wage of more than $105,000 in pharmaceuticals, the jobs created supply almost double the salary of the next highest group among all U.S.

manufacturing sectors, with $85 billion in tax revenue also created for local, state, and federal governments. The overall economic impact of the U.S. biopharmaceutical industry is estimated to be approximately $918 billion (Archstone Consulting & Burns, 2009; Battelle Technology Partnership Practice, 2011).

Even with these positive economic benefits, the pharmaceutical industry is often criticized for increasing overall healthcare costs through rising prescription drug prices. The exponential rise in direct-to-consumer advertising spending over the last 15 years has sparked the debate about its effect on increasing drug use and whether DTC advertising has created a world in which the company with the best ad agency—not the best drugs—gets the attention of consumers and prescribers. Empirical research suggests a positive correlation between DTC advertising spending and prescription drug demand and utilization, with an almost 40% increase in utilization from 1999 to 2009 and price increases over that same time span annually, on average, of 3.6% (Donohue, 2007; Kaiser Family Foundation, n.d.; Kravitz, 2005; Wilkes, 2000).

The pharmaceutical industry battles daily to try to overturn its negative public perception. For many years, the pharmaceutical industry has been at the bottom of the public approval list, typically rated as above only the tobacco industry (Arnst, 2005). The general consumer sees the large profits made by the pharmaceutical industry coupled with high and increasing prices (especially with brand medications) and does not view this favorably (FierceBiotech, 2007; Kaiser Family Foundation, 2008; Robinson, 2004).

The peak of general negativity toward the industry culminated with the removal of Vioxx (rofecoxib) from the marketplace. After a heavy DTC advertising and physician detailing campaign, the medication quickly became popular and sales soared (over 80 million doses prescribed during its time on the market). Amid mounting evidence of cardiovascular issues and media pressure, the product's manufacturer, Merck, removed the product from the market in September 2004. Numerous plaintiffs eventually took legal action against Merck, and in November 2007 Merck settled the lawsuits for $4.85 billion (Prakash & Valentine, 2007). This debacle led society to question the safety level within the pharmaceutical industry (Kaiser Family Foundation, 2008; Olsen & Whalen, 2009; Sillup & Porth, 2008).

Ethical Environment

Sell what I invent, or invent what I can sell? This question underlies the primary ethical dilemma within the pharmaceutical industry with respect to new drug discovery and the allocation of resources within the industry. As mentioned previously, pharmaceutical discoveries have saved, prolonged, and improved countless lives. However, as in any industry, the business exists to be profitable for itself and its shareholders in addition to existing over time. The pharmaceutical industry must work daily to find the right balance of profitability and not lose sight of its mission to discover new medications to alleviate pain and disease in the effort to offer consumers improved health and quality of life.

From a marketing perspective, the ethical issues and influencers within the industry center on the various communications by manufacturers. Whether it is sales reps or MSL interactions with physicians or advertising aimed at the general consumer, the pharmaceutical industry walks a fine line in promoting products yet still being able to promote the best healthcare decisions for patients. The following examples describe various ethical issues:

- *Interactions with healthcare professionals.* Many professions and professional organizations have guidelines on how to interact with the pharmaceutical industry, including, for example, the American College of Clinical Pharmacy (ACCP, 2008). The guidelines are primarily based on the PhRMA Code on Interactions with Healthcare Professionals (PhRMA, n.d.). Updated in 2009, the code lays out how pharmaceutical manufacturers should proceed ethically in their communications with all healthcare professionals. Areas covered include dealing with speakers, support of continuing medical education (CME), prohibition against entertainment and recreation (e.g., avoid offering trips or tickets to the big game to physicians or others), and representative training.

- *Off-label promotion/communication.* One area not covered directly by the PhRMA code is off-label communications. In all their communications, pharmaceutical manufacturers can discuss only approved indications; otherwise, they may (and have) become involved in a lawsuit by knowingly communicating and promoting a medication for non-FDA-approved uses. During the period from January 2001 to March 2009, pharmaceutical manufacturers paid almost $3 billion to settle cases involving off-label marketing/promotion of certain medications (Kesselheim, 2010).

- *Price reporting/communication.* As mentioned earlier, manufacturers must report to the pricing compendia prices that reflect values generally and currently paid in the marketplace (OIG, 2003). Failure to do so has led to numerous lawsuits from which payers have recovered billions from pharmaceutical manufacturers.

- *Publication practices.* Pharmaceutical manufacturers' relationships with providers, particularly physicians, must walk a fine line. This is especially true when it comes to the publication of clinical trial results. Clinical trials are conducted for new drugs to show safety and efficacy for FDA approval. Clinical trials are also typically published in the medical literature. Over the years, the publishing practices of pharmaceutical manufacturer–sponsored literature have been scrutinized, particularly with the issue of ghost writing. **Ghost writing** refers to the process when the work of an original creator or contributor is then credited to another author. In the pharmaceutical industry, outside writers (unaffiliated with the pharmaceutical company) often draft articles for publication in medical journals based on data provided by pharmaceutical manufacturers. Various guidelines exist for the publication process, including those from the International Committee of Medical Journal Editors and Wager et al. (2003) in *Current Medical Research and Opinion.*

Political and Legal/Regulatory Environment

Legal constraints and influences are also a part of the daily changes taking place in and around the pharmaceutical industry. Closely intertwined with this area is the political arena. Since the early 1900s, political leaders have enacted laws greatly affecting health care in the United States, including the original Food, Drug, and Cosmetic Act and its amendments and, most recently, the Patient Protection and Affordable Care Act signed into law in March 2010 and upheld by the Supreme Court. Prompted by citizen concern over access and quality, health care is typically always a part of state and federal political discussions and campaigns.

Not only do the legal and political environments affect the industry from a regulatory standpoint, but the government also functions as a large payer in the marketplace (through Medicare, Medicaid, and the Department of Defense), thus creating a situation in which politics and legislation could possibly be altered heavily given that role. State laws and regulations also influence the industry, chiefly with regard to how the Medicaid program is run in each state. Manufacturers are continually in contact with all state providers to ensure preferred formulary status for their medications. Overall, the political and legal environment in which the pharmaceutical industry exists has changed over time with regard to the manner in which drugs come to market, are distributed, and are dispensed.

CASE IN POINT 2-5
Pharmaceutical Manufacturers' Lobbying Efforts

Just as other entities and groups as profitable as the pharmaceutical industry do, pharmaceutical manufacturers spend big to protect their interests in the political arena. From 1990 to 2008, those in the industry contributed approximately $167 million to federal candidates' election campaigns. In addition, the industry's federal government lobbying efforts totaled more than $1.5 billion in the decade 1998–2008, with a ratio of two pharmaceutical lobbyists for each member of Congress (Americans for Campaign Reform, n.d.; Drinkard, 2005).

ISSUES UNIQUE TO PHARMACEUTICAL MARKETING

As discussed earlier, marketing is a process that works to create value for customers through the exchange process. Although all pharmaceutical marketers must recognize and work within the bounds of the unique nature of the external environment, they must differentiate in terms of how drugs are marketed based on classification, specifically whether a medication is prescription or over-the-counter (OTC) and whether it is a brand or generic medication. Each of these situations offers differing sets of primary customers and needs.

Prescription vs. Over-the-Counter Drugs

Given that both prescription and OTC drugs are medications used to treat many of the same conditions, one might assume the products are marketed using the same tactics and promotional ideas. However, although there are similarities to the underlying messaging, the primary customers and their needs are different for each type of medication. In the prescription environment, pharmaceutical manufacturer customers include physicians, consumers, pharmacies, wholesalers, and third-party payers. All customers work, albeit not necessarily together, to decide which product is ultimately dispensed. For OTC medications, however, the customer base is quite different.

The physician and third-party payer are not a primary concern to an OTC marketer. Even though a physician is usually aware of an OTC product (especially if it was previously a prescription product, such as Prilosec [omeprazole]), the OTC manufacturer typically does not detail or call on physicians because of physicians' low level of choice power. Instead, the OTC marketer focuses on the customer with the highest level of choice power: the general consumer.

Given the lack of an intermediary in the OTC market space (i.e., physician/prescriber), the OTC market behaves much like the traditional consumer goods market. Thus, the primary focus of the OTC product marketer is creating a recognizable and remembered brand, such as the "nighttime, sniffling, sneezing, coughing, aching, best-sleep-you-ever-got-with-a-cold medicine" or the "Mucinex in, mucus out" medication. As with other consumer goods, numerous private-label and store brands exist on the shelf right next to the branded product, with great price differences among them. For example, Sam's Club's "Simply Right" private-label brand loratadine costs approximately $13 for two 200-count bottles, while the brand-name Claritin costs approximately $35 for one 90-count bottle. From a marketing perspective, this situation is common in almost every consumer good category, and is why OTC marketers work hard to place their brand and its quality above reproach and to remove the price variable from the consumers' choice equation.

OTC marketing and promotions are focused on the consumer as well as the pharmacist. Given their accessibility within community pharmacies and mass merchandisers (the "place" for OTC products) and their role in product recommendation, it makes sense for OTC marketers to call on pharmacists and advertise in community pharmacy–focused magazines and publications such as *Drug Topics*.

Brand vs. Generic

In 1984, the Drug Price Competition and Patent Term Restoration Act (1984), better known as the Hatch-Waxman Act, gave rise to the modern-day generic pharmaceutical industry. No longer did generic manufacturers have to go through the same approval process as their innovator/brand counterparts, but could execute approvals in a fraction of the time. In fact, prior to the passing of the Hatch-Waxman Act, approximately 35% of innovator drugs had generics available even with an expired patent (Rouhi, 2002). Generic manufacturers now continue to climb the sales rankings even given the lower prices of their medications.

As noted earlier, the primary customer and marketing focus of brand manufacturers and innovator companies is the physician. In addition, general consumers and third-party payers are important target audiences so that specific drugs can develop brand loyalty and maintain preferred status on a given formulary.

However, in the generics industry, medications are considered to be a commodity (i.e., interchangeable), and thus the marketing of these products differs from that of other consumer goods because the focus of the marketing mix (i.e., the four Ps: price, place, product, and promotion) is on price. The other primary difference in generic manufacturers' customer and marketing mixes is the absence of the physician as a primary focus. The product selected by the physician is usually available from a number of manufacturers, each competing for market share. Although physicians still choose which medications patients need, pharmacy providers select the company that will supply the medication. Other members of the distribution channel can also affect the pharmacy's supplier decision by participating in buying groups and wholesaler source programs. Consequently, pharmaceutical manufacturers of generics focus their marketing efforts on pharmacy providers.

Regardless of product type, though, effective marketing in the pharmaceutical industry is based on being able to meet customer needs. For generic medications, pharmacy buyers must also seek consistency of supply and high product quality. Other product benefits, such as a company's ability to supply a full line of generic products, or "one-stop shopping," can also be important to generic pharmaceutical purchasers. Thus, price is the most salient evaluative criterion, and pharmacy providers seek out the lowest prices for products that meet quality requirements and

CASE IN POINT 2-6
Pfizer's Unique Strategy for Lipitor

Recently, in an effort to overlap the brand and generic pharmaceutical industries, Pfizer used a unique marketing strategy when its multi-billion-dollar blockbuster medication Lipitor (atorvastatin) was about to become generically available. To maximize profits as long as possible for the highly successful medication, Pfizer basically sold the medication to consumers using a $4 copay card backed up with a heavy DTC advertising campaign, as well as to insurers/payers through deep discounts and rebates. Although Pfizer still lost a large portion of market share, it lost it at a rate much slower than a typical blockbuster drug coming off patent. Given the financial success of Pfizer's marketing strategy, an increased use of this tactic is likely as many more blockbuster medications come off patent in the coming years (Fein, 2012; Silverman, 2011).

that can be adequately and consistently supplied. Commodity manufacturers, such as those in the generics industry, might hold to a more *product oriented* rather than *customer oriented* marketing philosophy. A customer (or market) orientation implies that a firm seeks to understand a market, develop an awareness of customer needs and wants, and then strive to develop a product or product line that satisfies these needs. A product orientation indicates that a generic manufacturer first produces a product, and then seeks to sell in the marketplace as much of the product as possible, recognizing that the focus in the marketplace is primarily on the price variable.

CASE IN POINT 2-7
How Does a Drug Get Its Names, Both Brand and Generic?

Lipitor, Viagra, Tylenol, and Prozac. Branding in the pharmaceutical industry is just as important as it is for any consumer good. But how does a chemical entity that started in the laboratory referred to as, for example, ABC-123, eventually become Ambien or Prozac? Further, where do the generic names, such as zolpidem and fluoxetine, originate?

First, a group known as the United States Adopted Name Council (USANC) initiates the generic/chemical name of a new drug (zolpidem and fluoxetine, in this example). This council is made up of five representatives, one each from the American Medical Association, United States Pharmacopoeia (USP), American Pharmacists Association (APhA), the FDA, and an at-large member (American Medical Association [AMA], n.d.b). When a manufacturer applies for a name, usually during Phase II clinical trials, the USANC works until a name agreeable to the council, manufacturer, and International Nonproprietary Names Expert Group is determined (World Health Organization, 2012). There can be only one name used around the globe for a generic/active ingredient.

The USANC considers three primary issues in the naming process: whether the name reflects the medication's mechanism, the name's ability to be translated to other languages, and the general ease of pronunciation of the name (AMA, n.d.a). In addition to the prefixes and infixes used to complete the name, the core component is the stem, which typically identifies the medication's class/group. For example, "oxetine" is the stem for *fluoxetine* and identifies the drug class known as selective serotonin reuptake inhibitors (SSRIs). Another example is "pril," which is the stem for the names of angiotensin-converting enzyme (ACE) inhibitors used for blood pressure and cardiovascular health.

To create brand and trade names of drugs, pharmaceutical manufacturers complete extensive marketing research to identify the most beneficial name. Their own marketing departments and/or market research firms identify and test dozens of names for consumer response.

For example, the name *Ambien* is formed from *am* (morning) and *bien* (good), aiming to enable the user to have a good morning after a great night's sleep. Premarin's name comes from where the product is derived: PREgnant MAre's uRINe. Although not every medication can be named as cleverly as Ambien or Premarin, at least an exhaustive list of possibilities is explored before a name is picked.

SUMMARY

The pharmaceutical industry and market in which it exists create a complex interaction of environmental factors, including government regulations; cultures and norms; high technological barriers to entry; multiple primary customers, each with their own needs; and competition. From a marketing perspective, the key is to understand the various roles of these environmental factors and to design pharmaceutical products consistent with consumer needs. Although the pharmaceutical industry as a whole continues to grow and be profitable, the high growth volume seen in the 2000s has been replaced by fewer blockbuster drugs, declining sales, shrinking workforces, and increased scrutiny by those external to the industry. Yet, the industry remains largely profitable.

Various opinions have surfaced on what the industry can do to recapture its growth (Chase, 2012; Denning, 2012). Perhaps the pharmaceutical industry must take a lesson from the experiences of one of its customers: the wholesale industry. While maintaining its core pick, pack, and ship business model, the industry has continued to grow with the provision of value-added services (including technology). Knowledge of the components of the pharmaceutical industry helps identify areas for growth and opportunity.

It is clear that new models of operation in the industry are desired. Given the success of pharmaceutical companies over the last 50 years, it seems clear this industry will continue to prevail in the face of rapidly changing environmental factors, new technology, and an aging and needy world population.

DISCUSSION QUESTIONS

1. Describe the differences between physician needs versus patient needs with regard to pharmaceutical products. Whose needs are more important?
2. What is meant by the term *directed demand,* and how does this concept affect most everything a pharmaceutical manufacturer does to promote its medications? Are there any similarities in the OTC market?
3. The pharmaceutical manufacturer invents and markets the drugs that doctors prescribe and patients take. Explain why an insurance company should or should not be involved in this exchange transaction.
4. Should the large number of U.S. physicians be considered a marketing opportunity or threat to pharmaceutical manufacturers? Why?
5. What are the pros and cons of a pharmaceutical manufacturer downsizing its sales force and increasing its medical science liaison presence?
6. Why can it be considered a "death knell" for a pharmaceutical product to be excluded from formulary coverage?
7. The rise in DTC advertising has provided information to consumers that they can use to recognize a problem, seek care, and gain awareness of diseases, vaccines, and treatments. These all seem to be positive aspects of DTC advertising. Describe some possible negative consequences of providing increased information to consumers through pharmaceutical marketing.
8. Considering your response to question 7 and the marketing implications, what would pharmaceutical manufacturers do to promote their products if the FDA banned DTC advertising? What if the FDA banned only television commercials?
9. Should pharmaceutical manufacturers be able to justify spending similar amounts on research and development compared to marketing expenditures? (*Hint:* Recall the three primary consumers and each consumer's unique needs.)
10. Comment on any ethical issues you might consider relevant to the funding of biomedical research by pharmaceutical manufacturers.

REFERENCES

ACCP. (2008). Pharmacists and industry: guidelines for ethical interactions. *Pharmacotherapy*, *28*(3), 410–420.

American Medical Association. (n.d.a). Generic naming. Retrieved from http://www.ama-assn.org/ama/pub/physician-resources/medical-science/united-states-adopted-names-council/generic-drug-naming-explained.page

American Medical Association. (n.d.b). United States adopted names. Retrieved from http://www.ama-assn.org/ama/pub/physician-resources/medical-science/united-states-adopted-names-council.page

Americans for Campaign Reform. (n.d.). Money in politics and prescription drugs. Retrieved from http://www.acrreform.org/research/money-in-politics-prescription-drugs/

Archstone Consulting & Burns, L. R. (2009, March). The biopharmaceutical sector's impact on the U.S. economy: Analysis at the national, state, and local levels. Retrieved from http://www.archstoneconsulting.com/biopharmapdf/report.pdf

Arnold, M. (2006). Merck image ad spend up. *Medical Marketing & Media*, *41*(6), 16.

Arnst, C. (2005, December 8). Big Pharma seeks an image cure. *Businessweek*. Retrieved from http://www.businessweek.com/print/technology/content/dec2005/tc20051208_397864.htm

Association of American Medical Colleges. (2011). 2011 state physician workforce data book. Retrieved from https://www.aamc.org/download/263512/data/statedata2011.pdf

Battelle Technology Partnership Practice. (2011, July). The U.S. biopharmaceuticals sector: Economic contribution to the nation. Retrieved from http://www.phrma.org/sites/default/files/159/2011_battelle_report_on_economic_impact.pdf

Baumer, D. L. (2005, September). Fee for service: Distribution of pharmaceuticals. Retrieved from http://www.iaccm.com/members/library/files/Fee_For_Service_White_paper%5B1%5D.pdf

Blumenthal, D. (2004). Doctors and drug companies. *New England Journal of Medicine*, *351*, 1885–1890.

Brownfield, E. D., Bernhardt, J. M., Phan, J. L., Williams, M. V., & Parker, R. M. (2004). Direct-to-consumer drug advertisements on network television: An exploration of quantity, frequency, and placement. *Journal of Health Communication*, *9*(6), 491–497.

Chase, D. (2012, July 28). IBM's reinvention should inspire flat pharma businesses. *Forbes*. Retrieved from http://www.forbes.com/sites/davechase/2012/07/28/ibms-reinvention-should-inspire-flat-pharma-businesses/

CodeBlueNow! (2008, May). Comparison of health care systems. Retrieved from http://conversations.psu.edu/docs/calkins_comparison.pdf

Deloitte. (n.d.). Taking a fresh look: The progression of the pharmaceutical marketing and sales model. Retrieved from http://www.deloitte.com/assets/Dcom-Global/Local%20Assets/Documents/SEA%20sales%20and%20marketing.pdf

Denning, S. (2012, March 28). What big pharma—and IBM—must rediscover: The customer. *Forbes*. Retrieved from http://www.forbes.com/sites/stevedenning/2012/03/28/what-big-pharma-and-ibm-must-rediscover-the-customer/

Donohue, J. M., Cevasco, M., & Rosenthal, M. B. (2007). A decade of direct-to-consumer advertising of prescription drugs. *New England Journal of Medicine*, *357*, 673–681.

Drinkard, J. (2005, April 25). Drugmakers go furthest to sway Congress. *USA Today*. Retrieved from http://www.usatoday.com/money/industries/health/drugs/2005-04 -25-drug-lobby-cover_x.htm

Fein, A. (2011, May 26). 2011 MDM market leaders: Top pharmaceutical wholesalers. *Modern Distribution Management*. Retrieved from http://www.mdm .com/2011_ pharmaceutical_mdm-market-leaders

Fein, A. J. (2012, March 15). Pfizer's Lipitor strategy and the 2012 generic monster. Drug Channels. Retrieved from http://www.drugchannels.net/2012/03/pfizers-lipitor -strategy-and-2012.html

FierceBiotech. (2007, January 9). Press release: Consumers and pharmaceutical companies far apart on views of pharma industry. Retrieved from http://www.fiercebiotech.com /node/5167

Food and Drug Administration (1999, August). Guidance for industry: Consumer-directed broadcast advertisements. Retrieved from http://www.fda.gov/downloads /RegulatoryInformation/Guidances/ucm125064.pdf

Harris, K. D. (2008, December 3). The average wholesale price litigation: A report from the front lines. Retrieved from http://www.amcp.org/WorkArea/DownloadAsset .aspx?id=11395

Kaiser Family Foundation. (n.d.). United States: Prescription drugs. Retrieved from http://www.statehealthfacts.org/profileind.jsp?sub=66&rgn=1&cat=5

Kaiser Family Foundation. (2008, April). Views on prescription drugs and the pharmaceutical industry. *Kaiser Public Opinion Spotlight*. Retrieved from http://www.kff.org /spotlight/rxdrugs/upload/rx_drugs.pdf

Kaiser Family Foundation. (2010, May). Prescription drug trends. Publication No. 3057-08. Retrieved from http://www.kff.org/rxdrugs/upload/3057-08.pdf

Kesselheim, A. S., Studdert, D. M., & Mello, M. M. (2010, May). Whistle-blowers' experiences in fraud litigation against pharmaceutical companies. *New England Journal of Medicine, 362*(19), 1832–1839.

Kravitz R. L., Epstein R. M., Feldman M. D., Franz C. E., Azari R., Wilkes, M. S., et al. (2005). Influence of patients' requests for direct-to-consumer advertised antidepressants. *Journal of the American Medical Association, 293*(16), 1995–2002.

Office of Inspector General. (2003, May 5). OIG compliance program guidance for pharmaceutical manufacturers. *Federal Register, 68*(86), 23731–23743. Retrieved from http://oig.hhs.gov/authorities/docs/03/050503FRCPGPharmac.pdf

Olsen, A. K., & Whalen, M. D. (2009). Public perceptions of the pharmaceutical industry and drug safety: Implications for the pharmacovigilance professional and the culture of safety. *Drug Safety, 32*(10), 805–810.

Pharmaceutical Research and Manufacturers of America. (n.d.). Code on interactions with healthcare professionals. Retrieved from http://www.phrma.org/about /principles-guidelines/code-interactions-healthcare-professionals

Pharmaceutical Research and Manufacturers of America. (2012, April). *Pharmaceutical industry profile 2012*. Washington, DC: Author. Retrieved from http://www.phrma .org/sites/default/files/159/phrma_industry_profile.pdf

Prakash, S., & Valentine, V. (2007, November 10). Timeline: The rise and fall of Vioxx. NPR. Retrieved from http://www.npr.org/templates/story/story .php?storyId=5470430

Robinson, A. R., Hohmann, K. B., Rifkin, J. I., Topp, D., Gilroy, C. M., Pickard, J. A., et al. (2004). Direct-to-consumer pharmaceutical advertising: Physician and public opinion and potential effects on the physician–patient relationship. *Archives of Internal Medicine, 164*(4), 427–432.

Rouhi, A. M. (2002, September 23). Beyond Hatch-Waxman: Legislative action seeks to close loopholes in U.S. law that delay entry of generics into the market. *Chemical and Engineering News, 80*(38), 53–59. Retrieved from http://pubs.acs.org/cen/coverstory /8038/8038biogenerics2.html

Sataline, S., & Wang, S. S. (2010, April 12). Medical schools can't keep up. *Wall Street Journal.* Retrieved from http://online.wsj.com/article/SB10001424052702304506904575180331528424238.html

Schiller, J. S., Lucas, J. W., Ward, B. W., & Peregoy, J. A. (2012). *Summary health statistics for U.S. adults: National Health Interview Survey, 2010.* National Center for Health Statistics. *Vital Health Statistics, 10*(252). Retrieved from http://www.cdc.gov/nchs /data/series/sr_10/sr10_252.pdf

Sillup, G. P. & Porth, S. J. (2008). Ethical issues in the pharmaceutical industry: An analysis of US newspapers. *International Journal of Pharmaceutical and Healthcare Marketing, 2*(3), 163–180.

Silverman, E. (2011, December 1). What managed care thinks of Pfizer and its Lipitor strategy. *Forbes.* Retrieved from http://www.forbes.com/sites/edsilverman/2011/12/01 /what-managed-care-thinks-of-pfizer-and-its-lipitor-strategy/

Surescripts. (2011). The national progress report on e-prescribing and interoperable health care, year 2011. Retrieved from http://www.surescripts.com/about-e-prescribing /progress-reports/national-progress-reports.aspx/

Voreacos, D. (2012, February 28). Mylan to pay $57 million to settle drug overpricing claims. *Bloomberg.* Retrieved from http://www.bloomberg.com/news/2012-02-28 /mylan-to-pay-57-million-to-settle-drug-overpricing-claims-1-.html

Voreacos, D., & Fisk, M. C. (2012, January 4). Actavis will pay $118.6 million to end drug-pricing claims. *Bloomberg Businessweek.* Retrieved from http://www .businessweek.com/news/2012-01-06/actavis-will-pay-118-6-million-to-end -drug-pricing-claims.html

Wager E., Field, E. A., & Grossman, L. (2003). Good publication practice for pharmaceutical companies. *Current Medical Research and Opinion, 19*(3), 149–154.

Wilkes, M. S., Bell, R. A., & Kravitz, R. L. (2000, March). Direct-to-consumer prescription drug advertising: trends, impact, and implications. *Health Affairs, 19*(2), 110–128.

World Health Organization. (2012). International nonproprietary names. Retrieved from http://www.who.int/medicines/services/inn/en/

Products in the Pharmaceutical Industry: Trends, Identification, Approval, and Monitoring

Brent L. Rollins, PhD, RPh, Randall Tackett, PhD, and Matthew Perri, PhD, RPh

LEARNING OBJECTIVES

1. Discuss how the pharmaceutical industry and its product base and pipeline have evolved over time.
2. Assess how the pharmaceutical industry identifies a good product for development and the pros and cons with each identification method.
3. Identify and describe the various pieces of legislation that affect the pharmaceutical industry and product development.
4. Identify and describe the New Drug Application (NDA) process, including compound identification and acquisition and preclinical, clinical, and postmarketing surveillance.
5. Differentiate the generic and over-the-counter (OTC) drug approval process from the prescription approval process and the impact of the difference.
6. Describe the necessary components of a prescription drug label and analyze their impact on the product's marketing efforts.

7. Characterize how research, clinical science, and medical practice affect the development of pharmaceutical products.
8. Analyze the role of marketing during the drug development and approval process, including how it influences research and development.

Since the Middle Ages, apothecaries and chemists have offered natural remedies and other "products" to those seeking relief from varying disease symptoms. Treatment with medicines was based on anecdotal evidence and tradition at best. The modern pharmaceutical industry, whose roots date back only to about the middle of the 19th century, now takes a different approach by targeting patient needs and finding solutions to their health problems. Thus, from a marketing perspective, the "product" is the result of extensive research and development of chemicals that might become medicines. This, along with investigation of what patients need, has marked the path to success.

Focusing on the discovery, research and development, testing, and marketing of new chemical entities has led to many important therapeutic advances to treat diseases such as hypertension, diabetes, asthma, and rheumatoid arthritis. For some of these innovations, the results have been impressive, leading to what have been called "blockbuster" drugs—drugs with annual sales of more than $1 billion. These include products such as the very first "blockbuster," Merck's Tagamet (cimetidine) introduced in the late 1970s; Eli Lilly's antidepressant Prozac (fluoxetine); and Pfizer's anticholesterol drug Lipitor (atorvastatin).

PRODUCT AND INDUSTRY EVOLUTION

Historically, manufacturers have been able to rely on the research and development pipeline to identify promising chemical entities. Recently, however, larger manufacturers have seen fewer successes and shrinking pipelines, and advances in technology have enabled smaller companies to excel in product discovery. These factors, as well as the overall increased level of competition, have led to an industry where manufacturers have sought to enhance pipelines and product offerings through mergers, acquisitions, and extensive consolidation.

While Pfizer's acquisition of Wyeth represents one of the largest over the past 15 years or so, from 2000 to 2009 the industry as a whole saw more

CASE IN POINT 3-1
Pfizer Acquires Wyeth

In early 2009, Pfizer, Inc., announced its $68 billion acquisition of Wyeth, Inc., which created one of the largest and most diversified companies in the global pharmaceutical industry. For Pfizer, this merger enhanced its product offerings in specific disease areas such as Alzheimer's disease, inflammation, oncology, pain, and psychosis while also improving the company's competitive position in biotherapeutics and vaccines (Pfizer, 2009).

than 1,300 mergers and acquisitions, totaling approximately $700 billion in exchanged capital (FierceBiotech, 2010). Other specific examples include Merck's $41 billion acquisition of Schering-Plough (2009), Roche's $47 billion merger with Genetech (2009), and Pfizer's $56 billion acquisition of Pharmacia Corporation (2002) (Abkowitz, 2009). Furthermore, the trend is not just limited to branded medication manufacturers because the generic pharmaceutical industry has also seen an increasing number of consolidations, including Teva Pharmaceutical Industries' acquisitions of fellow generic manufacturers Barr Pharmaceuticals (approximately $9 billion in 2008) and Ivax Corporation (approximately $8 billion in 2005) (FierceBiotech, 2010).

However, regardless of who discovers a medication, the process for bringing a new entity to market has not changed. Products are identified in scientists' laboratories and must eventually progress to the prescriber's prescription pad. This process is highly regulated, and complex scientific discoveries must be translated into practical solutions or applications. Working together, research, manufacturing, and marketing translate drug discoveries into useful medicines. In the pharmaceutical industry, for maximal success, information flows both from basic scientists to practitioners and from these practitioners back to the basic scientists about what works and what does not.

The process is not without problems and some controversy, such as the time it takes for new drugs to be reviewed or the total cost of the approval process. The U.S. Food and Drug Administration (FDA) Center for Drug Evaluation and Research (CDER) plays a major role in evaluating drugs before they are made available to the public and ensuring the safety of these products (Food and Drug Administration [FDA], 2010). Although responsible for evaluation of new products, the CDER does not conduct research related to new product development; this is the responsibility of the pharmaceutical manufacturer. Thus, using the data from manufacturers to evaluate submitted medications, the CDER employs physicians, statisticians, chemists, pharmacologists, and other scientists to review New Drug Applications (NDAs), the core document submitted to initiate the approval process.

Pharmaceutical manufacturers work within the New Drug Approval process described in this chapter to create new and innovative therapeutic entities to alleviate symptoms, provide overall improvements in patients' quality of life, and, hopefully, cure diseases. Manufacturers with this kind of patient (or customer)-oriented focus effectively manage the product variable through innovation in areas of unmet need and continuous quality improvement. Marketers who are strategically aligned with unmet patient (customer) needs are ideally positioned to compete in the modern pharmaceutical industry.

IDENTIFYING A GOOD DRUG TARGET FOR MARKETING

There are two basic components to the identification of an agent with commercial potential. Although not always aligned in this particular order, manufacturers can identify a chemical entity with promising activity and determine where it might fit into treatment regimens. Alternatively, a manufacturer can identify a promising drug for marketing by developing an understanding of a particular disease state, hormone, or neurotransmitter and breaking the disease process into components where treatments are needed, known as **rational drug discovery**. For example, angiotensin was known to be involved in the disease process related to high blood pressure, or hypertension. Through understanding the biochemistry of angiotensin formation, scientists were able to identify specific drug targets such as the enzyme responsible for its creation and the specific receptor that could be stimulated or blocked with new drug therapy. These targets became the basis for the angiotensin-converting enzyme inhibitors (ACE-I, e.g., Zestril [lisinopril] and Altace [ramipril]) and the angiotensin receptor blockers (ARBs, e.g., Diovan [valsartan].)

In another example, the statins represent a drug target identified through understanding the biochemistry of atherosclerosis and the effects of cholesterol. The enzyme HMG Co-A reductase is the rate-limiting enzyme in cholesterol synthesis. Therefore, inhibition of this enzyme was perceived as potentially effective in reducing cholesterol and treating atherosclerosis. Further, Remicade (infliximab), a monoclonal antibody used to treat rheumatoid arthritis (RA), was developed based on research in the academic arena. Inflammatory cytokines were identified as having a significant role in arthritis, and monoclonal antibodies that could inhibit these cytokines were then developed and proved to be effective in RA treatment.

In addition to new medications with unique mechanisms of action, a number of drugs on the market today are referred to as **"me-too"** drugs, or drugs with the same mechanism of action as the innovator/first-in-class medication. The pharmaceutical industry as a whole has learned that improvements to the innovator can be extremely profitable, sometimes even exceeding the innovator. The improvements on the succeeding drugs usually involve increased efficacy and effectiveness, more convenient dosage forms, a change in the duration of action, and/or a purported improvement in the side-effect profile. Any drug class with the same mechanism of action and multiple products within the class serves as an example of the me-too phenomenon, such as the ACE inhibitors and ARBs mentioned earlier.

CASE IN POINT 3-2
Therapeutic Improvement vs. Innovation

The statins, or HMG-CoA reductase inhibitors, have emerged as one of the most significant medication classes in history. These drugs work by inhibiting the enzyme responsible for the production of cholesterol in the liver and greatly reduce the incidence of future cardiovascular events. Early entrants to the market (e.g., Lescol [fluvastatin], Mevacor [lovastatin], and Pravachol [pravastatin]) were characterized by less efficacy and greater side effects. Patients and physicians readily accepted these early drugs as a means to lower cholesterol, but sought greater efficacy, fewer drug interactions, and less risk of serious side effects. The knowledge and experience gained from these early drugs paved the way for extremely successful drugs such as Zocor (simvastatin), Crestor (rosuvastatin), and Lipitor (atorvastatin), which is currently the most successful pharmaceutical product in terms of sales in the industry's history.

CASE IN POINT 3-3
The Viagra Story

Synthesized in 1989 and originally identified as UK-92,480, Viagra (sildenafil) was initially tested in clinical trials as a possible agent to treat high blood pressure and angina. Through a series of clinical trials in the early 1990s, sildenafil's effects on blood pressure and angina were found to be minimal and not significant enough for further development in these disease states. In addition, the drug had to be administered three times a day because of its short action time in the body. However, after penile erection was noticed to be a common side effect in these early trials and based on the literature of the mechanism of erectile dysfunction (ED), the first clinical trial examining sildenafil's use in ED occurred in late 1993. After 21 separate trials showed the medication's promise as a safe and effective ED treatment, Pfizer sought and gained FDA approval for sildenafil in 1998. Through savvy marketing and the realization of unmet patient needs, Viagra became a household name and one of the most successful products of its time (Ghofrani, Osterloh, & Grimminger, 2006).

THE FDA AND LEGISLATIVE HISTORY

As the result of public concern regarding unsanitary food packaging and the sale of dangerous and ineffective medications, the Food and Drug Administration (FDA) Act was passed in 1906. Among other things, this legislation established the requirement that drugs must meet certain standards regarding their purity and strength. However, this legislation focused on the actual labeling of the drug rather than testing and approval before marketing. Over time, in addition to the original 1906 FDA Act, various pieces of legislation and important time points have worked to shape what was once known as the Bureau of Chemistry into today's FDA, including the 1938 Food, Drug, and Cosmetic Act (FD&C Act), the 1951 Durham-Humphrey Amendment (to the FD&C Act), the 1962 Kefauver-Harris Amendment, and the 1984 Hatch-Waxman Act, among others. The legislative influence over time on the FDA is further highlighted in **Table 3-1.**

Table 3-1 Important Events That Shaped the Current FDA

Legislation (Year), Event, Regulations, or Term	Impact or Meaning
Pure Food and Drug Act (1906)	The first law passed regulating drugs, which came into being as a result of public outrage in response to unsafe and unsanitary conditions in the meat packing industry largely brought to the public's attention by Upton Sinclair's novel *The Jungle*. The book explained in detail the gory conditions under which the nation's meat supply was processed and handled and resulted in a boycott of meat by the American public, pushing Congress to act on President Roosevelt's wish for a pure food bill, which he requested in December 1905. The law prohibited **misbranded** and **adulterated** foods, drinks, and drugs in interstate commerce.
Food and Drug Administration (1930)	The Pure Food and Drug Act was initially enforced by the Bureau of Chemistry in the Department of Agriculture, which became the Food and Drug Administration (FDA) in 1930. The FDA, an agency within the U.S. Public Health Service under the umbrella of the Department of Health and Human Services, was founded to regulate the approval of new foods and health-related products and is charged with ensuring the safety of the country's food and drug supply.
Federal Food, Drug, and Cosmetics Act (1938)	This act was passed by the legislature after a tragedy involving an elixir used to treat throat infection in children. It contained the sweet-tasting diethylene glycol, and caused kidney failure and the death of several children. The FD&C Act required that pharmaceutical manufacturers/marketers prove their drugs were safe and required the submission of a New Drug Application (NDA) by the sponsor to the FDA for review and approval prior to placing the drug in commerce.
Durham-Humphrey Amendment (1951)	This amendment defined the kinds of drugs that could not be used safely without medical supervision and, therefore, created sale by prescription only.
Kefauver-Harris Amendment (1962)	This amendment to the original FD&C Act occurred after the thalidomide scare, in which the commonly used thalidomide caused numerous, severe birth defects in pregnant women in Europe. The amendment required that sponsors prove their drug to be both safe and effective, thus establishing the basis of the current regulatory system for review and drug approval. In addition, this update also gave the FDA jurisdiction over prescription drug marketing, expanding the FDA's scope to products for both human and animal use, including foods, cosmetics, medicines, biologics, and medical devices.

(continues)

Table 3-1 Important Events That Shaped the Current FDA (*continued*)

Legislation (Year), Event, Regulations, or Term	Impact or Meaning
Drug Price Competition and Patent Term Restoration Act (1984)	Also referred to as the Hatch-Waxman Act, this act expedited the availability of lower cost generics by permitting the FDA to approve generic applications without having to repeat safety and efficacy trials. This act also provided for manufacturers to apply for up to 5 years of additional patent protection to make up for time lost in the FDA review process.
The Prescription Drug User Fee Act (1992)	This act established fees for review of drug applications with a goal to increase revenue for the FDA that could be used to hire additional support staff and upgrade information technology, which would facilitate faster reviews of drug applications.
FDA Modernization Act (1997)	This act codified a number of changes that had been emerging, including guidelines for submission of abbreviated drug applications (ANDAs), reauthorization of the Prescription Drug User Fee Act (PDUFA), promotion of pediatric drug trials by extending patent exclusivity, and provisions for fast-track approval of drugs for treating life-threatening diseases.

Source: Food and Drug Administration. (2010, October 14). Significant dates in U.S. food and drug law history. Retrieved from http://www.fda.gov/AboutFDA/WhatWeDo/History/Milestones/ucm128305.htm

THE NEW DRUG APPROVAL PROCESS

In the United States, for a drug to be approved by the FDA, a pharmaceutical manufacturer must go through a lengthy series of FDA-required research studies and application processes to prove the medication is safe and effective, which typically can take anywhere from 10 to 15 years to complete and cost in excess of $1 billion (Pharmaceutical Research and Manufacturers of America [PhRMA], 2012).

The series of studies and applications (represented graphically in **Figure 3-1**) includes preclinical research, clinical testing (Phases I, II, and III), submission of the New Drug Application (NDA), and then postmarketing surveillance and monitoring if the medication is approved by the FDA.

Preclinical Discovery and Research

To discover and eventually develop a medication, scientists are constantly working to understand fully the different disease processes so that they can find a specific focus area for a potential medication. When they find a target area for a potential medication and determine it can be altered by a drug (e.g., a receptor or

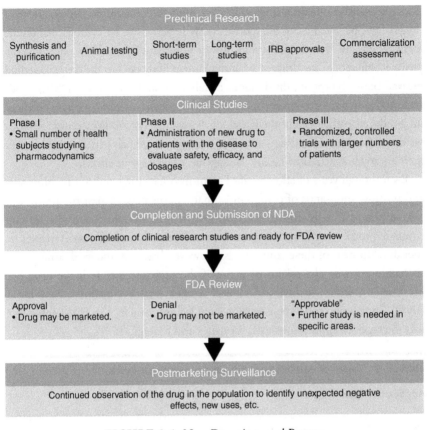

FIGURE 3-1 New Drug Approval Process

enzyme blockage), basic scientists methodically screen thousands of compounds in hopes of finding something with therapeutic potential. Scientists find compounds through many avenues, such as natural sources or genetically engineered biotechnology products. On average, approximately only five out of the thousands of tested compounds make it to clinical trials and only one eventually receives FDA approval (PhRMA, 2012).

When a set of compounds is identified, preclinical studies are conducted to determine the compounds' viability as medications, the drug's basic mechanism of action, and, most important, the potential toxicity that could occur if administered to humans. **In vitro**, or test tube–based, studies are frequently employed to determine the new drug's receptor-binding properties as well as predict its pharmacologic and toxicologic actions. Animal testing is usually done in two or more species of animals with at least one nonrodent species. Additionally, if a suitable animal model for the targeted disease is available, the drug is tested in these models. For example, antihypertensive drugs might be tested using the spontaneously hypertensive rat as an animal model for hypertension. These animal studies provide important information concerning the pharmacokinetics of the drug, or what the human body does to the drug, including bioavailability/absorption, distribution, metabolism, and excretion (ADME). Both acute and long-term studies are conducted with particular attention given to potential drug-induced pathologies of the blood, cardiovascular system, liver, central nervous system, and kidneys. The drug also is given to pregnant animals to determine whether there are any potential carcinogenic, mutagenic, or teratogenic effects.

Even though years of effort might be put into screening and testing hundreds and possibly thousands of compounds, many never make it past the preclinical testing phase. Usually, this stems from low or minimal pharmacologic activity compared to existing drugs on the market and/or toxic side effects deterring further development of these compounds. However, based on the marketing analysis combined with the scientists' input, if the manufacturer feels the drug has promise and wishes to invest in clinical studies, an Investigational New Drug (IND) Application must then be submitted for approval by the FDA. **Table 3-2** lists the types of applications used for drugs and biologicals.

Table 3-2   Types of Applications for Drugs and Biologicals

Application Type	Purpose
Investigational New Drug (IND) Application	Used in early product development, the IND allows the FDA to evaluate whether a product is reasonably safe and has promising pharmacologic activity. This usually contains information on animal pharmacologic studies and toxicology data, manufacturing information, and clinical protocols to be used in early studies.
New Drug Application	This is the primary application used to evaluate a drug's safety and efficacy fully based on clinical trials.
Abbreviated New Drug Application	ANDAs contain data the CDER uses to review and approve generic products. Generic products approved in this manner are generally not required to conduct the clinical testing, but rather test for bioequivalence (the time it takes the generic medication to reach the bloodstream).
Therapeutic Biologic Applications	This is the approval process for biological products such as monoclonal antibodies, growth factors, thrombolytics, proteins extracted from animals or microorganisms, immune modulators, and other nonvaccine therapeutic immune therapies.
Over-the-Counter (OTC) Drugs	The CDER reviews product applications for over-the-counter use, or use that does not require recommendation or prescription. These products are deemed safe for consumer self-selection.

Investigational New Drugs

The IND format, dictated in Section 21 of the *Code of Federal Regulations*, generally includes all the preclinical data and their analyses. Additionally, the manufacturer must describe the drug's indication, route of administration, dosage, proposed clinical trials, chemical composition, and how it will be manufactured. The FDA can do one of three things with a manufacturer's IND Application (FDA, 2012b):

- Approve the IND, allowing the manufacturer to initiate clinical trials
- Reject the IND completely
- Require additional information or studies before approval, typically by placing any work done by the manufacturer on **clinical hold**

A clinical hold is a stoppage of the trials required by the FDA. If trials under an IND remain on clinical hold for longer than 1 year, the FDA might then place the IND under inactive status.

Clinical Studies

Once the FDA approves the IND Application, the pharmaceutical manufacturer can initiate clinical studies and conduct them in distinct phases, each establishing important pharmacologic and safety parameters for the subsequent studies, with the end goal of gaining full FDA approval and ability to market. For each of the proposed clinical trials, the protocol, investigators and their qualifications, and the investigation site(s) must be presented and approved. Additionally, each clinical trial must also be approved and overseen by an institutional review board (IRB).

CASE IN POINT 3-4
Financial Implications of Drugs Placed on Clinical Hold

Not only do stakeholders in the pharmaceutical industry pay close attention to the actions of the FDA and the various sanctions or penalties it places on pharmaceuticals, but so does Wall Street and financial advisors/investors. In 2011, once the FDA decided to lift a clinical hold on Icagen's antiepileptic drug under trial, Icagen's stock price rose 31% and has continued to rise as the drug works its way through clinical trials and the approval process (Sengupta, 2011).

Phase I

The initial clinical trials are labeled as Phase I studies and conducted in a small number of healthy subjects. Based on the information from preclinical studies, small doses are usually given to approximately 20 to 100 individuals so that pharmacokinetic data, including the product's absorption, distribution, metabolism, and excretion (ADME), can be determined in humans. Also, Phase I studies allow for the determination of potential safety problems that can arise, and, if tolerated in the healthy subjects, results are then used to design Phase II studies.

Phase II

In Phase II studies, the new drug is evaluated in a larger number of patients (100–300) who have the disease the drug will be used to treat. Researchers examine tolerability in addition to further defining and analyzing dosing and ADME data. Phase II studies frequently encompass several hundred patients and are either single- or double-blinded and instrumental in defining the drug's risk–benefit ratio.

Phase III

Phase III studies are the large randomized, double-blind, controlled trials that involve several hundred or thousands of patients at multiple clinical sites. In these studies, the drug can be compared to placebo and/or another drug. For drug approval, the FDA generally requires a minimum of two well-controlled, randomized studies. However, based on the FDA Modernization Act of 1997, the FDA might allow the efficacy of a drug to be approved at its discretion based on one adequate and well-controlled study, often referred to as the **pivotal trial**.

New Drug Application

Upon completion of Phase III studies demonstrating the drug is safe and effective, the manufacturer can submit a **New Drug Application (NDA)** to the FDA for approval to manufacture and market the drug. The NDA presents a compilation of the data obtained from the IND as well as data from all the drug's clinical trials and a comprehensive analysis of the drug's chemistry, pharmacology, and toxicology. The manufacturer must also describe the manufacturing site and process with the assurance the marketed product complies with existing good manufacturing processes (GMPs) and submit the proposed drug labeling. The FDA then evaluates the NDA with regard to the drug's chemistry, biopharmaceutics, pharmacology, statistics, and medical information. If the drug is an antibiotic, an additional microbiology review is conducted.

FDA Approval and Postmarketing Surveillance (Phase IV Studies)

Following the full FDA review process, which can take several months to years, the FDA takes one of the following actions:

- Approves the NDA, allowing the manufacturer to market the drug in the United States
- Deems the NDA unapprovable, indicating significant deficiencies
- Deems the NDA "approvable" (but not provided with approved status), which usually requires additional studies to demonstrate the level of safety and efficacy considered necessary by the FDA

Once an NDA is approved, a manufacturer can begin to market the drug for a specific indication, dosage, and use in a particular population, representing the only conditions evaluated by the FDA.

CASE IN POINT 3-5
Merck's Vioxx

In May 1999, Merck began marketing Vioxx (rofecoxib), a medication approved for pain and arthritis. With a heavy dose of direct-to-consumer (DTC) advertising and physician detailing behind it, the medication quickly became popular with patients and physicians and sales soared. Postmarketing studies were later published questioning its safety and showing an increased risk of cardiovascular problems. Amid mounting pressure and evidence of cardiovascular issues, Merck removed the product from the market in September 2004. Given the product's popularity (more than 80 million doses prescribed during its time on the market) and the heavy DTC advertising campaign, overall public backlash against the pharmaceutical industry ensued and legal action was eventually taken against the company by numerous plaintiffs. In November 2007, Merck settled the lawsuits for $4.85 billion (Prakash & Valentine, 2007).

Postmarketing surveillance, or Phase IV studies, is conducted after FDA approval of the NDA, and often these studies are suggested by the FDA during the approval process. These studies as a whole have become recognized as providing important information concerning rare side effects that were not detected during the Phase I, II, or III clinical trials because of the small patient numbers. In addition, Phase IV studies can be done to detect drug interactions or other adverse events that might occur when the drug is used in real-world settings and often provide important new safety information communicated through labeling changes. Given the dynamic nature of drug safety, the significance of these studies has increased. Several drugs have had significant label changes (e.g., black box warnings) or even been withdrawn from the market because of findings in postmarketing studies.

GENERIC DRUGS

In the 1960s, Medicaid and Medicare amendments moved generic drugs to the forefront as a means to reduce healthcare costs. Initially, though, generic drugs were required to go through the same review and approval process as brand-name drugs, which changed in 1984 with the passing of the Drug Price Competition and Patent Term Restoration Act (better known as the Hatch-Waxman Act). This legislation significantly shortened the drug approval process by allowing generic drug manufacturers to rely on the preclinical and clinical studies previously performed by the brand-name/innovator manufacturer on the original NDA (also known as the **reference listed drug [RLD]**). Generic drug manufacturers were then allowed to submit an **Abbreviated New Drug Application (ANDA)**, which made the manufacturer primarily have to show the medication was **bioequivalent** to the brand-name medication.

In the ANDA, the generic manufacturer demonstrates pharmaceutical equivalence by showing the medication meets the same batch requirements for dose form, purity, strength, and quality as the branded medication. This bioequivalence is determined in 24 to 36 healthy volunteers who are given the branded medication and then the generic drug after an appropriate washout period in a cross-over study to determine two pharmacokinetic parameters—the maximum plasma concentration of the drug (C_{max}) and area under the curve (AUC), which must be shown with statistical confidence to be therapeutically equivalent to the brand-name medication. Even with these criteria, concerns still exist with whether there are significant variations between brand and generic drugs or even among different generic drugs. This is of particular concern with drugs that have

CASE IN POINT 3-6
Six-Month Exclusivity

From a marketing perspective, and to best serve its customers, generic pharmaceutical manufacturers focus on providing high-quality and consistently supplied generic products at low prices. Generic manufacturers monitor the marketplace and identify possible branded targets, looking at raw materials supply issues, production issues (such as difficult-to-produce chemical entities), manufacturing and packaging capabilities, size and durability of market demand, and profitability to drive the decision of which branded products to pursue. To stay ahead of the competition, generic firms must strategically plan and analyze well in advance which specific brand medications they want to reproduce so as to eventually be the first generic to penetrate the market for a given product.

As a result of the 1984 Hatch-Waxman Act, in the generic industry being the first to file an ANDA successfully and gain paragraph IV approval brings a 6-month (180-day) exclusive period for the filing manufacturer (FDA, 2009b; Rumore, 2009). A paragraph IV filing contends the patent is void and begins a judicial process to determine its validity prior to the patent's expiration. Once approved and the patent expires, the first ANDA is granted the above exclusivity period (Rumore, 2009). This means that once the innovator's patent has expired and generic equivalents can begin to be on pharmacy shelves and be dispensed, the generic manufacturer has a 6-month period to penetrate the market and maximize profits without having to worry about another generic competitor in the marketplace. During this period, exclusive generics might be priced close (usually with about a 10% discount) to the branded product. Once the 180-day exclusivity period ends, other generic manufacturers with approved ANDAs can enter the marketplace, which almost immediately drives product pricing down, sometimes discounting prices by as much as 90% from the brand product. This price erosion creates an ultra-competitive market situation in which buyers typically focus on price as the most important, and sometimes only, evaluative criterion.

a narrow therapeutic index, such as lithium, digoxin, anticonvulsants, and warfarin, because small variations in plasma concentrations can result in significant adverse effects.

In addition to demonstrating bioequivalence, the generic manufacturer must document an assurance the medication will be manufactured according to **good manufacturing practices (GMPs)**. The medication's labeling when submitted in the ANDA must mirror the brand medication. In terms of timing, generic drug manufacturers can initiate the ANDA just prior to a brand medication's patent expiration so that they are poised to market the generic drug almost immediately after the patent expires. In the United States, the innovator company has patent protection for 20 years with the patent—usually filed during the preclinical testing period. Thus, given that the NDA drug approval process usually takes anywhere from 10 to 14 years, an innovative, brand-name product can expect approximately only 6 to 10 years of effective patent protection before generic versions can begin their approval process and be produced (FDA, 2011).

OVER-THE-COUNTER DRUGS

The second class of medication products available to consumers/patients is over-the-counter (OTC) drugs, or those available without having a prescription from an authorized prescriber. OTC medications are not to be confused with dietary supplements or medical foods, which are labeled as foods and not regulated for safety and efficacy by the FDA in the same manner as an OTC medication. Dietary supplements and medical foods do not require FDA approval before they can be marketed, but they are subject to FDA labeling requirements as well as good manufacturing practices to ensure their safety and quality.

Even though OTC medications do not require a prescription, they still must be approved by the FDA through CDER's Office of Nonprescription Drugs and have the following characteristics:

- A wide safety and efficacy margin given their use is not overseen by a licensed practitioner (hence, a consumer can self-diagnose, treat, and manage)
- Low misuse and abuse potential
- Labeling inclusive of all the necessary information an average consumer would need (Christl, n.d.)

Most approved OTC medications have already gone through an NDA process very similar to that of prescription products; however, a number of OTC drugs were marketed before the FDA required proof of safety and efficacy. The ingredients and labeling of these drugs have been evaluated by the FDA and OTC monographs established. The monographs describe the acceptable ingredients, doses, formulations, and labeling of the drugs. The monographs are continually being updated. Drugs that conform to the monograph can be marketed without prior approval of the FDA. Otherwise, a drug must go through the NDA process as described earlier.

Prescription-to-OTC Switch

Recently, many drugs approved for OTC status initially had been approved as prescription medications and, thus, originally submitted an NDA that was reviewed for safety and efficacy. As a result, a significant amount of experience has been gained with these drugs regarding efficacy and safety. To gain approval for OTC use of a previously prescription drug, a manufacturer submits another NDA, which is often referred to as an Rx-to-OTC switch application.

The decision as to whether to allow a drug to switch from prescription to OTC is based on a number of factors. Because it was initially marketed as a prescription, there is usually significant experience to demonstrate an acceptable margin of safety and wide therapeutic index for the drug. It is also important that the indication for which the drug is intended can be recognized and treated by the patient with minimal or no supervision by a physician. The drug must also be safe and effective when used without a prescription and the potential for abuse and misuse of the drug is minimal or none. Many OTC drugs are available at lower dosages than the prescription counterpart. To assess this, manufacturers conduct usage studies to determine whether consumers can use the drug appropriately. Additionally, they conduct label comprehension studies to determine whether consumers can read and understand the labeling of the OTC drug.

Over the last 30 years, numerous prescription medications have made the switch from prescription-only status to OTC status. This is a tremendous opportunity for marketers in that previously untapped markets can be accessed when former prescription drugs are made available for sale without a prescription. Some of the most notable "switched" medications are Benadryl (diphenhydramine), Sudafed (pseudoephedrine), Claritin (loratadine), Zyrtec (cetirizine), and a number of other antihistamines, decongestants, and combination products. Medicines to treat acid reflux and indigestion have also created significant market opportunities for products such as Zantac (ranitidine), Prilosec (omeprazole), and Prevacid (lansoprazole). When products are switched, the perception is that a potent medication is now available because of the drug's safety and efficacy and consumers can identify their own need for the drug without physician assistance. Switches can effectively extend a product's life cycle by creating new markets for self-medication.

DRUG LABELING

All drugs are required to have FDA-approved labeling (i.e., the package insert) that provides the essential information necessary for a prescriber, or the consumer in the case of OTC drugs, to use the drug safely and effectively. The information in the label is based on the data in the NDA, and the FDA dictates that a specific format is used, as outlined in the *Code of Federal Regulations* Title 21, Part 201 (FDA, 2012a). The FDA also requires the label to be informative and accurate while not being promotional, false, or misleading. Although the FDA must approve the label, the content is based on the information obtained by the manufacturer and, as such, it is the manufacturer's responsibility continually to make sure the label remains accurate. This is an important duty of the manufacturer because drug safety can and often does change as the drug is used in real-world conditions. Thus, when new safety information arises after marketing, the manufacturer must change the label to reflect the new safety information. The format of the prescription label/package insert is as follows (e.g., see www.berlex.com/html /products/pi/fhc/YAZ_PPI.pdf):

- *Chemistry.* Includes the chemical class, active ingredient, excipients, dyes, and product fillers.
- *Clinical pharmacology.* Includes the mechanism of action (pharmacodynamics) and clinical efficacy.
- *Pharmacokinetics.* Absorption, distribution, metabolism, and excretion data.
- *Uses in special populations.* Such as older adults, children, or ethnic groups.
- *Safety and efficacy.* Data supporting use for a specific indication or indications.
- *Dosing.* Specific dosage ranges recommended by the clinical data.
- *Contraindications.* Conditions in which the drug should not be used because it puts the patient at severe risk of serious or life-threatening adverse events.
- *Warnings.* Describes any serious side effects or drug interactions that the drug might cause, including any specific monitoring that could be required or symptoms that might occur.

- *Precautions.* Provides general precautions users should follow (and drug interactions to avoid) to use the drug safely and effectively, including recommended lab tests that should be performed to monitor use of the drug.
- *Adverse reactions.* Adverse events that occurred during the clinical trials are of particular importance because they occurred in the closely monitored and controlled conditions of Phases I–III and are likely to occur in patients once the drug is marketed. The label lists adverse events that occurred at an incidence of 1% or greater and other adverse events that occurred at an incidence of less than 1%. Further comments include whether the drug has the potential to be abused or produce dependence and recommended overdosage treatment. Finally, the label lists the approved dosage and route of administration, how the drug is supplied, and photographs of the drug product.
- *Pregnancy use.* Follows the current risk categorization of either A,B, C, D, or X. A drug with an X should not be used during pregnancy because there is strong evidence that there is a risk to the fetus. Category D includes drugs in which there is a risk to the fetus, but the benefit of using the drug might outweigh the risk. Most drugs fall into Category C, which means they show evidence of fetal risk in animal studies or there are no studies in which risk has been assessed. Category A includes drugs for which no risk has been demonstrated.

In addition, some drugs contain a black box warning positioned at the top of the label and prominently displayed in a bold black box. **Black box warnings** are designed to bring to the prescriber's attention any special problems that could lead to serious injury or death as a result of taking the drug. The black box warning must be approved by the FDA and is placed on any material that describes the use of the drug by healthcare providers. Information in the black box describes the particular adverse event, its frequency or incidence, the symptoms that occur, and what should be done. Often, black box warnings on drugs arise through postmarketing surveillance and discoveries/reports of adverse events when the drug was introduced into the real world. In some cases, the black box warning is a class warning, which means that all drugs in the class have the warning. In other cases, the black box warning is specific to a particular drug and not the entire class of drugs.

As described, the product label/package insert contains a large amount of information, different pieces of which might be difficult to find even though the

CASE IN POINT 3-7
Chantix Black Box Warning

On July 1, 2009, the FDA issued a requirement to Pfizer, the manufacturer of Chantix (varenicline), a smoking cessation medication, to add a black box warning to its labeling and develop patient medication guides stressing the associated risks. Through postmarketing surveillance and adverse event reporting, the FDA discovered the medication could cause severe neuropsychiatric symptoms, including, but not limited to, suicidal thoughts and behaviors, agitation, and altered mood—even in those without a previous history of psychiatric disorders (FDA, 2009a). Although black box warnings do not preclude a drug from being prescribed, they do bring extra negative attention to the medication and might alter its future potential.

format is standardized. It is also important to recognize that the product label is written for the prescriber and not for the patient. The FDA responded to this criticism of the old format and implemented a new format that has an executive summary or highlights section of the important information with a contents section that refers the reader to more detailed information in the label. The highlights section provides an overview of the benefits and risks of the drug, the approval date of the drug, and a notation as to whether there have been any recent changes to the label (FDA, 2012a).

Off-Label Medication Use

When marketed drugs are prescribed for other conditions outside of the product's FDA-approved indications, this is referred to as **off-label prescribing**. This does not mean the drug is necessarily dangerous or should not be used for these purposes, only that the FDA has not evaluated and approved the medication for the use in question. Off-label prescribing cannot be promoted by pharmaceutical manufacturers, and instead is usually identified in academic and professional literature based on either the drug characteristics' theoretical efficacy or the physician's actual experience with a drug. Following approval, manufacturers might decide to seek approval for new indications, such as those identified through off-label use, new dosage forms, or new delivery systems. In some cases, manufacturers

CASE IN POINT 3-8
Mental Health Medications

Since the development of medications such as Clozaril (clozapine) and Risperdal (risperidone) in the early 1990s, physicians have noted that in some patients the second-generation antipsychotic agents (which now include numerous products such as Zyprexa [olanzapine], Seroquel [quetiapine], Abilify [aripiprazole], Fanapt [iloperidone], Saphris [asenapine], Geodon [ziprasidone], and others) have improved symptoms associated with mood and anxiety. Physicians have prescribed antipsychotic medications for these symptoms off-label. Manufacturers, recognizing the market potential in these areas, conducted studies and some have sought and obtained approval from the FDA for these additional indications.

study and seek FDA approval to use a drug in a special patient population, such as children or adolescents. The process for obtaining new indications includes supplementing the original NDA with additional studies and the submission of a supplemental NDA (sNDA).

PHARMACOVIGILANCE

In general, FDA approval simply means that based on the data presented by the manufacturer, the FDA deems the drug safe and effective at that time. However, this can and often does change as more patients are exposed to the drug under different circumstances. More important, rare and serious side effects likely are not seen during preapproval clinical trials because these trials are not powered with enough patients to detect these unusual side effects. **Pharmacovigilance** is the discipline that looks for and assesses safety signals indicating there might be problems/adverse events with a medication's use, blending, pharmacology, and epidemiology. These safety signals are detected by collecting adverse event data from various sources such as pharmaceutical manufacturers, the FDA, and the World Health Organization (WHO). In the United States, adverse events are collected by the FDA using the MedWatch system, implemented in 1993 as a means of increasing adverse event reporting (Michele, 2008). Manufacturers are required to monitor, assess, and report adverse events that occur in their clinical trials as well as after the drug is approved and marketed. The FDA is particularly interested in any new side effects that are not in the label, any serious side effects, or an increase in adverse event frequency. These data are then put into the Adverse Event Reporting System (AERS) database for analysis.

When emerging safety information is detected, this information should be incorporated into the product label and the risk communicated to prescribers and/or consumers. This can be done through the MedWatch system through email alerts, Dear Doctor or Dear Healthcare Provider letters, and label changes. The FDA can also require the manufacturer to develop package inserts to communicate this new safety information to patients.

MARKETING'S ROLE DURING PRODUCT DEVELOPMENT

From the moment a viable chemical entity is identified, effective and successful pharmaceutical manufacturers involve the marketing department or marketing professionals, depending on the firm's size. Whereas larger firms typically have a whole department of marketing professionals, smaller (e.g., biotechnology) firms might have only a few marketing professionals or even subcontract out to market research firms.

Why is the marketing department important as the company prepares the product to be tested in Phase I and further clinical trials? Although many associate marketing with sales efforts and promotions such as television and print advertisements, the marketing department is a firm's primary business research unit. Ideally, marketers consider the following issues and complete the following tasks throughout the development and approval process:

- Identify key areas of unmet need and market potential, in particular the potential sales a product could expect. Although any market for a new drug can seem appealing, marketing assesses the viability of a market by answering certain market-specific questions, such as the following:
  - Who would be the product's customers and what do they specifically need and want? (Measurable)
  - What is the overall size of the market? (Substantial)
  - How similar are needs, wants, and demands on the part of customers in the market? (Homogenous)

- o Can customers (e.g., specialty physicians) be reached? (Accessibility)
- o Are there other new innovations in development that could change the market dynamics? (Durability)
- o What are the current market dynamics from a competition perspective?
- o What is the existing product customer loyalty level?

- Develop a vision for the potential product, typically based on its key attributes and value drivers. How will this product be differentiated from others in the marketplace? Are there product features or uses the manufacturer needs to focus on to penetrate physicians' thought process? How will this drug be positioned in customers' (both physicians' and consumers') minds? What do key opinion leaders (KOLs) in the specified field say about the product and its key attributes and potential market share?

- Identify early the product market, including the minimum clinical and pharmacoeconomic outcome levels to achieve success. This centers on the idea of market analysis. Specifically, when examining early-stage clinical trials, the manufacturer must have an understanding of the current market the product could potentially enter, particularly if it is an already competitive market or the product is a "first-in-class." This is especially important in clinical trial design and execution leading up to the initial NDA. Marketing and R&D must work cohesively to identify and pursue the appropriate initial indication for the product. For example, what level of reduction in mm Hg for high blood pressure or cost-effectiveness ratio would be necessary to have clinical significance and drive market share toward the product under development?

- Identify and assess commercial interests, including issues related to pricing, insurance coverage (formularies), and reimbursement. A new drug that cannot achieve preferred status (i.e., covered) or that is excluded from coverage on insurance formularies cannot be expected to capture market share and, therefore, will be less profitable than a product viewed as safer or more cost-effective. Further, if the product is entering an already crowded medication class, certain typical limitations on reimbursement (cost-containment measures) such as prior authorization, quantity limits, or generic-first protocols, could negatively affect product adoption and result in lower market share potential and sales.

Table 3-3 summarizes these points, including where on the approval process timeline they typically fall.

Table 3-3 Marketing and Research and Development Overlap

Development Stage	Marketing's Role
Compound identification and screening	• Disease-focused research and analysis • Size of the disease market/market potential • Competition within the disease state/target market • Disease population trends and future
Preclinical	• Further in-depth market analysis • Product vision and strategy • Identification of product's possible key marketable attributes • Needs, wants, and demands of potential customers (physicians and patients)
Phases I and II	• Identification of market segments and determination of positioning strategy for those various segments • Development of market entry and pricing strategy, which depend on type of competitive environment entering ("me-too" versus "first-in-class," etc.) • Identification of minimally acceptable levels of clinical and pharmacoeconomic (e.g., cost-effectiveness) significance • Determination of optimal initial primary product indication • Initial identification and targeting of key opinion leaders in the disease field
Phase III	• Determination of product name • Publication strategy • Engaging the identified key opinion leaders • Finalization of pricing and reimbursement strategies • Final preparation for ultimate approval and launch
Post-FDA approval	• Continual evaluation of all product movement, strategies, and dynamics • Continual analysis of usage and adoption statistics, leading to identification of possible new indications, claims, and so forth • Continual evaluation of pricing and reimbursement strategies • Continual interaction with manufacturing so as to avoid possible customer issues/complaints

SUMMARY

In the pharmaceutical industry, the linkage between the marketing department and research and development (R&D) scientists is critical to long-term success. Basic scientists discover chemical entities with pharmacologic activity and marketers determine the potential for these entities to be brought to market to become the next blockbuster drug. With potentially thousands of chemicals to be screened for each new drug developed, the continual and early flow of information between R&D and marketing over time contributes to a more focused research effort and more productive marketing.

DISCUSSION QUESTIONS

1. The process of bringing a new chemical entity to the marketplace involves staggering costs and is lengthy to ensure safety and efficacy. With effective patent life shortened by the length of time a drug can be under review at the FDA, what are some possible ways a pharmaceutical manufacturer can effectively extend patent life for new products?

2. Although off-label marketing, or marketing a drug outside its FDA-approved indications, is illegal, off-label prescribing is not. Why and how is off-label prescribing beneficial to patients, physicians, and manufacturers?

3. Is it ethical for pharmaceutical manufacturers to fund studies investigating a drug's side effects, alternative uses, or uses in pediatrics if the primary goal is to support off-label prescribing? Would it be ethical if the primary goal was to provide data for a new indication for the drug?

4. Postmarketing surveillance can provide additional safety and efficacy information from large numbers of patients using a medication after it has been approved and used by the medical community. Why can this be a double-edged sword for pharmaceutical manufacturers?

5. The 1951 Durham-Humphrey Amendment changed the landscape for pharmaceutical products. Using the intent of this legislation as a backdrop, how have Rx-to-OTC switches and drugs that do not require a prescription but that must be obtained from a pharmacist created opportunities for pharmacists and pharmaceutical manufacturers?

6. Is key opinion leader acceptance of a new product critical to the product's success? If not, how would a pharmaceutical manufacturer strategically market its product without acceptance from key opinion leaders?

7. Is a black box warning a positive or negative from the perspective of the FDA? Consumers? Prescribers? Manufacturers?

8. Comment on the following statement: "Generic drugs do not have to prove they are safe or effective—all they have to do is prove they are bioequivalent. That must mean some generic drugs are not safe and effective."

9. To bring a new drug to market, Phase I, II, and III studies together provide information to determine whether a drug is safe and effective.

Yet, some medical foods and dietary supplements do not require this rigorous testing. Discuss the pros and cons of enhancing the regulatory requirements for medical foods and dietary supplements.

10. From a product perspective, pharmaceutical manufacturers, and the industry in general, have always been associated with a tangible medication/drug/pill. As we move forward, what other "products" might eventually be associated with pharmaceutical manufacturers? In other words, will diversification of the product lineup ever extend outside of the medication/drug/pill model?

REFERENCES

Abkowitz, A. (2009, March 12). Big pharma's new landscape. CNNMoney. Retrieved from http://money.cnn.com/2009/03/11/news/companies/pharma.fortune/index.htm

Christl, L. (n.d.). Introduction to nonprescription products. CDER Forum for International Drug Regulatory Authorities. Retrieved from http://www.fda.gov/downloads/Drugs/NewsEvents/UCM182551.pdf

FierceBiotech. (2010, March 25). Ten-year data on pharmaceutical mergers and acquisitions, from DealSearchOnline.com, reveals top deals and key companies. Retrieved from http://www.fiercebiotech.com/press-releases/ten-year-data-pharmaceutical-mergers-and-acquisitions-dealsearchonline-com-reveals-to

Food and Drug Administration. (2009a, July 1). Drugs: Information for healthcare professionals: Varenicline (marketed as Chantix) and Bupropion (marketed as Zyban, Wellbutrin, and generics). Retrieved from http://www.fda.gov/Drugs/DrugSafety/PostmarketDrugSafetyInformationforPatientsandProviders/DrugSafetyInformationforHeathcareProfessionals/ucm169986.htm

Food and Drug Administration. (2009b). Drugs: Small business assistance: 180-day generic drug exclusivity. Retrieved from http://www.fda.gov/Drugs/DevelopmentApprovalProcess/SmallBusinessAssistance/ucm069964.htm

Food and Drug Administration. (2010, April 23). How drugs are developed and approved. Retrieved from http://www.fda.gov/Drugs/DevelopmentApprovalProcess/HowDrugsareDevelopedandApproved/default.htm

Food and Drug Administration. (2011). Drugs: Frequently asked questions on patents and exclusivity. Retrieved from http://www.fda.gov/Drugs/DevelopmentApprovalProcess/ucm079031.htm

Food and Drug Administration. (2012a). Title 21—*Food and Drugs: Chapter I—Food and Drug Administration, Department of Health and Human Services Subchapter C—Drugs: General.* 21CFR. Retrieved from http://www.accessdata.fda.gov/scripts/cdrh/cfdocs/cfCFR/CFRSearch.cfm?CFRPart=201

Food and Drug Administration. (2012b). Title 21—*Food and Drugs: Chapter I—Food and Drug Administration, Department of Health and Human Services Subchapter D—Drugs for Human Use: Part 312: Investigational New Drug Application.* 21CFR312. Retrieved from http://www.accessdata.fda.gov/scripts/cdrh/cfdocs/cfcfr/CFRSearch.cfm?CFRPart=312&showFR=1&subpartNode=21:5.0.1.1.3.3

Ghofrani, H. A., Osterloh, I. H., & Grimminger, F. (2006, August). Sildenafil: From angina to erectile dysfunction to pulmonary hypertension and beyond. *Nature Reviews Drug Discovery*, 5(8), 689–702.

Boyer, M. (2008, June 4). History of the Food and Drug Administration (FDA). US RecallNews. Retrieved from http://www.usrecallnews.com/2008/06/history-of-the-food-and-drug-administration-fda.html

Pfizer. (2009, January 26). Pfizer to acquire Wyeth, creating the world's premier biopharmaceutical company. Retrieved from http://media.pfizer.com/files/investors/presentations/Acquisition_Press_Release_012609.pdf

Pharmaceutical Research and Manufacturers of America. (2012, April). Pharmaceutical industry profile 2012. Washington, DC: Author. Retrieved from http://www.phrma.org/sites/default/files/159/profile_2012_final.pdf

Prakash, S., & Valentine, V. (2007, November 10). Timeline: The rise and fall of Vioxx. NPR. Retrieved from http://www.npr.org/templates/story/story.php?storyId=5470430

Rumore, M. M. (2009, August 15). The Hatch-Waxman Act—25 years later: Keeping the pharmaceutical scales balanced. *Pharmacy Times*. Retrieved from http://www.pharmacytimes.com/publications/supplement/2009/genericsupplement0809/generic-hatchwaxman-0809

Sengupta, K. (2011, February 2). Update 2—FDA lifts clinical hold on Icagen's drug; shares up. Reuters. Retrieved from http://www.reuters.com/article/2011/02/02/icagen-idUSSGE7110BD20110202

CHAPTER 4

Pharmaceuticals and Pricing

Matthew Perri, PhD, RPh, and Brent L. Rollins, PhD, RPh

LEARNING OBJECTIVES

1. Identify the issues and trends that affect pharmaceutical product pricing.
2. Evaluate the role of pricing as a part of the marketing mix and understand the economic factors affecting prices.
3. Integrate industry trends with the process of developing a pricing strategy.
4. Evaluate pricing strategies used with pharmaceuticals.
5. Describe the role of various stakeholders in pharmaceutical pricing, including the role of reimbursement on pricing decisions.
6. Illustrate how a pricing strategy can change through the product life cycle and the market factors that might possibly cause the change.
7. Describe how price can function as a promotional variable and discuss the possible consequences of this action.
8. Apply pricing strategy decisions to a newly approved medication and the future pharmaceutical market.

Pharmaceutical marketing is the application of universal marketing principles and practices to the pharmaceutical industry and the process by which medicines and the value they bring to patients and society are actualized. It is this value

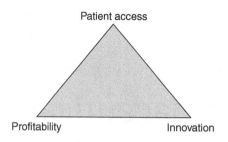

FIGURE 4-1 Competing Goals and Price Strategy

that pharmaceutical marketers must reveal to the marketplace for any pricing strategy to be effective. Given that medicines can be necessary to sustain life, pharmaceutical marketers must recognize a special challenge in pricing pharmaceuticals: Pricing strategy must meet business objectives while maintaining patient welfare.

Balancing the competitive ends (**Figure 4-1**) of patient access to medications, profitability, and continued innovation provides a challenge to the pharmaceutical marketers' pricing dilemma: What price is too much? For branded products, there is the temptation to price at the highest level that can be economically justified. This is a value proposition, and the answer depends on who is making the decision and if that decision maker is willing to evaluate total cost of care or is just concerned with medication costs. In the quest to estimate where this price level might be (effectively leaving no money on the table), pharmaceutical manufacturers should and have studied the opinions and preferences of payers, prescribers, and patients to determine optimal pricing levels. Pricing that is sensitive to these stakeholders should enable the pharmaceutical marketer to balance revenue needs, production capabilities, and profit maximization with anticipated patient demand.

PRICE AND POSITIONING

Pricing is a key marketing mix variable (along with place, product, and promotion) because of the impact price has on product positioning (**Figure 4-2**). Setting price is, however, a complex decision process focusing on issues relevant to a variety of stakeholders. These stakeholders (e.g., state Medicaid programs, Medicare, other government entities, regulators, legislators, patients, insurers, prescribers, and even advocacy organizations) each bring to the table needs and wants requiring the pharmaceutical marketer to price at a level that ensures profits, ensures access to medications, and satisfies ever-increasing demands of prescribers for innovation, thereby creating demand for their products.

Although the impact of the various stakeholders in creating demand for a manufacturer's product is obvious, in many cases these stakeholders are not in direct competition and serve different customers or patient populations. Pricing

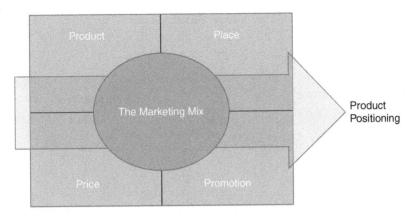

FIGURE 4-2 Marketing Mix and Positioning

for separate customers in various **classes of trade,** or the customer's business category, such as hospitals or chain pharmacies with their own drug warehouse, can be challenging, and pharmaceutical manufacturers must monitor competition and price sensitivity in these groups.

It is well understood that prices can vary greatly between classes of trade; for example, prices for hospitals might be significantly lower than prices for wholesalers that distribute to retail pharmacies. From a marketing perspective, pricing lower to hospitals makes good sense. Given relative equivalence between competing products, when lower pricing makes a product more attractive to a hospital it is likely the drug will become a part of that hospital's formulary. This formulary status increases utilization of the drug in the hospital setting. Patients who receive a medication while in the hospital will likely continue to use that medication after discharge to manage their disease and symptoms. However, even with an understanding of this issue, payers might not be satisfied when other market segments, that is, classes of trade, receive lower prices.

In addition to the actual level of price established, the level of price sensitivity of decision makers for prescription medications is a critical factor in setting price strategy. This price sensitivity, known as **price elasticity,** is a measure of the responsiveness of the quantity of the product demanded by customers when there is a change in price. For most products, increases in price are generally met with decreases in the quantity demanded (**Figure 4-3**). However, for prescription medications this is not always true.

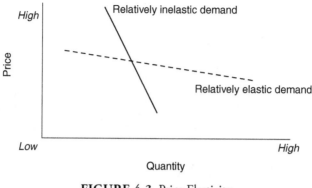

FIGURE 4-3 Price Elasticity

Because medications might be necessary to cure a disease, alleviate a symptom, or even sustain life, many prescription medications have relatively inelastic demand. In other words, marketers can expect only minor changes in the quantity of medication demanded as the price changes. The implication for the pharmaceutical manufacturer is that under these conditions, namely, **inelastic demand**, products can be priced at higher levels without significant reductions in expected sales levels.

Whereas this is true for some branded products with little competition, the demand for more crowded therapeutic categories where there are competing therapeutic alternatives or generic equivalents can be highly elastic. This means changes in price are met with larger changes in the quantity demanded. Understanding the degree of price elasticity is a primary goal of the pharmaceutical marketer. To better understand price elasticity, pharmaceutical marketers use a variety of methods to assess price elasticity, including retrospective data analysis, **qualitative research** (e.g., focus group discussions), and **quantitative research** (e.g., conjoint analysis and willingness-to-pay studies) evaluating the impact of various price levels on prescription demand.

THE COST OF PHARMACEUTICAL INNOVATION

Another major factor to consider in any discussion of pricing for pharmaceutical products is the total cost to bring a new chemical entity to the marketplace. Although estimates vary, the total cost to bring a drug to market has been estimated to be in excess of $1 billion. (Despite estimates that vary year by year and the considerable debate about the true cost to bring an innovative pharmaceutical product to market, it is estimated this cost ranges between $800 million and $1.5 billion. See, for example, Adams & Brantner [2006]; Collier [2012]; DiMasi, Hansen, & Grabowski [2003]; and Gayura [2012]). Obviously, this expense cannot be overlooked, and recovery of these costs must be built into any pricing strategy.

The cost to bring a drug to market influences the product's price variably depending on the length of the remaining patent life. So, for a drug that gets to market relatively quickly, there is a longer period of time from which to recover the research and development costs (lower impact on initial pricing). Similarly, drugs that take longer to bring to market (e.g., drugs that take longer to move through the FDA new drug approval process) have a shorter time period from which to recover research and development costs (greater impact on initial pricing). However, in the short run, the manufacturer's product cost considerations will likely yield to other factors in determining product price. For example, an upper limit on price might be created by the presence of similar or alternative products already available or prescribers' preferences and price perceptions. In such cases, price points can be limited, which significantly affects profitability.

DEVELOPING AN EFFECTIVE PRICE STRATEGY

Pricing decisions, including the creation and assessment of competing strategies, are made at a variety of levels, with final decision making generally resting with executive management. At the brand level, **pricing or commercialization committees** (composed of, for example, brand managers, market researchers, manufacturing, regulatory affairs, and pharmacoeconomics/outcomes researchers) serve to gather the information to create pricing policy and make recommendations. These recommendations must be based on extensive market analysis and careful attention to desired product position in the market.

Ultimately, the pharmaceutical industry is focused on innovation. This quest for innovation has created an environment where no single pricing strategy can be effective across products, therapeutic categories, or customer groups. Although pharmaceutical marketers repeatedly face certain issues, the unique nature of each new product innovation means price strategy must be tailored to the individual product. For example, when the second-generation antipsychotic agents (e.g., Clozaril [clozapine] and Risperdal [risperidone]) began to emerge in the early 1990s, dissatisfaction with existing treatments allowed

CASE IN POINT 4-1
Makena

KV Pharmaceutical of St. Louis, Missouri, was granted governmental approval to market (by Ther-Rx, a KV subsidiary) Makena, a weekly progesterone injection used during pregnancy to prevent preterm births. Prior to approval, the drug could be obtained for about $10–$20 per injection from compounding pharmacies.

KV has invested approximately $100 million (and over time possibly up to hundreds of millions of dollars) in this orphan drug. Orphan drug status means KV's Ther-Rx will be the sole source of the drug for 7 years. However, the FDA will continue to allow compounding pharmacies to produce the drug.

KV's price was set to be approximately $1,500 per dose, but after public comment (and even outrage), price was reduced by about 55% to $690 per injection. For a typical pregnancy, 36 weeks of treatment could be required, costing about $25,000 compared to approximately $400 per pregnancy for the compounded version of the drug.

KV expects that 85% of patients will be able to access the drug for $20 or less per dose through various measures, including, for example, insurance coverage, **rebates**, and patient assistance programs. KV justifies the new, higher price by citing the savings to patients and insurers of preventing the high costs incurred to care for premature infants, perhaps as much as $50,000 or more per premature birth (Grogan, 2011; Lowe, 2011; Stobbe, 2011).

Discussion Questions

1. Can this price of $690 per injection be justified?
2. Will insurers, including Medicaid, continue to cover this medication?
3. Will patients pay out of pocket for this medication?
4. Have pricing decision makers correctly assessed the impact of price elasticity on Makena sales?
5. What might patient advocacy organizations have to say about this pricing decision? Was this a good business decision?

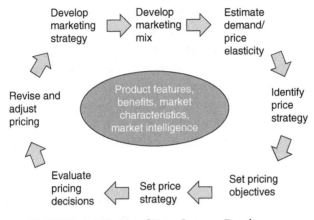

FIGURE 4-4 Stages of Price Strategy Development

premium pricing strategies for these drugs to be successful. Other product categories might enjoy this same kind of pricing flexibility, such as oncology or certain rare diseases. Conversely, for product categories where there are many comparable alternatives, such as hypertension or depression, pricing options are likely limited. Thus, no simple decision algorithm can ensure success. Pricing decision makers must consider a variety of key variables when formulating price strategy and setting price levels. The general stages to develop a pricing strategy are presented in **Figure 4-4**.

MARKET ASSESSMENT: A STARTING POINT

Understanding the marketplace is the starting point in developing a price strategy. This should include information on the competition as well as factors internal to the manufacturer. The goal of this market assessment is to develop the desired position in the marketplace for the product, based on the capabilities and limitations of the firm, the product, and customer needs. Many questions that influence pricing strategy development must be considered, including the following:

- Is the market perceived as one where there is significant need for additional treatment options? How well do existing treatments work? How are these other treatments priced? At what point in therapy is drug therapy initiated?
- What is the potential size of the market? Is the market stable or changing? Is future growth expected?

- How will product benefits and features affect the ability of the drug to gain market share? Does the product stand out from the competition? Is there competition close to entering the market?
- How unique or innovative is the new product? Does it represent a significant improvement over other, existing treatments? How is the product used (e.g., a single-dose injection or a once-daily continual use oral medication)?
- How sensitive are decision makers to price in this market?
- If there are nondrug therapies, how will the cost of these alternatives factor into pricing decisions?
- Can a higher medication price be justified if long-run costs are minimized? Will pharmacoeconomics analyses support the use of the product?
- What is the time frame and expected impact of generic substitution?
- Is counterfeiting or reimportation a likely concern for this product?

How these questions, and others, are answered provides the basis for identifying possible pricing strategy options.

ROLE OF DECISION MAKERS: PATIENTS AND PRESCRIBERS

In the past, pharmaceutical manufacturers exclusively targeted physicians to generate demand for their products. Now, with more than 30 years of direct-to-consumer (DTC) advertising and new models of care where patients play a more active role in drug product selection, pharmaceutical marketers must understand both the physician and consumer. Whereas patients have traditionally shown interest in and concern over the cost of prescription medications, this has not always been true for physicians. However, prescribers' views of prescription prices are changing because it seems physicians are increasingly aware of the medication costs, and pharmaceutical manufacturers have also noticed this trend. Physicians are especially sensitive to the price issue for patients who pay for prescription medication out of pocket and patients with chronic medical conditions. In fact, physicians might prioritize managing out-of-pocket costs over total medication costs (Shrank et al., 2006). For some physicians who administer medications, such as those in oncology, price has direct implications when these physicians purchase and administer drug therapy.

Further complicating price perceptions on the part of prescribers are the issues of preferred drug lists and formularies. A prescription drug formulary, sometimes referred to as a preferred drug list (PDL), is a complete listing of medications

CASE IN POINT 4-2
A Statin Goes Generic

In 2007, as patent protection for Merck's Zocor (simvastatin) drew close to ending, Merck offered prescription plans significant price reductions on Zocor in exchange for preferred formulary status for its combination cholesterol-lowering product Vytorin (simvastatin/ ezetimibe). The rationale for this price reduction strategy was to maintain sales of Zocor, albeit at a much lower price, and keep patients from switching to a generic form of simvastatin. In exchange for the price concessions, Merck asked for preferred formulary status for its alternative cholesterol-lowering product Vytorin. Taken together, these two strategies would serve to maintain total revenue. It was notable that during the same time period, Merck utilized a well-known direct-to-consumer advertising campaign focusing on Vytorin, using a split screen to show a person and a food item, making the point that cholesterol comes from two sources: food and the body's own production.

Even more recently, when Pfizer's Lipitor (atorvastatin) lost patent protection (December 2011), Pfizer effectively chose to become the generic producer of Lipitor by offering to meet or beat the price of any competitor. Pfizer also used a DTC advertising strategy to inform current and possible consumer users they could receive Lipitor prescriptions for as little as $4 through a patient copay/coupon card promotion.

Discussion Questions

1. Given Pfizer's strategy with Lipitor, will this now become the preferred strategy for blockbuster brands coming off patent?
2. Would third-party payers prefer this strategy over usage of generic medications?

that have been approved for use within a prescription drug plan. Medications listed on the formulary or PDL are generally available for use by patients, while drugs not listed either might be associated with higher costs to patients or have limited access for patient use. When choices are limited, economic considerations might override a prescriber's diligent consideration of the patient, the patient's condition, and the available options. This presents an opportunity for the pharmaceutical marketer when clinical and economic factors lead a product to preferred agent status in a therapeutic category. It also poses a significant threat when preferred formulary status is not achieved. This marketplace factor will only increase over time as insurers, prescribers, and patients negotiate formulary and preferred drug list restrictions, higher copays and deductibles, donut holes, and incentives for generic use.

To patients and prescribers, preferred status usually translates into lower patient cost, which decreases the impact of the price variable. When medications in a therapeutic class are seen as largely similar in clinical safety and efficacy, price becomes the salient evaluative criterion in determining formulary status. Pricing decision makers must realize the value to be obtained through preferred status, namely, market share and increased revenues. As consumers pay more out-of-pocket, price sensitivity in the pharmaceutical marketplace will continue to increase.

THE NEW DECISION MAKERS

As noted previously, pricing strategy development requires pharmaceutical pricing decision makers to consider the impact of their pricing decisions on the new key decision makers: those who develop and manage formularies and preferred drug lists. With a majority of all prescriptions being paid for through some form of prescription insurance, premium pricing can significantly impact sales when payers are not satisfied with price levels.

Once any clinical concerns about a drug are resolved, the level of payer satisfaction with price can generally be inferred from formulary status. Payers use tiered levels of preference that affect patient copayments, prior authorization requirements, and step therapy (such as fail-first on a generic requirements) to limit choice and drive market share toward preferred products. For competing products that have been deemed clinically or therapeutically equivalent, price becomes the only meaningful variable to payers. Pharmaceutical marketers then evaluate the cost and economic impact of offering a lower price in exchange for a higher formulary position.

Decisions made at this level, that is, to offer a lower price with the expectation of preferred formulary status, are generally the result of price negotiation and contracting. For some programs, such as state Medicaid programs, this also includes mandatory rebates to states that cover a manufacturer's products. Although these rebates might be a cost of doing business, they exert a negative impact on revenue for pharmaceutical manufacturers.

Therefore, an effective pricing strategy must carefully evaluate payer experience and willingness to work with manufacturers in innovative ways. Prescription insurance plans are leaving "silo thinking" (focusing only on drug costs and not total healthcare costs) behind and balancing cost concerns with patient outcomes. As plan administrators continue to better understand and use pharmacoeconomic data (e.g., cost–benefit, cost–utility, cost–effective, or comparative–effectiveness research) in formulary decision making, especially for high-utilization or high-cost classes of drugs, the goal of the pharmaceutical marketer will be to determine what constitutes valuable evidence to payers.

ECONOMIC ASPECTS OF PRICING STRATEGIES

As mentioned, the economic cost of bringing a new chemical entity to the market is significant. Manufacturers must consider the total cost of innovation, production, sales, and marketing in determining product price. However, the ability to recoup these costs quickly is dictated by a variety of other economic factors. Pharmaceutical marketers must consider these factors, such as patient/prescriber preferences, prices of competing products, and how changes in price affect demand for their products (price elasticity). Whereas it is generally assumed the demand for innovative products is relatively inelastic, where changes in price do not result in much change in demand, this might not be true when patients and physicians have other options, such as therapeutic substitutes or even nondrug therapies.

In most cases, innovation means patent protection and the ability to set price at a level indicative of the monopoly enjoyed by the company. Further, truly innovative products will have few, if any, substitutes. In cases where there are multiple drug therapies and formulary or PDL considerations, price sensitivity is generally expected to be higher. In addition, patients with acute conditions and their physicians might be less sensitive to price because of the urgency of prescribing and limited choices. Specialists who prescribe might also be more likely to have less price sensitivity than general practitioners because of the highly specialized nature of their practices: treating patients with more serious problems.

Whereas pricing power is greatest when a product has no competition, the reality of the pharmaceutical marketplace is that when the cost of a medication presents an insurmountable barrier for a patient, the patient simply chooses to forgo the prescription. The result is patient nonadherence, and the impact of patients not taking their medications presents a significant problem for pharmaceutical manufacturers, patients, and society (National Council on Patient Information and Education, 2007). This same thinking can extend to drug formulary decision makers. When there are multiple choices within a therapeutic class, all with similar actions, all with potential side effects and precautions, selection of a higher price can result in nonpreferred status or even formulary exclusion.

PRICING STRATEGY AND MARKETING GOALS

Pharmaceutical marketers need clear marketing goals to formulate and evaluate alternative pricing strategies. For example, if a manufacturer's goal is to capture

CASE IN POINT 4-3
Hyperlipidemia and the Growth of a New Market

For many years, cholesterol problems were treated with diet, exercise, and inexpensive over-the-counter medications such as garlic or niacin. At the same time, prior to the advent of new medications capable of reducing cholesterol levels to prevent heart attacks, physicians viewed a total cholesterol (TC) level of less than 300 mg/dL to be a normal TC level.

In 1987, with the entry of Mevacor (lovastatin), the first HMG-CoA reductase inhibitor (also known as a statin) for treating high cholesterol, physicians now had a tool for combating cardiovascular disease. Based on studies examining the link between high cholesterol and cardiovascular disease, new total cholesterol target goals (< 200 mg/dL) for therapy were identified.

By 1991, the first competition entered the market, and by 1997 there were six statins on the market, collectively reducing the incidence of fatal and nonfatal heart attacks by an estimated 20–30%. Even though these products were significantly more expensive than existing treatments, statin use gained wide acceptance in the prevention of cardiovascular disease. According to the Medical Expenditure Panel Survey, statin utilization had reached more than 173 million by 2005, and this number continues to grow (Stagnitti, 2000). The statins, priced at a premium level, had created a new market for prevention of heart disease.

market share, a market penetration pricing strategy that enables the product to compete more effectively on the price variable will likely be effective. Practices such as couponing or bundling (discussed later in the chapter) can be effectively employed to assist in reaching this kind of marketing goal. If market expansion is the goal, more extensive promotion (such as direct-to-consumer advertising) and a premium pricing strategy using price to position the product more uniquely can be required. The key is that whatever price strategy is selected, it must be consistent with desired product positioning and strategic marketing goals.

Recent experience in the treatment of patients with high cholesterol demonstrates how premium pricing can facilitate market expansion. (See Case in Point 4-3.) Specifically, manufacturers utilized both branded and nonbranded DTC marketing to increase awareness of hyperlipidemia, effectively increasing the size of the overall market within this therapeutic category, while pricing these products at a higher level than existing treatments.

PRICING STRATEGY OPTIONS

Traditional product marketers have at their disposal a variety of pricing strategies (**Table 4-1**) that can be employed to meet a host of price objectives. The strategy selected depends on the specific goals of the manufacturer (revenue, profits, market share, product position, etc.) and the nature of the product, such as how innovative the product is or if it is similar to drugs already on the market. (See **Table 4-2**.) The term *me-too* refers to medications that are structurally similar to others already on the market but sometimes carries a negative connotation. However, me-too products create competition and drive prices down. Whereas a significant therapeutic innovation, where product demand is expected to be

---

Table 4-1 Selected Pricing Strategies Relevant in the
Pharmaceutical Industry

Pricing Model/ Strategy	Description	Comments
Cost-plus	A determination is made of the cost of producing the product and a percentage (profit) is added to that price to give the selling price.	A critical issue resulting from the high cost to bring a pharmaceutical product to market. Depending on price levels, the time to recoup these costs varies significantly.

(continues)

Table 4-1 Selected Pricing Strategies Relevant in the Pharmaceutical Industry (*continued*)

Pricing Model/ Strategy	Description	Comments
Skimming	Products are priced at premium levels with the knowledge that this will decrease demand but maximize revenue in the short run.	A firm might use this to regain high product development costs early in the product life cycle, especially for drugs with significant improvements over existing therapies. Most appropriate when demand is expected to be relatively inelastic.
Market-oriented pricing	Marketers set a price based on analysis and research compiled from the target market. Price is set based on research results, including customers and competitors.	Requires significant qualitative and quantitative research to determine prescribers, patients, and payers' price sensitivity and appropriate price levels.
Penetration pricing	Establishing a low introductory price to capture greater market share.	Most useful when demand is expected to be highly elastic or in a crowded market where market share is the primary goal.
Premium pricing	Premium pricing sets the price of a product or service artificially high to stimulate more favorable perceptions among buyers, based on the price.	This strategy can be effective where there is a strong perception that higher price is equated with a significant therapeutic innovation.
Contribution margin–based pricing	Contribution margin (CM)–based pricing incorporates expected changes in demand based on product price and maximizes the profit derived from an individual product. This is based on the difference between the product's price and variable costs (CM per unit) and on one's assumptions regarding the relationship between the product's price and the number of units that can be sold at that price. The contribution to total profit is maximized when a price is chosen that maximizes the following: CM per unit × Number of units sold.	This strategy is useful where the relationship between price and expected demand can be accurately estimated.

Pricing Model/ Strategy	Description	Comments
Price leadership	When a company sets the level of pricing for the product category and competitors.	Most useful when the company is the dominant competitor, for new therapeutic categories, and for significant new product innovations.
Target pricing	Target pricing sets the selling price for a product to produce a specific revenue or profit target at a specific volume of production. Total revenue = Price × Volume.	This approach allows for more stable revenue flows even when demand changes.
Marginal cost pricing	This is the practice of establishing price at a level equal to the extra cost of producing an additional unit of output.	This strategy is most commonly seen where there are multiple market segments with varying levels of price sensitivity, in particular, where customers in some segments have high price sensitivity.
Value-based pricing	Pricing a product based on the perceived value of the product to customers rather than production costs or other factors.	This "leave no money on the table" strategy can be most effective where there are few if any competing products or therapies or where the existing treatments carry significant cost, morbidity, or mortality.
Profit maximization	Setting price at a level producing the highest profit while taking into account revenue and costs.	This strategy can result in lower long-term profits.
Revenue maximization	Seeks to maximize current revenue with no regard to profits.	An effective strategy for ensuring revenue flows. With this strategy, there is the secondary objective of maximizing long-term profits by increasing market share and lowering costs.

relatively inelastic, could benefit from a skimming pricing strategy, a me-too product in a crowded market might benefit from a penetration pricing strategy.

The interaction of price and other marketing mix decisions should also be considered. For example, oncology medications generally use a distribution system different from that of other medications (e.g., hypertension or asthma). In determining the appropriate pricing strategy, the impact of this channel variation must be evaluated (e.g., its impact on elasticity of demand, patient access, or reimbursement methods). Alternatively, a new product with a significant story to tell might be a good candidate for direct-to-consumer advertising. This

Table 4-2 Internal and External Market Factors

Internal	External
Product	Customers/target markets
Place	Competition
Promotion	Technology
Resources	Economic environment
Personnel	Legal
Strategic advantages (e.g., first to	Social
market, price)	Political
Other	Other

advertising could result in more rapid diffusion and adoption, providing greater revenue streams earlier in the product life cycle and affecting the levels of prices needed to achieve revenue or profit goals.

BUNDLING AND COUPONING

Over time, bundling and couponing have emerged as two additional marketing strategies that directly influence pharmaceutical pricing. **Bundling** involves offering multiple products for sale in one combined pricing deal. A manufacturer might choose to bundle a well-accepted product with a less popular one in an attempt to maintain or even increase sales levels of the latter. In the same manner, bundling can also be used to leverage formulary status. The benefits of bundling for the manufacturer are obvious; however, purchasers might not view this practice favorably. Bundling limits the ability of purchasers to negotiate on each individual product. Depending on the nature of the bundle, it might or might not represent a good economic value for purchasers.

At the consumer level, drug manufacturers interested in gaining market share through price reductions have used discount cards and **couponing** for prescription medications. These promotions directly affect price and include options such as free trials, reduced copayments, and discounts on refilled prescriptions.

Coupons for prescription medications work by attracting consumers' attention and creating interest in the product as a result of the impact on price and, in general, can circumvent traditional decision making. Most consumers process information in a stepwise fashion, but with coupons it can be different. Without a coupon or discount card, when consumers are exposed to and attend to an ad, they comprehend and evaluate alternatives before they make a decision. With a coupon or discount card, consumers might not so diligently evaluate the product. Consumers might select products, whether superior or not, just based on the offer of savings. When this occurs, manufacturers using a coupon strategy can see increased trial of products and more brand loyalty. Consumers who use coupons reduce their out-of-pocket expense, thereby changing price sensitivity. Coupons influence prescription insurers by shifting utilization away from a preferred agent, causing difficulty for plan administrators in managing medication use.

EVALUATING, REVISING, AND ADJUSTING PRICES

Over the last decade, drug prices at the retail level have grown annually by about 8% (Schondelmeyer & Purvisa, 2011). Although the retail prices of brand-name drugs do change over the product life cycle, these prices can increase at a higher rate just prior to patent expiration. This is largely because of price competition from generics and expected market share losses and the resulting impact on revenues. The pricing strategy at this point is to increase price to maintain revenues and profits. Therefore, contrary to expectations, the prices of brand-name

CASE IN POINT 4-4
Product Life Extension

The process of making minor modifications to an existing product to apply for and obtain new patents is a form of product life extension known as **evergreening**. Although sometimes controversial, a good example of evergreening involves the acid-reducing (proton pump inhibitor) drugs Prilosec (omeprazole) and Nexium (esomeprazole). When faced with generic competition, Prilosec's manufacturer introduced a modified chemical entity very similar to Prilosec called Nexium, which then became the focus of physician marketing/detailing.

Other examples of evergreening include products that are reformulated, for example, to an extended-release version or from tablets to capsules, patches, or other methods of drug delivery to extend patent life. Alternatively, medications can be combined, such as with Vytorin, a combination of ezetimibe (Zetia) and simvastatin (Zocor), or Caduet, which is atorvastatin (Lipitor) and amlodipine (Norvasc). In each case, pricing is set based on expected demand, revenues, and profits. The ultimate goal is to maintain a desired revenue stream.

products generally do not decline after generic competition emerges. In fact, pharmaceutical marketers employ a variety of strategies to extend the useful product life and maintain revenues.

PRICING GENERIC MEDICATIONS

In many cases, pharmacy providers operate under mandatory generic substitution laws requiring the use of generics when possible. Further, PDLs and formularies might also require the use of generic medications before a branded product. For multisource generic medications, whose use might be mandated by insurers or regulation, marketing mix decision making is different from branded product decision making. In the case of a generic medication, the product selected by the physician is usually available from a number of manufacturers, each competing for market share. Although physicians still choose which medication patients need, the pharmacy provider selects the company that will supply the medication. Consequently, generic pharmaceutical manufacturers focus their marketing efforts on pharmacy providers.

It should be noted that some generic manufacturers do make sales calls on physicians to encourage the use of their products. This is common when generic companies give a generic medication a brand name in the hope of creating name or brand recognition and encouraging sales. Also, other members of the distribution channel can also influence choice of supplier through buying groups and wholesaler source programs.

TRANSFORMING THE PRICE VARIABLE INTO A PROMOTIONAL VARIABLE

Between about 1990 and 2005, the prices established by some pharmaceutical manufacturers for generic medications increasingly drew the attention of government regulators, sparking significant state and federal litigation referred to as the "Average Wholesale Price (AWP) Litigation." In these cases, the government generally alleged that generic manufacturers violated the False Claims Act by establishing, reporting, and marketing inflated average wholesale price (AWP) or wholesale acquisition cost (WAC) to increase profits for providers at the expense of third-party payers.

Background

Third-party payers reimburse pharmacies based on a variety of mechanisms, including reimbursement formulas, usual and customary prices, and other means, such as reimbursement based on the lower of a series of potential reimbursement rates, a maximum allowable cost (MAC), and an upper limit on product cost (also called a federal upper limit, or FUL). Third-party reimbursement to pharmacies is based on prices created by pharmaceutical manufacturers and published for third-party payers to use in reimbursement formulas. These prices, sometimes referred to as benchmark prices, include the AWP and WAC. Typically, third-party reimbursement formulas take the form of either one of the following:

Reimbursement = AWP – % Discount + Dispensing fee
Reimbursement = WAC + % + Dispensing fee

Generic manufacturers know pharmacy buyers want low prices, consistency of supply, and quality. Other product benefits, such as a company's ability to supply a full line of generic products, or "one-stop shopping," can also be important to some generic pharmaceutical purchasers. However, because in many cases generic products are viewed as commodities, price is the most important evaluative criterion, and pharmacy providers seek out the lowest prices for products that meet quality requirements and that can be adequately and consistently supplied.

These market characteristics led to intense sales price competition and price erosion with respect to generics. As a result, manufacturers had to lower sales prices to attract new customers or even maintain existing business. This price competition and the reduction in product prices meant pharmacy providers paid less for generic products over time.

Third-Party Reimbursement

At the time of a new generic product launch, some generic manufacturers have chosen to establish AWPs for products that are approximately 10% below the AWP for competing brand-name products. It should be noted that setting AWP at this level serves at least three purposes. First, it ensures the generic status for any given product with the pricing compendia responsible for establishing generic status. Second, it provides the highest reimbursement level for pharmacies being reimbursed by third-party payers. Finally, setting AWP at approximately 10% below the AWP for the comparable brand product provides the lowest possible savings to insurers and consumers, who either reimburse or pay for medications based on AWP prices. Further, when AWPs are maintained at these levels, the AWPs do not reflect declining market prices despite generic manufacturers' expectations that generic prices will decline in the marketplace.

Third-Party Reimbursement: Pricing and the Reimbursement Spread

A somewhat unique aspect to pricing in the pharmaceutical industry is the requirement for pharmaceutical manufacturers to report product prices for their products to be eligible for reimbursement in prescription insurance programs. Specifically, manufacturers that wish for their products to be reimbursed by public and private insurers must report AWP and/or WAC to the national pricing databases. These databases are also referred to as the pricing compendia and include Medi-Span, a product of Wolters Kluwer Health, and First DataBank, which is owned by the Hearst Corporation. The prices reported to these databases are then used by insurers and providers to determine the product cost portion of reimbursement for prescriptions.

When marketers set an artificially high AWP this creates higher payments to pharmacy providers and increases costs to third-party payers. In setting an inflated AWP, the manufacturer effectively transforms the price variable of the marketing mix into a promotional variable. The promotional value is the higher reimbursement "spread" created from the inflated AWP (or WAC). This translates into increased revenues for pharmacy providers and can offer a competitive advantage to products with larger reimbursement spreads, at no cost to the manufacturer.

When faced with purchasing decisions, pharmacy providers seek products with the lowest cost and highest level of reimbursement. Creating value for the customer through larger reimbursement spreads provides incentive for prescription providers to use products with the best reimbursement spreads rather than the lowest prices. In fact, wholesalers and buying groups make available to pharmacy providers purchasing software that enables pharmacists to identify the lowest price and best spread options in an automated fashion.

Marketing the Spread

By setting artificially high AWPs and WAC prices and selling to customers at low contract prices, well below WAC or AWP, generic manufacturers create attractive reimbursement spreads for their products. Through this process, manufacturers were able to transform the price variable of the marketing mix into a promotional variable through the value to customers of the reimbursement spread.

GENERICS' IMPACT ON BRAND PRICING

Pricing for generic medications poses more of a dilemma to the brand name being imitated than to the generic manufacturer. For the generic manufacturer, the goal is to enter the market with generic status for reimbursement purposes and to satisfy the price demands of customers. Traditionally, generic manufacturers accomplish this by establishing list (usually AWP or WAC) pricing that is no more than 90% of the branded product's list price. The Hatch-Waxman Act also allows generic products that are first-to-market an exclusivity period of 6 months during which time competition is blocked so that the first generic has time to gain a market presence. This period also allows generic manufacturers to enter the market with a higher initial list price. However, after the exclusivity period, generic pricing is marked by increasing competition and consistent price erosion.

For branded products, the price response to generic competition can be a difficult decision. As noted earlier, branded product prices generally do not decline in the face of generic competition. Instead, price might increase in an effort to maintain revenues. Recently, pharmaceutical manufacturers have started lowering prices on branded products essentially to preempt generic competition. This strategy makes sense in situations where research and development costs have been recouped or the marginal costs of production, based on current volumes of sales level, result in maximization of total revenues.

SUMMARY

Pricing is a complex issue in the pharmaceutical industry that requires intensive market intelligence. With the knowledge gained from the marketplace, pharmaceutical manufacturers must balance patient access to medications with profitability and innovation. Without sufficient profits, innovation will languish and ultimately result in decreased patient outcomes. Sound pricing strategies are based on understanding and appealing to the needs and wants of the key decision makers who direct the demand for manufacturers' products. Understanding the growing role of the patient and insurers as new decision makers is critical to pharmaceutical manufacturers developing an effective pricing strategy.

DISCUSSION QUESTIONS

1. What is the impact of prescription insurance on prescription pricing decision making?

2. How does a highly inelastic demand function affect pricing decisions?

3. Consider a new oral cancer medication that has traditionally been administered intravenously. Although not a new chemical entity, the new formulation reduces doctor office expense for patients and insurers. How could this influence potential pricing for the new agent?

4. Zelsmith Pharmaceuticals has brought a new antihypertensive, Preslow, to the market. Although it is a new chemical entity, it has a number of therapeutic substitutes, which all have essentially the same mechanism of action and side-effect profile. Preslow usually needs to be dosed twice a day, but some patients can achieve good results with once-a-day dosing. One of Preslow's chief competitors is a branded product, Depress, which is indicated for once-a-day dosing and sells for $100 for a 30-day supply. Several other competitors are indicated for twice-a-day dosing (less convenient) and are available generically for about $30 per 30-day supply. How should Zelsmith position this product from a pricing perspective? Would a premium strategy designed to position Preslow to compete primarily with Depress be a better option than pricing in the generic price range? Why or why not? Should Zelsmith consider other factors with respect to pricing Preslow?

5. Why is it possibly not feasible to ensure future innovation when pricing is at suboptimal levels?

6. Although numerous pricing strategies can be applied to pharmaceutical products, skimming has traditionally provided good results for significant new innovations. How might innovative status affect the choice of a pricing strategy?

7. Why is establishing clear marketing goals the starting point for establishing product pricing?

8. Relative to generic pricing, is there an optimal price relative to the branded product that should be used as a benchmark for pharmaceutical pricing?

9. Because total revenue (R) is equal to the price (P) of the product times the quantity sold (Q), why might pharmaceutical prices frequently increase after the introduction of a generic in the marketplace?

10. Given the increasing numbers of blockbuster medications coming off patent, the saturation of certain chronic disease treatment areas, and the increasing focus on genetics and pharmacogenomics, how might pharmaceutical manufacturers alter their pricing strategy with the new medications they bring to market in the near future?

REFERENCES

Adams, C. P., & Brantner, V. V. (2006, March–April). Estimating the cost of new drug development: Is it really 802 million dollars? *Health Affairs, 25*(2), 420–428.

Collier, R. (2009, February 3). Drug development cost estimates hard to swallow. *Canadian Medical Association Journal, 180*(3), 279–280. Retrieved from http://www.ncbi.nlm.nih.gov/pmc/articles/PMC2630351

DiMasi, J., Hansen, R., & Grabowski, H. (2003). The price of innovation: New estimates of drug development costs. *Journal of Health Economics, 22*, 151–185.

Gavura, S. (2011, April 14). What does a new drug cost? Science-Based Medicine. Retrieved from http://www.sciencebasedmedicine.org/index.php/what-does-a-new-drug-cost/

Grogan, K. (2011, April 4). KV halves price of Makena but controversy rages on. Pharma Times Online. Retrieved from http://pharmatimes.com/Article/11-04-04/KV_halves_price_of_Makena_but_controversy_rages_on.aspx

Lowe, D. (2011, March 24). KV Pharmaceuticals' pricing for Makena. Seeking Alpha. Retrieved from http://seekingalpha.com/article/260029-kv-pharmaceuticals-pricing-for-makena

National Council on Patient Information and Education. (2007). *Enhancing prescription medication adherence: A national action plan.* Rockville, MD: Author. Retrieved from http://www.talkaboutrx.org/documents/enhancing_prescription_medicine_adherence.pdf

Schondelmeyer, S., & Purvis, L. (2011, March). Rx price watch report: Retail prices for widely used brand name drugs increase considerably prior to generic competition. AARP Public Policy Institute. Retrieved from http://assets.aarp.org/rgcenter/ppi/health-care/i49-rx-2011.pdf

Shrank, W. H., Joseph, G. J., Choudhry, N. K., Young, H. N., Ettner, S. L., Glassman, P., … Kravitz R. L. (2006). Physicians' perceptions of relevant prescription drug costs: Do costs to the individual patient or the population matter most? *American Journal of Managed Care, 12*, 545–551.

Stagnitti, M. (2000). Statistical brief 5: Medical care and treatment for chronic conditions. Agency for Healthcare Research and Quality. Retrieved from http://meps.ahrq.gov/mepsweb/data_files/publications/st5/stat05.pdf

Stobbe, M. (2011, March 9). Premature labor drug spikes from $10 to $1,500. NBC News.com. Retrieved from http://www.msnbc.msn.com/id/41994697/ns/health-pregnancy

CHAPTER 5

Place: The Pharmaceutical Industry Supply Chain

Brent L. Rollins, PhD, RPh, and Matthew Perri, PhD, RPh

LEARNING OBJECTIVES

1. Describe the evolution of the pharmaceutical wholesale industry from distributive and financial perspectives.
2. Characterize how issues in the pharmaceutical industry supply chain ultimately affect patient health outcomes.
3. Identify the wholesale industry's primary customer base, explain the various supply chain models, and describe the dynamics of the different models and relationships.
4. Distinguish the different issues unique to the pharmaceutical wholesale industry from pricing, negotiating, and reimbursement perspectives.
5. Analyze how the dynamics of the wholesale industry affect the pharmaceutical manufacturer marketer.

Recently, the pharmaceutical industry has been marked by a drastic increase in drug shortages. Numerous injectables (including the emergency medication epinephrine), pain, attention deficit disorder (ADD), and, in particular, cancer medications have not been consistently supplied to local hospitals, pharmacies, and clinics that dispense them. Thus, with a shortage of chemo-therapeutic agents in hospitals, cancer patients might not get the essential medications they need for survival and providers are forced to identify and execute alternate treatment routes/methods. Since 2010, these shortages have cost an estimated $216 million in additional healthcare labor costs (Gatesman, 2011). The problem escalated to the point that President Obama issued an executive order to examine the trouble (Salahi, 2011) and the Food and Drug Administration (FDA) has created a site dedicated to drug shortages (Food and Drug Administration, 2012).

The topic of drug shortages brings full circle the issues that can arise within the pharmaceutical industry supply chain. *Supply chain* is the practical term associated with the marketing four Ps *place*, which refers to any activity designed to create value and utility by making the product(s) available in the market-place. Like many large-volume industries, the pharmaceutical industry sup-ply chain is quite dynamic and complex because prescriptions are dispensed at approximately 140,000 different venues in the United States (Handfield & Dhinagaravel, 2005). In its simplest form, the supply consists of pharmaceutical manufacturers making and then shipping medications to wholesalers, who, in turn, distribute products to community pharmacies, pharmacy benefit manager (PBM)–owned mail-order pharmacies, hospitals, long-term care facilities, and various clinics.

To fully understand the impact of the pharmaceutical industry supply chain, though, one must understand how the links in the chain ultimately affect patients and health outcomes. Consider a pharmacy owner in a rural area who owns a pharmacy in each of two neighboring small towns. This pharma-cist needs to purchase medications at the best possible price to ensure she can profitably stay in business. Further, she needs the purchased products delivered in an efficient and timely manner so as not to inconvenience her customers or possibly lose them to competitors. Within the supply chain, the pharmacist cannot negotiate directly with the various manufacturers because they do not provide the necessary distribution services. Thus, the pharmacist must negoti-ate with a wholesaler that she hopes can provide the best possible combina-tion of price and distribution services. Without the wholesaler providing its vital distribution function in the pharmaceutical supply chain, many pharma-cies across the country would not be able to serve their customers/patients. In the worst-case scenario, those patients could possibly have to survive without vital medications such as insulin, pain, blood pressure, or thyroid medications, among others.

CASE IN POINT 5-1
Supply Chain Issues in Other Industries

Supply chain issues can damage a brand reputation or image very quickly if unresolved. Recently, Apple, Inc., was made aware of working condition issues in one of its primary suppliers in China: Foxconn, an electronics manufacturer that handles products such as the iPad and iPhone for Apple. Consider the business ramifications if Apple, the leading U.S. technology company, had to delay shipments or availability of its two primary products for any period of time (Burnson, 2012; Gupta & Grenon, 2012; Kropp, 2012). For most electronics consumers, this is an unthinkable situation. Now, consider the implications for patients if the pharmaceutical distribution system fails to provide medications needed to sustain life and alleviate the symptoms of disease.

EVOLUTION OF THE PHARMACEUTICAL WHOLESALE INDUSTRY

In the 1960s and 1970s, pharmaceutical wholesaling was primarily a retail business driven by sales representatives who made daily or weekly sales visits and called in medication orders to the warehouse. Once the order was placed, the product would then be delivered within a few days. Thus, the core business for wholesalers revolved around the pick, pack, and ship model. As technology advanced and brought ordering and delivery to an efficient and quick turnover/next-day process, wholesalers began to evolve and expand their service offerings into, for example, reimbursement, packaging, and consulting services, otherwise known as value-added services.

As a buyer of medications and customer of the pharmaceutical industry, wholesalers consistently need the best available pricing and a consistent supply of medications. Given the continual pricing pressures applied by manufacturers and purchasing pharmacies, the years have brought constant price and margin erosion within the core pick, pack, and ship model. In addition to the price and margin erosion, the wholesale industry was marked by increasing competition in the marketplace, leading to the same fate as the pharmaceutical manufacturer industry—increased consolidation and mergers. As a result of these consolidations

CASE IN POINT 5-2
Technology Products Offered by Wholesalers

While still remaining a pharmaceutical wholesaler at its core with the pick, pack, and ship model, the wholesale industry has quickly evolved as a major player in the health information technology business. Companies continue to expand their reach in this area and make quality, user-friendly information and distribution solution products available to healthcare providers throughout the United States. McKesson, for example, has become a leader in automation, bar-coding, and integration technologies for hospital pharmacies, hospitals, and health systems in general. McKesson offers numerous other solution systems, including financial and clinical information systems, hospital information systems (for efficient and clear integration throughout the health system), and electronic health record (EHR) solutions for physicians.

over time, the wholesale industry is currently dominated by three large, multi-billion-dollar firms that have combined to eliminate or buy a majority of the competition: AmerisourceBergen, Cardinal Health, and McKesson Corporation. At this point, the "Big 3" wholesalers control approximately 85–90% of the market share in the United States (Britt, 2007; Fein, 2011).

In addition to the consolidation within the industry on a macro level, the business model of the wholesale pharmaceutical industry has evolved on the micro level. Prior to the mid-2000s, pharmaceutical wholesalers worked off a prospective buying system, also known as a **buy-and-hold system**. Wholesalers purchased medications from pharmaceutical manufacturers in extreme bulk, and then sold the medications at a later date, counting on prices going up from the time of purchase and, thus, creating their profit margin.

However, the pricing pressures and margin erosion, as well as the rise in prominence of generic medications, forced the wholesale industry to change its business model. In the mid-2000s, the industry abandoned the buy-and-hold model in favor of the current fee-for-service (FFS) model (Handfield & Dhinagaravel, 2005). In the FFS model, wholesalers charge manufacturers for the services rendered, including distribution, inventory management, customer service, and financial administration (chargebacks, which are discussed later).

From a pharmaceutical manufacturer's marketing perspective, the FFS model has led to increased market intelligence in the form of timely and accurate data from wholesalers. The pharmaceutical marketer can then use this information to help in forecasting and customer service if any issues arise.

PRIMARY CUSTOMERS AND INDUSTRY DYNAMICS

With the evolution in the wholesale pharmaceutical distribution system, virtually any provider of medications (e.g., hospitals, pharmacies, medical clinics, health departments) has become a customer of the pharmaceutical wholesaler. However, unlike the consumer-driven evolution toward shared decision making in the pharmaceutical industry where the general consumer/patient has become a primary customer for the industry, the wholesale industry typically does not concern itself with the general consumer population as a customer base. Given the laws and regulations of the pharmaceutical industry and that pharmaceutical products are sold by prescription only, general consumers cannot purchase medications directly from pharmaceutical wholesalers. Therefore, the "buy direct from the wholesaler" model seen in many industries, such as the furniture industry, does not exist with pharmaceuticals. From a marketing perspective, even though this lessens the burden on pharmaceutical wholesale marketers in terms of the analysis and reach needed to form a relationship with its customers, there are still challenges within the industry and its customer base.

One of the primary challenges within the wholesale industry is the interaction/dynamics between the manufacturer and wholesaler. Manufacturers (and pharmaceutical marketers) must work to match the wholesaler's volume and packaging demands with their own production processes and forecasts (includes quantities, package sizes, etc.; that is, product-specific needs). The advent of **just-in-time (JIT) inventory**, an inventory system in which goods are only delivered when needed as opposed to prospectively or after the fact, has greatly helped to overcome this obstacle and created better inventory control and more physical efficiency in the distribution system.

Financial challenges also exist with the **upstream customers** (wholesaler to manufacturer) and **downstream customers** (wholesaler to pharmacy/dispensing outlet) customers. Working upstream, wholesalers must budget accordingly to take advantage of payment incentives offered by manufacturers and be efficient in their recording for chargeback purposes. From the downstream perspective, because the wholesaler–pharmacy relationship depends on the type of pharmacy (large chain or mail-order pharmacy with its own warehouse vs. regional chain without its own warehouse vs. small independent pharmacy), wholesalers must show pharmacy customers how they can help them increase their own inventory and financial efficiency.

SUPPLY CHAIN MODELS

Generally speaking, the pharmaceutical supply chain functions as depicted in **Figure 5-1**. The pharmaceutical manufacturer discovers, produces, and ships medication to the wholesaler, who, in turn, distributes to the thousands of pharmacies, hospitals, and clinics nationwide. As discussed, this process is vital for the survival of small, independently owned pharmacy businesses in smaller, more rural areas.

Even though wholesalers distribute to numerous pharmacies and hospitals, other entities within the supply chain and industry in general have worked to exclude the wholesaler (the middle man) and increase their own efficiency levels and profits. The first entity is the large chain pharmacy. Consider Wal-Mart Pharmacies: With thousands of pharmacy outlets that need medication delivered on a consistent basis, a large international warehouse and distribution system, including one of the largest private trucking fleets in the world, why would this company need a middle man such as the pharmaceutical wholesaler?

FIGURE 5-1 General Pharmacy Supply Chain Model

Larger, nationwide chain pharmacies (e.g., CVS, Walgreens, Rite Aid) and grocery chain/mass merchandisers (e.g., Wal-Mart, Kroger) have worked for quite some time to establish their own efficient and cost-reducing supply chain. An additional benefit to this method is these larger chain pharmacies negotiate and buy directly from the pharmaceutical manufacturers, typically leading to better pricing, given their ability to move market share. Although this model primarily excludes the wholesaler, large chain pharmacies still have contracts and services in place with the wholesaler to handle inventory needs not met by their own warehousing operations (**Figure 5-2**). Many chain pharmacies, for example, have medications delivered from their warehouse to the various stores either daily, once weekly, or once every other week, depending on store volume and company logistics. A wholesaler then serves to handle inventory needs not covered by the pharmacy warehouse during the weekdays. From a practicing pharmacist perspective, the various chain pharmacies do not prefer that medications be ordered from a wholesaler when the medication is available in the pharmacy warehouse because of the pricing differentiation.

In addition to the large national chain pharmacies, mail-order pharmacies bypass the wholesaler as much as possible. Mail-order pharmacies are pharmacies servicing members of a pharmacy benefit plan. Mail-order pharmacies rely on economies of scale created by dispensing as many prescriptions as possible to continually lower their cost of dispensing. With fewer, more regionalized facilities, mail-order pharmacies dispense massive numbers of prescriptions per facility compared to an individual chain pharmacy store. Further, just as their large chain pharmacy counterparts, mail-order pharmacies can purchase medications

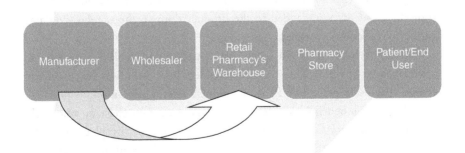

FIGURE 5-2 Large Retail Pharmacy Supply Chain Model

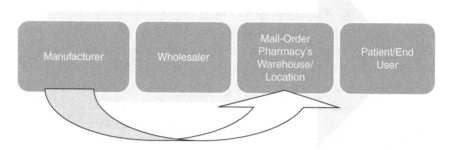

FIGURE 5-3 Mail-Order Pharmacy Supply Chain Model

directly from the manufacturer and greatly enhance their buying power, but still have contracts and receive some product from the wholesaler for those needs not met through direct purchasing (**Figure 5-3**).

ISSUES UNIQUE TO THE PHARMACEUTICAL WHOLESALE INDUSTRY

Pricing and Terms

Pricing at the pharmaceutical wholesale level has evolved over time. As mentioned previously, the wholesale marketplace has become more concentrated (fewer, larger wholesalers), price competition has become significantly more intense (in part because of a significant rise in the utilization of generic products), and greater efficiency has been demanded in the distribution chain (pick, pack, and ship component). Pharmacy customers pay wholesalers for the pharmaceutical product and the value added to the product through the warehousing and distributive functions provided.

Wholesalers have employed a few basic methods to achieve a reasonable return on investment. Traditionally, wholesalers have set prices based on the **average wholesale price (AWP)** of a product, offering discounts to purchasers based on this benchmark price. When wholesalers purchase at **wholesale acquisition cost (WAC)**, which has traditionally been set by pharmaceutical manufacturers at 25–30% below AWP, the size of the discount to the pharmacy purchaser could be negotiated within this range. Another method for pricing that has been used successfully is **WAC-plus pricing**. With WAC-plus pricing, the pharmaceutical wholesaler passes on the WAC to the pharmacy purchaser and charges an additional markup percentage, providing the desired profit to the wholesaler. Pharmacy wholesalers have also used line fees in conjunction with **AWP-minus pricing** or WAC-plus pricing. **Line fees** are simply a monetary charge for each line item ordered by the pharmacy purchaser, encouraging more efficient purchasing by customers (efficiency is obtained when customers order greater quantities of individual products fewer times).

An additional and common practice for wholesalers is the participation in programs where the pharmaceutical manufacturer contracts directly with purchasers (e.g., regional chain pharmacy without a warehouse), yet uses the wholesaler for the distribution function. In these cases, manufacturers and purchasers establish prices and wholesalers purchase under their normal terms (usually WAC-minus). Wholesalers provide the distributive function and sell to the purchaser at the lower contract price. Then, when the competitive contract price to the purchaser is lower than the price paid by the wholesaler (e.g., WAC-minus), manufacturers provide the wholesaler with a **chargeback** amount to make the wholesaler whole on the purchase. The chargeback amount can also be

CASE IN POINT 5-3
Chargebacks

Even though it is a smaller, regional chain, Shelly's Pharmacies can move significant market share for its most commonly dispensed medications. Although not large enough to operate its own warehouse operation, Shelly's is large enough to negotiate directly with manufacturers to get more attractive pricing than is available through the major national wholesalers. As a result, Shelly's has negotiated a contract price with Watson Pharmaceuticals for several products, including a commonly prescribed birth control product called Leena. The contract price for Leena is $2.25 less than the wholesaler's best price for Leena. Shelly's orders Leena directly from its wholesaler, which then passes along the contract price savings of $2.25 to Shelly's. The wholesaler then bills a chargeback to Watson to cover the difference.

negotiated and generally represents the difference between what the wholesaler paid and the lower price the manufacturer has negotiated with the customer. The wholesaler submits a chargeback request to the manufacturer on a regular basis (daily or weekly). Each chargeback request can contain thousands of line items for review. A typical drug manufacturer processes millions of chargeback requests per year and transfers hundreds of millions of dollars per year in chargeback payments. These programs are common with large pharmacy customers such as chains, hospitals, and larger independent pharmacies that have the ability to direct significant amounts of market share.

Although these methods seem straightforward, issues external to the wholesalers have created additional factors influencing the ability to earn profits through the wholesale function. These include the following:

- Expansion of the generic market and the associated intense price competition and price erosion this has created.
- Intense competition at the wholesale level, requiring pharmaceutical manufacturers to offer wholesalers additional discounts and incentives.
- Third-party prescription reimbursement systems adding downward price pressure in the marketplace.

Generic Prices and Price Erosion

For pharmaceutical products in general, prices to customers are established by manufacturers based on development, production, and marketing costs in combination with the level of prices among competitors, or "what the market will bear." Manufacturers typically set net prices; contract, list, or invoice prices; WAC; and AWP. With respect to price levels established by manufacturers, contract prices are the lowest, followed by WAC or sometimes list price. As noted, the exact nature of the relationship among each of these prices depends on the discounts and incentives manufacturers use to create attractive net prices for customers, including wholesalers.

For generics in particular, the U.S. generic drug market is characterized by intense sales price competition and **price erosion**. This means that over time, manufacturers must lower sales prices to maintain business or attract new customers in an effort to maintain or gain market share. In the cost-plus world of the pharmaceutical wholesaler, these lower prices also affect the wholesaler's ability to earn profits as lower-priced products dominate the marketplace, ultimately resulting in lower profit margins for wholesalers.

Price erosion also creates the expectation from customers that prices will continue to decline, resulting in increased customer demands for lower pricing. Although this price erosion obviously affects the prices of generics, it also exerts downward pressure on the prices of branded products in two ways. First, lower prices of generics create a larger gap between the branded and generic price, further incentivizing the use of generics over branded products. Second, lower prices for generics translate into a lower-cost treatment option that can influence pricing of new branded products that must still compete therapeutically with older, less expensive generics.

Incentives

Given the level of price competition in the wholesale marketplace, pharmaceutical manufacturers offer wholesalers a variety of ways to reduce product cost, serving to both increase profits to wholesalers and provide them with the ability to offer lower prices to pharmacy purchasers. These incentives have included, for example, competitive, market-based contract prices; cash or **prompt payment discounts**; **market share–based bonuses** or **rebates**; and **volume discounts**. Although each of these pricing practices offers a different mechanism to reduce prices to wholesalers, the net effect is the same: to reduce product acquisition cost to the customer, in this case, the wholesaler. Reductions in acquisition costs to wholesalers allow wholesalers both to pass along part of the savings to customers and generate desired levels of net profit.

CASE IN POINT 5-4
Wholesalers and Incentives

XYZ Wholesaler has negotiated a contract with a generic manufacturer to provide four high-volume products: lisinopril, hydrochlorothiazide, citalopram, and amoxicillin. List pricing for each of these products will be based on the WAC with a flat 5% discount and additional terms **2/10 net 30**. The additional terms mean that if XYZ pays its bill within 10 days, it receives a 2% discount (i.e., prompt-pay discount), with the full balance due within 30 days. In addition, the contract specifies that if a monthly volume of 20,000 units of each product is obtained, an additional 5% discount will be applied to all prices.

Source Programs and Buying Groups

In addition to various incentives within the pricing structure of a wholesaler contract, other entities and dynamics in the industry exist to lower prices and increase margins for both pharmacies and the wholesaler. For example, in Case in Point 5-4, to reach the volume terms of its contract with the manufacturer and receive the 5% discount, XYZ Wholesaler would designate this generic manufacturer's products as the preferred generics by adding them to its "source" program. A **source program** is a comprehensive listing of products where similar deals have been negotiated to increase wholesaler profits and pass along part of the savings to purchasers (i.e., essentially functioning as a preferred drug list). Pharmacy purchasers know that generic source program products often carry the lowest acquisition costs because of the incentives offered to wholesalers by manufacturers, so these purchasers, in turn, choose these products to take advantage of the competitive pricing.

Also working with the wholesaler as a customer is **buying groups** or **group purchasing organizations**. Buying groups are numerous pharmacies (typically independent pharmacies) that band together in their contracts with a wholesaler and, in turn, exclusively use the contracted wholesaler. The primary purpose is to increase buying power in their drug-purchasing negotiations. Consider again the small pharmacy owner discussed earlier in the chapter. If she were to negotiate directly with the wholesaler, purchasing medications for her two stores, the wholesaler would not view her volume as sufficient enough to provide significant price breaks, primarily because her relatively small operation cannot move overall market share. However, if she joins forces with a group of 3,000 other pharmacies (a retail buying group), this group collectively can significantly alter market share and volume. The wholesaler would then be very willing to negotiate with the buying group and likely alter the pricing structure. This is a relatively good situation for both the wholesaler and pharmacies, even though the wholesaler makes some pricing concessions. The pharmacies gain buying and negotiating power, leading to better prices and, hopefully, greater profits, while the wholesaler gains 3,000 exclusive customers. Some examples of buying groups include Independent Pharmacy Cooperative and American Associated Pharmacies, among others. **Figure 5-4** includes these examples and others, in addition to their primary wholesaler.

Third-Party Reimbursement

An additional external market force that affects wholesalers is third-party reimbursement. Third-party payers reimburse pharmacies based on a variety of

Buying Group	Participating Pharmacies	Primary/Preferred Wholesalers
Independent Pharmacy Cooperative	3,300	McKesson
Independent Pharmacy Alliance	2,300	AmerisourceBergen, Kinray
American Associated Pharmacies	2,000	Cardinal Health
Pace Alliance	1,700	Multiple wholesalers
American Pharmacy Cooperative, Inc.	1,650	McKesson
EPIC Pharmacies	1,400	Multiple wholesalers

Source: *The 2010–11 Economic Report on Pharmaceutical Wholesalers, 23.*
Available at http://www.pembrokeconsulting.com/wholesale.html.

FIGURE 5-4 Wholesale Buying Groups

CASE IN POINT 5-5
GeriMed, RxMed, and IVMed

A signature example of a group purchasing organization (or buying group) is GeriMed. Established in 1983, GeriMed is a leading group purchasing organization focused primarily as a buyer for pharmacies servicing long-term care (LTC) facilities, such as nursing homes and assisted-living facilities. In addition, they have a buying unit focused on aiding retail/independent pharmacies (RxMed) and one focused on home infusion pharmacies (IVMed).

---

mechanisms, including reimbursement formulas, usual and customary prices, reimbursement based on the lower of a series of potential reimbursement rates, a maximum allowable cost (MAC), and an upper limit on product cost (also called a federal upper limit, or FUL). As insurers have sought to control prices and reduce reimbursement rates, pharmacy purchasers have sought additional discounts on product costs, adding further competitive pressure to wholesalers' prices.

SUMMARY

The wholesale industry functions as the centerpiece of the pharmaceutical industry supply chain and the place denominator from a marketing viewpoint.

Primarily, though, from the manufacturers' perspective, the Big 3 wholesalers make up a large and important customer base. Thus, the pharmaceutical marketer must continually be in touch with the needs and wants of the wholesale industry to best serve it as a customer. In addition to providing the best possible price and payment terms, pharmaceutical marketers must make sure their own manufacturing processes are in tune with the desires of the wholesaler and pharmacy. The wholesaler, in turn, can provide unique data to the manufacturers on market share, volume, and any logistical issues in the distributive process so as to avoid any disruptions in product delivery and eventual sale.

DISCUSSION QUESTIONS

1. Explain why consolidation from many pharmaceutical wholesalers into the Big 3 makes sense from a business perspective. What benefits does this consolidation provide for retail pharmacies and hospitals? Pharmaceutical manufacturers? Patients?

2. Describe the difference between relying on a pick, pack, and ship model and a value-added model. How does this shift in the wholesale business model affect pharmaceutical marketers and retail pharmacies?

3. Consider the large national chain pharmacy with its own warehousing operation. Does it make sense for this chain to also contract with one of the Big 3? Why or why not?

4. What are some services that a pharmaceutical wholesaler can provide that would fall into the category of value added? Is there overlap between these services and the pick, pack, and ship model?

5. What advice would you give to a pharmacy operation that is not a member of a buying group and that purchases directly from one of the Big 3 pharmaceutical wholesalers using a just-in-time inventory management system (in other words, the pharmacy orders its inventory to arrive just in time to be utilized, with little reserve inventory)?

6. Describe the dynamics of generic pricing that result in price erosion, usually to levels that are only about 10% of initial launch prices, and how this affects the wholesaler.

7. Describe the value of the following value-added wholesale pharmaceutical services and rank their importance in the healthcare industry:
   a. Daily delivery of products
   b. Reimbursement consulting

   c. Consistent product supply

   d. Product quality

   e. Low prices

8. In your opinion, how valuable is the market intelligence provided by pharmaceutical wholesalers (which primarily come from retail pharmacy sales) as compared to the data that can be obtained from commercial market research firms such as IMS Health, Inc., which can track physicians' prescription-writing habits?

9. Pharmaceutical wholesalers are an integral part of the industry, providing the majority of the distribution function. For many years, there has been a consolidation in the wholesale industry and greater emphasis placed on economic efficiency. How does the wholesale distribution chain positively and/or negatively affect the marketing mix variables (price, place, product, and promotion)?

10. Given how the wholesale industry has thrived even in the face of low profit margins in its core pick, pack, and ship business model, how might pharmaceutical manufacturers learn from this and possibly expand their business model?

REFERENCES

Britt, R. (2007, May 30). Growing share of 'Big Three' gets federal attention. Market Watch. Retrieved from http://articles.marketwatch.com/2007-05-30/news/30788055_1_wholesale-drug-market-reimportation-mckesson-and-cardinal

Burnson, P. (2012, February 3). Apple's supply chain problem. Market Watch. Retrieved from http://articles.marketwatch.com/2012-02-03/commentary/31029194_1_supply-chain-apple-products

Fein, A. (2011, May 26). 2011 MDM market leaders: Top pharmaceutical wholesalers. *Modern Distribution Management.* Retrieved from http://www.mdm.com/2011_pharmaceutical_mdm-market-leaders

Food and Drug Administration. (2012). Drugs: Drug shortages. Retrieved from http://www.fda.gov/Drugs/DrugSafety/DrugShortages/default.htm

Gatesman, M. L., & Smith, T. J. (2011, November). The shortage of essential chemotherapy drugs in the United States. *New England Journal of Medicine, 365*(18), 1653–1655.

Gupta, P., & Grenon, A. (2012, January 27). Apple not turning "blind eye" to supply chain problems: CEO. Reuters. Retrieved from http://www.reuters.com/article/2012/01/27/us-apple-supply-idUSTRE80Q20T20120127

Handfield, R. B., & Dhinagaravel, V. (2005, November 4). Future trends in pharmaceutical and biotech distribution. Supply Chain Resource Consortium, NC State University. Retrieved from http://www.supplychainredesign.com/publications/trends-pharma-biotech.pdf

Kropp, R. (2012, April 12). Learning from Apple's supply chain management mistakes. GreenBiz.com. Retrieved from http://www.greenbiz.com/blog/2012/04/12/learning -apple-supply-chain-mistake

Salahi, L. (2011, October 31). Obama issues executive order to ease drug shortages. ABC News. Retrieved from http://abcnews.go.com/Health/Wellness/presidents-executive -order-drug-shortage-draws-mixed-reactions/story?id=14852829#.UFIDcFE_KHs

CHAPTER 6

Promotional Marketing Activities and Practices

Dee Fanning, PharmD, Brian Mitchell, MBA, MPH,
and Julie Brideau, PharmD

LEARNING OBJECTIVES

1. Explain the roles of commercial operations and how key personnel disseminate information regarding the company's products.
2. Define, describe, and recognize fair balance in pharmaceutical promotion.
3. List and describe the three primary marketing tactics used by pharmaceutical manufacturers.
4. Describe and give examples of the promotional formula of "Right Message, Right Frequency, and Right Reach."
5. Differentiate between co-promotion and co-marketing.
6. Distinguish the three factors that have resulted in a large reduction in the number of U.S. drug reps over the past 5 years and the impact this has had on the pharmaceutical industry.
7. Explain the events that led to the blockbuster era and the subsequent decline of said era.
8. Apply these principles to a marketing campaign of a newly FDA-approved product.

As one of the traditional marketing mix Four Ps, promotion serves as the communication arm of marketing, imparting on the customer the product's features and benefits to initiate purchase and exchange. In the case of the pharmaceutical manufacturer, for the company to survive and grow, more of the actual pharmaceutical product must be sold. Thus, all divisions of a pharmaceutical manufacturer work toward, and are ultimately responsible for, the success of the company and its products.

Pharmaceutical companies use promotional marketing tactics to communicate their products' features and benefits to their customers—typically, physicians, or other prescribers, but also patients and third-party payers. Medical journals, scientific conferences, peer discussions, and independent research are all means that physicians use to stay informed about treatment options. However, more often than not, the primary source of information about pharmaceutical products is the pharmaceutical manufacturer itself. The data provided to physicians by pharmaceutical manufacturers about their products and related disease states provide a venue for an exchange of information that might not otherwise exist. Pharmaceutical marketers are then focused on understanding how prescribers learn about the medications they prescribe. They seek to answer questions such as how providers keep up with the changing pharmaceutical landscape and how they decide which product to prescribe for a patient when several similar choices exist.

The primary promotional tactics used are sales visits to physicians (known as **detailing**), public relations (PR) messaging, and direct-to-consumer (DTC) advertising. At its most fundamental level, a pharmaceutical company's marketing strategy is not very different from that of other types of companies: to create or raise the awareness, trial, and usage of a given product. However, unlike most other types of companies, pharmaceutical companies market products that have a direct impact on human health, and, therefore, their marketing practices are heavily regulated by the Food and Drug Administration (FDA). Unlike the world of consumer product marketing where claims need not be substantiated, every written or spoken word claiming a benefit of a marketed pharmaceutical product is required to be authenticated by scientific data. Claims of efficacy, safety, and improvements in quality of life must be reinforced by clinical evidence so that physicians and patients are not misled or put at risk. In addition, disclosure of common side effects and risks must accompany pharmaceutical product promotion. This risk information must provide a **fair balance** to the beneficial claims, which is why television commercials for pharmaceutical products always include information regarding the product's risks. Promotional marketing tactics are also used to raise awareness of the prevalence of a disease state or condition.

Whereas the nature of these responsibilities are not all *promotional* in the traditional sense of the word, examples of the various divisions responsible for the "product" include manufacturing, clinical development, research and development, commercial operations, and medical affairs, just to name a few. This chapter focuses on the commercial division, but remember as you read: The interaction of all these divisions is a vital part of the marketing process and, ultimately, the success of a company's products.

COMMERCIAL OPERATIONS

In most pharmaceutical companies, the commercial operations division includes departments such as Sales, Marketing, and Managed Markets. In general, departments that have a primary goal of generating revenue to the company through the sales of its products fall under commercial operations (analogous to a profit center in accounting terms). The promotional materials used by these departments are typically developed in-house with the help of advertising agencies, go through an extensive review process (often referred to as Advertising and Promotional Review—described later in the chapter), and are regulated by the FDA, or, in some situations, the **Federal Trade Commission (FTC)**.

The commercial operations team uses numerous types of promotional materials targeted to physicians or other healthcare providers (HCPs) with prescriptive authority and/or directly to patients or consumers (DTC). These can include, but are not limited to, help-seeking/disease awareness ads (e.g., "ask your doctor"), coming soon ads (e.g., "Drug XYZ will be available in 20xx"), institution ads (e.g., "Company ABC is researching important new treatments in the area of cardiovascular health"), reminder ads or items (e.g., pens, calendars—these items are no longer allowed, though, and will be discussed later in the chapter), and full product pieces (e.g., journal ads, detailing aids, product websites). Full product pieces, whether DTC or targeted toward HCPs, must be fair balanced, meaning if they include product claims, they must also include appropriate risk information to present a fair balance of information to prescribers and/or patients so they can make a fully informed product decision. The intent of the information disseminated with the aid of these promotional materials is proactive in nature with the outcome or deliverable measured by sales numbers, and thus the FDA or FTC regulates them all.

Detailing

For decades, pharmaceutical sales representatives, commonly known as "drug reps," have been the primary messengers for branded pharmaceutical products. Companies use a variety of complex implementation strategies for sending their representatives into the field. However, the tried-and-true formula for effective sales promotion in this industry is "Right Message, Right Frequency, and Right Reach."

- The message refers to the features and benefits of the product, and **right message** means the information must be both factual and compelling to a prescriber.
- The frequency refers to the number of times the message is delivered to the physician. A number of factors, such as the product's age or physicians' familiarity with the product's therapeutic category, determine how frequently a prescriber needs to hear a message before he or she develops a preference for a particular product. The **Rule of Seven** is often used in pharmaceutical and other types of marketing. As its name implies, this approach assumes that customers do not fully understand a marketing message until they have heard it at least seven times, which is the **right frequency** (Domanski, 2007; Stenberg, 2008).
- Reach describes the number and type of physicians targeted by the pharmaceutical company for a given brand. A company with a new treatment for diabetes, for example, might instruct a representative to achieve a **right reach** of at least 80% of the endocrinologists in that rep's sales territory each month.

Pharmaceutical companies view the sales representative and physician as the constants in this formula. By making adjustments to the variables of the message, reach, and frequency based on a product's life cycle and/or its competitive landscape, companies can optimize their investment of sales representative time and expense. When detailing efforts appear to be successful, companies often increase those efforts until they experience diminishing returns.

Detailing physicians has been extremely successful for the pharmaceutical industry and largely responsible for its growth during the **blockbuster** era that has existed since the beginning of the 1990s. A blockbuster drug is one that generates more than $1 billion in annual sales for the company. At the height of the blockbuster era in 2005, 94 medications met the blockbuster threshold, accounting for 36% of global pharmaceutical sales (Cutler, 2007). Examining Pfizer's statistics from that same year show three of their blockbuster medications (Zoloft [sertraline], Norvasc [amlodipine], and Lipitor [atorvastatin]) accounted for approximately 40% of their total sales (Cutler, 2007).

At its peak, the number of drug reps in the United States exceeded 100,000, with many of the largest pharmaceutical companies employing "pods" of representatives detailing the same products to the same set of physicians. Although this tactic might appear wasteful and redundant, there was rapid adoption and dramatic growth of several commonly prescribed products during this time. In fact, entire therapeutic categories such as depression, erectile dysfunction, and hypercholesterolemia have been affected by this approach to product detailing. Although pharmaceutical companies rarely apply the pod approach today, the reason is not its lack of effectiveness, but rather its cost in terms of dollars and public perception.

Smaller pharmaceutical companies also use product detailing as a promotional tool, but without the vast resources of their larger counterparts these companies often apply more creative approaches to detailing than the brute force of an army of representatives. One common approach smaller pharmaceutical companies use is the partnership model, or **co-promotion**. Co-promotion is when small companies partner with larger, more established companies to promote their products jointly as long as no conflict of interest exists. This co-promotion can benefit both parties in terms of resource optimization, specifically in the ability to increase reach with an experienced sales force with known relationships and therapeutic knowledge. For example, in 2005, Solvay Pharmaceuticals entered into a co-promotional agreement with ICOS Corporation, a biotechnology firm eventually acquired by Eli Lilly. ICOS representatives were already detailing urologists on the drug Cialis (tadalafil) for the treatment of erectile dysfunction. Under this agreement, ICOS reps would also detail these same physicians on the appropriate use of AndroGel (testosterone gel) 1% for the treatment of low testosterone in men. The tactic of co-promotion is not to be confused with **co-marketing**, the less popular model. Co-promotion involves joint sales and/or marketing of the same branded product (or synergistic brands), usually with the same objectives, whereas in a co-marketing agreement, the sales and marketing are performed separately and the objectives of the two companies might not be the same.

Another approach smaller companies frequently take is the utilization of **contract sales organizations (CSOs)**. These organizations employ sales professionals who are skilled at calling on physicians and simply require training on the specific features and benefits of the hiring company's product. Partnering with a CSO, such as Advocos, provides an advantage for a pharmaceutical manufacturer because it is much less expensive to do than hiring and maintaining a dedicated sales team. This has led to the growth of the CSO industry as a pharmaceutical industry offshoot.

As effective as pharmaceutical detailing has been—and still is—the industry has become less reliant on this tactic in recent years. The number of drug reps in the United States peaked in 2007 at approximately 102,000. At the end of 2012, this number is estimated to be approximately 75,000, a decrease of more than 25% (O'Reilly, 2009). Although that might still seem like a large number, getting there has required drastic layoffs by companies of all sizes. The negative public perception of pharmaceutical companies and their large sales forces is as high as it has ever been. Patient advocacy groups, politicians, the media, and others have increased their criticism of the nature of the industry's relationships with its physician customers. These groups and individuals have also sought to connect the expense associated with the practice of detailing to the cost of branded pharmaceuticals and health care overall.

Although pharmaceutical companies take such criticisms seriously, the downsizing of the sales representative and the decreasing role of detailing should not be viewed as a reaction to these external efforts. Three factors, each internal to the pharmaceutical industry, have been the primary contributors to the large reduction in the number of U.S. drug reps over the past 5 years and moving forward in the future: fewer blockbuster products to sell, less physician time or access, and emergence of new technologies.

Fewer Blockbuster Products to Sell

The rise in the number of blockbuster products between 1990 and 2005 was not merely a function of successful detailing efforts. The legions of drug reps were armed with FDA-approved products for the treatment of a wide variety of prevalent conditions. During this time period, it was not unusual for large pharmaceutical companies to gain approval for multiple new products with significant sales potential in a single year. Companies were becoming quite efficient at navigating the regulatory landscape once they had a molecule through the **proof-of-concept** stage. A proof-of-concept study is a clinical trial designed to establish the safety of drug candidates in the target population and to explore the relationship between the dose and desired activity, as measured directly or by means of a surrogate (e.g., PharmaNet, n.d.). Once a company gets a molecule through this stage, the marketing department then gets involved so as to begin to analyze the potential market and sales of a given product.

When large companies entered into large markets with their large sales forces, the results were predictably large sales. Success in a therapeutic area by one company (e.g., Eli Lilly's success with Prozac [fluoxetine] for depression) was soon followed by attempts to duplicate that success as closely as possible with similar products by competitor companies (in the case of the prior example, Pfizer with Zoloft [sertraline] and GlaxoSmithKline with Paxil [paroxetine hydrochloride]). This created a **me-too** dynamic within a few product categories, or a situation in which multiple pharmaceutical products mechanistically act in the same manner with similar side effect profiles but are still different chemical entities. The COX-2 anti-inflammatory class is another prime example. The events surrounding the approval, marketing, and eventual withdrawal of Merck's Vioxx (rofecoxib) had effects reaching far more broadly than its manufacturer. The FDA was the target of as much negative sentiment from the public as was Merck when Vioxx was in the news (see Case in Point 6-1).

This public pressure and the facts from the Vioxx ordeal, including that more than 80 million people worldwide had been prescribed the drug in the 5 years it was available, led the FDA to adopt a much more conservative position on approving new medications. The rate of approvals slowed dramatically, and the

CASE IN POINT 6-1
Merck's Vioxx

On the last day of 1998, the FDA approved Celebrex (celecoxib), the first cyclooxygenase-2 (COX-2) inhibitor, for the treatment of various types of arthritis. Shortly thereafter, in May 1999, Merck received approval for Vioxx (rofecoxib), the second COX-2 inhibitor. With a heavy dose of DTC advertising and physician detailing behind it, both medications quickly became popular with patients and physicians and sales soared. However, the clinical trials behind Vioxx's rise were being questioned, in particular, the cardiovascular risks associated with using the product. After other studies were published questioning Vioxx's safety and showing the increased risk of cardiovascular problems, Merck removed the product from the market in September 2004. Given the heavy DTC advertising campaign for the medication, backlash against the pharmaceutical industry ensued. Subsequent legal action was taken against the company by numerous plaintiffs. Eventually, in November 2007, Merck settled these lawsuits for $4.85 billion (Prakash & Valentine, 2007).

CASE IN POINT 6-2
Blockbusters

A blockbuster drug is defined as a product that achieves $1 billion or more in annual global sales. For decades, the profits of blockbuster drugs have been the staple for many major pharmaceutical companies. In the 1970s and 1980s, collaboration with universities and academic science centers was a common business model for the pharmaceutical companies. As a result, many drugs were discovered during that time, resulting in many of the blockbuster drugs that dominated the market over the last 25 years.

An example of a blockbuster drug is Lipitor (atorvastatin). Pfizer, a New York–based pharmaceutical company, launched Lipitor as a cholesterol-lowering drug in 1997. Prior to its patent expiration in December 2011, the drug achieved more than $100 billion in sales, making it the best selling medication of all time.

However, since 2000, the market has seen fewer blockbuster drugs. One reason for this is fewer new therapeutic classes have been discovered because an increasing number of new products approved are me-too drugs. In addition, the time between the launch of an innovator product (first in class) to the launch of a me-too has decreased significantly over the last 40 years as a result of increased technology, both in the areas of discovery and manufacturing. For example, in 1970, a product had approximately a decade of market exclusivity before a me-too was introduced. The time frame decreased to just over 1 year in the late 1990s, and this decrease in market exclusivity decreased the amount of time the innovative manufacturer had to recoup the millions of dollars spent on research and development.

The future of blockbuster medications is certain to change for many reasons. Many of the drugs that once dominated a therapeutic field have already lost or will be losing their patent by 2013, which, based on 2009 data for 10 of the largest pharmaceutical companies, will equate to approximately $95 billion in lost revenue as a result of these patent expirations (Ledford, 2011). Also, many experts speculate that if personalized medicine becomes the norm, it will be unlikely that the blockbuster model, that is, a one-size-fits-all product, will prevail (Cutler, 2007; Dimasi & Paquette, 2004; Ledford, 2011; Lessons from Lipitor, 2011).

number of studies required—thus, expense for the pharmaceutical company—increased as well. This dynamic still exists today and creates a significant barrier to entry for many potentially viable products. This results in fewer blockbuster products for companies to sell.

Less Physician/Prescriber Time and Access

Physicians have always been busy professionals. The demands on their time range widely from treating patients, clinical research, continuing education, service in medical organizations, and administrative activities, among others. As the amount of information and number of resources at their disposal have risen over time, so have the number of patients and the variety of their demands. Our population is aging, requiring more doctor visits. Patients are more informed about their healthcare choices and options, also leading to more doctor visits. As these two dynamics continue to move in this direction, doctors are increasingly being forced to make trade-offs with regard to how they spend their time.

A seemingly easy trade-off to make is spending less time seeing pharmaceutical representatives. The value to a prescriber of the time spent with a drug rep is far less than the value of the same amount of time spent with a patient. If a prescriber feels that he or she can get the same level of product information from a mobile device, for example, this trade-off is made even easier. In addition, factors such as rising administrative costs and lower reimbursements lead to this decision.

The demands on prescribers' time are no longer simply a challenge to a drug rep's creativity (lunch appointments or early morning visits were often used to battle this); physicians are increasingly and aggressively banning drug reps from their offices altogether. So-called no see physicians were once few and far between but are now the rule rather than the exception. Sales operations specialty firms such as ZS Associates have created sophisticated tools to identify and rank physicians in terms of their "accessibility" in addition to their prescribing potential. The challenge is significant and has had a considerable impact on the role of detailing in recent years. The declining number of drug reps is consistent with this phenomenon. However, it is a bitter pill for drug companies to swallow (pun fully intended) because of the role of professional detailing in the growth and prosperity of the industry.

In the late 1990s and early 2000s, a trend emerged as many academic medical centers started the partial or complete elimination of sales representative access to practitioners within the clinics, hospitals, or affiliated professional office settings (Winter-Sperry, n.d.). This "blockade" has significantly reduced the number of individuals who may call upon nurses, pharmacists, physicians, and other healthcare professionals in these settings. Also affected are medical residents and others in various stages of training within these institutions. A previously common strategy used by the pharmaceutical industry was to educate and build relationships with future prescribers to influence their patient care behaviors during their formative years. With access limited or eliminated, new methods must be employed to accomplish the same goal: impact prescribers.

Emergence of Effective Technologies

Prescriber reliance on new sources and media for medical information has created opportunities as well as challenges for pharmaceutical companies. Like all companies, pharmaceutical firms are constantly seeking ways to operate more efficiently without losing effectiveness. Mobile technologies, including smartphone applications, streaming audio/video capabilities, and ubiquitous Internet access all combine to create platforms for delivering marketing messages to physicians without the presence of a sales representative while achieving and maintaining adequate **share of voice**, or the percentage of advertising each brand contributes to a particular category.

Initially, pharmaceutical companies were not rapid adopters of these technologies because of the effectiveness of their professional salespeople and prescriber resistance to these media. However, the declining access and role of the representative combined with the increasing need for physicians to rely on new technology and the relative affordability of using this technology have created a perfect storm on the practice of pharmaceutical detailing. Product messages can now be delivered to a physician's personal device with the desired frequency and reach, and without the associated expense of a sales representative. These messages can be altered in real time and vary from simple reminder advertisements to full-length streaming video. The technology has also reached the point where a two-way exchange is possible, enabling drug companies to collect a large amount of data fed back from physicians, ranging from how long they spend viewing a particular message to detailed customized notes with their thoughts. This information is not only less expensive to collect, it is also delivered in a more timely, organized, and objective fashion. This allows for analytics-based decisions on a variety of other marketing tactics.

These new realities and possibilities for the pharmaceutical industry affect the concept of personal detailing. Additionally, they can also open new avenues of regulatory risk for companies as they navigate how to ensure compliance with promotional regulations, adverse event reporting, and product complaints that might show up on **social media** sites.

Public Relations

Whereas pharmaceutical detailing is intended to inform physicians specifically, pharmaceutical companies go to great lengths to inform other **stakeholders** as well. Increasingly, well-informed patients and/or caregivers such as family members or loved ones influence decisions about which medications are prescribed. One frequently used tactic for helping these stakeholders become well informed about pharmaceutical choices is through consumer-directed public relations (PR) campaigns.

While companies often issue press releases to communicate with stockholders regarding clinical study results, or healthcare practitioners to relay new product approval information, consumer-directed PR campaigns rarely mention or discuss specific products, unless the product itself is a newsworthy breakthrough. These campaigns are most frequently, and effectively, used to raise awareness of a certain condition in addition to the range of treatment options and are commonly referred to as **disease awareness campaigns**. For example, pharmaceutical companies with products indicated for the treatment of type 2 diabetes spend millions of dollars each year on PR campaigns related to the condition. Other examples include campaigns that highlight the increasing prevalence of a condition, the serious nature of the condition's complications, or ways to prevent or manage the condition.

PR campaigns can be very effective at encouraging patients to speak with their doctor about a specific condition/disease and its management. Campaigns can include press releases, nonbranded websites, and brochures educating patients and caregivers about the disease and its treatment. For example, type 2 diabetes PR campaigns might include tips on how to increase exercise and follow a healthier diet. By coupling PR campaigns effectively with product-specific detailing efforts, pharmaceutical companies seek to create a **push and pull marketing dynamic**—pushing product information to physicians while patients pull those same physicians to treat their illnesses. This approach can be effective for large and small companies and products because PR campaigns and detailing efforts can be broad or narrow, depending on their objectives. Highly targeted PR campaigns aimed at very specific audiences can be far more cost-effective than are massive, broad campaigns without losing their impact. Press releases or other sources of information can be made available online, making it easy for patients or other interested stakeholders to search for, and find, information on uncommon disease states or conditions.

Another benefit of using PR as a marketing tactic is that the information is often picked up and shared by large, reputable news outlets such as newspapers and television reporters. Patients who view these outlets as more credible than pharmaceutical companies might look to them as they seek information on a

CASE IN POINT 6-3
Novartis Public Relations Campaign

In 2004 and 2005, Novartis worked with Ketchum, a large global public relations agency, to develop an educational campaign for its overactive bladder treatment Enablex (darifenacin). Enablex was the sixth product to enter the market for overactive bladder and, as such, the campaign needed to increase awareness of overactive bladder and encourage patients to seek product-specific treatment. The educational campaign focused on travel and the inevitable dilemma facing sufferers of overactive bladder, "where am I going to go to the restroom?" The travel expert, Arthur Frommer, developed a book titled *Where to Stop & Where to Go: A Guide to Traveling with Overactive Bladder in the United States* that became the cornerstone of the campaign, for both patient- and prescriber-directed pieces. More than 104 million consumers were reached during the media campaign, both in print and on television. In addition, more than three-quarters of the stories included Novartis's name and number, which resulted in a 1,000% increase in call volume and increased website traffic by 318%. Requests for guides reached approximately 24,000 and included almost 13,000 people requesting Enablex-specific information. As a result, the sales of Enablex surpassed two of its competitors during the launch year (Ketchum, n.d.).

condition and make decisions about potential treatment options. For these reasons, public relations agencies are important strategic partners for pharmaceutical companies. Pharmaceutical marketing teams work closely with their PR agencies to develop responsible campaigns that can be effective in reaching intended audiences far beyond their prescriber customers.

Direct-to-Consumer Advertising

Of all of the marketing tactics used by pharmaceutical companies, direct-to-consumer (DTC) advertising is by far the most widely recognized and criticized. This tactic is sometimes referred to as "direct-to-*patient*" advertising, which is the source of both its popularity with pharmaceutical companies and its unpopularity with some physicians. DTC advertisements include any ads that are intended to reach the end user of a given product, including newspaper, magazine, Internet, mobile, and radio ads. Of course, the tactic is most obviously and closely connected to advertisements that appear on television, still the most widely used information and entertainment delivery tool in the world. Since the rapid and dramatic adoption of DTC advertising as a pharmaceutical marketing tactic in the 1990s, the terms *erectile dysfunction*, *irritable bowel syndrome*, *GERD*, and many others have become familiar to millions of people who are neither physicians nor affiliated with the pharmaceutical industry. This familiarity has translated into prescriptions and dollars for pharmaceutical companies because it has been proven that DTC advertising is an effective means of generating awareness and trial of specific products (Spake & Mathew, 2007).

The FDA describes three types of DTC advertisements (U.S. Department of Health and Human Services, Food and Drug Administration, Center for Drug Evaluation and Research, Center for Biologics Evaluation and Research, & Center for Devices and Radiological Health, 2004):

- *Product claim advertisements:* The most common of the three, these typically include both the brand name and the condition the drug treats. They also describe the risks and benefits associated with taking the medication.
- *Help-seeking advertisements:* Also known as disease-awareness or nonbranded communications, these mention the disease or health condition but not the name of the drug that treats it. The purpose of this type of advertisement is to create an awareness of symptoms or conditions among consumers (GAO, 2002). These advertisements are not required to provide risk information and are not FDA regulated if done correctly. The types of materials that often make up a consumer-directed public relations (PR) campaign can fall in this category as well, such as nonbranded, disease-specific consumer websites and brochures.
- *Reminder advertisements:* This type of advertisement, which is exempt from risk disclosure requirements, names the drug and dosage form or cost information. It does not mention the condition it treats or make claims or representations about the product.

DTC advertising has various implications for pharmaceutical companies, patients, and physicians because the industry has clearly embraced the tactic due to its effectiveness. Between 1997 and 2005, the industry more than quadrupled its spending on DTC advertisements from approximately $1 billion to more than $4 billion (U.S. Government Accountability Office [U.S. GAO], 2006).

By investing at this level, pharmaceutical companies attempt to generate product awareness, trial, and usage. Although this is no different from the goal of any consumer product's advertising, the end users of pharmaceutical products, that is, patients, are not the direct customers of pharmaceutical companies or individuals who actually prescribe the medications. Therefore, the call to action in the advertisement for the potential patient is to "ask your doctor" about the condition and/or medication. If the advertisement is effective at influencing a potential patient to ask for a specific pharmaceutical product by name, physicians might be compelled to prescribe that product as a result (U.S. GAO, 2002). There is a strong business case supporting this dynamic because it is not unusual for pharmaceutical companies to expect and generate at least a 2:1 **return on investment** for DTC advertising campaigns (U.S. GAO, 2006). In other words, the $4 billion spent on pharmaceutical DTC advertisements in 2005 returned more than $8 billion in revenue to the industry.

Pharmaceutical DTC ads also have implications for patients. Some advertisements serve to educate patients about their health concerns, symptoms, and available treatments, empowering them to become active participants in their own care (Bradford & Kleit, 2006). For example, an advertisement can inform people experiencing persistent thirst that this is a symptom of diabetes and the advertised product can be an effective treatment option. Early detection is another potential benefit of DTC on patients. These advertisements can foster important doctor–patient conversations about a patient's health concerns that might otherwise not happen (Pharmaceutical Research and Manufacturers of America, 2005).

The implications of DTC advertising on physicians are the subject of continuous debate. Some physicians agree there are benefits for patients to this type of awareness generation as long as the ads do not diminish the role of the prescriber as the healthcare provider (U.S. GAO, 2002). However, many physicians (and some advocacy groups) disapprove altogether of patients requesting pharmaceutical products by name (Lazarus, 2008). Some contend this practice creates inflated demand for the advertised products and could potentially harm patients. Furthermore, skeptical physicians indicate that DTC advertisements do not provide sufficient information about the cost, alternative treatments, or side effects of the advertised product (Robinson et al., 2004). In fact, despite the affinity that pharmaceutical companies have for this tactic, the majority of physicians maintain a generally negative response to the increase in advertising prescription drugs directly to consumers (Murray, Lo, Pollack, Donelan, & Lee, 2003).

PHARMACEUTICAL PROMOTION IN PRACTICE

Promotional materials, including advertisements, are typically developed by the marketing team, often with the aid of advertising agencies.

CASE IN POINT 6-4
Ad Promo Review

Brand A is approved for the treatment of moderate pain and aggressively marketed by Company X. The drug was launched 3 years ago, and the marketing team would like to "refresh" the campaign with a new look as well as data from a small, recently completed Phase IV study that included patient-reported outcomes, such as degree of pain and feelings of well-being as secondary endpoints. The product manager enlists the aid of the brand's advertisement agency at substantial cost and time to create a new visual aid to be used by the sales force in detailing to healthcare providers that includes new formats for presenting safety and efficacy data along with the patient-reported claims. Several related pieces are also created, including an email campaign and a major update to the product's branded healthcare practitioner website.

Representatives from the medical affairs, legal, and regulatory departments, along with marketing, are present during the review meeting. The medical reviewer questions the new data display for the efficacy results from the registration trials because the results have now been pooled, even though one of the three studies used a different dosing regimen and the population was not similar. During labeling negotiations, the FDA had not allowed such pooling and required Brand A's package insert to present the data from each study separately. Additionally, the regulatory reviewer points out the fact that the data from the Phase IV study does not fulfill the requirements of substantial evidence and, therefore, would be false and misleading to include. The legal reviewer also has concerns with potential product liability should the patient-reported outcomes be presented because they overpromise the extent and length of pain relief patients could expect from the data included in the package insert.

After a long, frustrating meeting, it becomes clear the product manager wasted much time, effort, and money on a campaign that cannot be salvaged. Thus, it is a best practice to hold a concept meeting with the review team and the advertising agency to discuss major revisions or brand new campaigns prior to moving forward with development.

Leading Up to the Sign-Off Meeting

Several months, and sometimes years, are spent developing advertising pieces to ensure that the final product is both compelling and accurate. This is true for promotional marketing tactics that are used for all modes of delivery. Whether the tactic is intended to inform physicians (e.g., sales representative tools) or patients (e.g., television commercials), the process for ensuring a fair and balanced presentation is similar.

Because promotion is fundamentally a piece of the marketing process, creating promotional materials begins with the pharmaceutical company's marketing department, which works with its advertising partners to determine the desired creative concept and message. Some promotional items were intended simply to remind physicians of the product's existence and dosing. These items (pens, pads, etc.) did not typically carry promotional messaging and were used to keep the product's share of voice high in competitive categories. Note that these reminder items are not used today as a result of the Pharmaceutical Research and Manufacturers of America (PhRMA) code on interactions with healthcare professionals.

On the other side of the promotional spectrum, selling tools and commercial advertisements are intended to be persuasive to their target audiences by describing the features and benefits of branded products. The features and benefits are expressed as the efficacy, safety, and improvements in a patient's quality of life. Each claim must be substantiated by scientific evidence, and the process for checking and balancing the messages involves the marketing, medical, regulatory, and legal departments of the pharmaceutical company. This is an iterative process designed to make certain that promoted products do not misrepresent their potential benefits in any way. Patient safety is the priority, and although the details of the process differ with each individual company, all pharmaceutical companies employ a process like this to mitigate medical risks to patients and regulatory and legal risks to the company itself.

These materials, with all supporting references, are then submitted to an internal review team. (Different names for the teams include copy review, legal medical regulatory [LMR], medical/regulatory [med/reg], and advertising and promotional [ad promo] review.) This team typically consists of personnel from medical affairs, regulatory, legal, and marketing. Depending on the type of piece, ad hoc members might also be included in the review, such as public relations for press materials and training personnel for training and development pieces. Each member has a specific role on the committee. The role of the medical reviewer is to check medical accuracy of the data and claims presented and to ensure that appropriate references are used. The legal reviewer is primarily concerned with protection of the company's intellectual property, copyright and patent issues, and litigation concerns. It is the regulatory reviewer's responsibility to ensure that pieces fulfill the requirements outlined in the advertising and promotional regulations.

SUMMARY

From physician detailing to public relations to direct-to-consumer advertising, pharmaceutical manufacturers use a variety of means to inform their customers about their products. This chapter examined the structure, issues, and practice of promotion within the pharmaceutical industry. As fewer blockbusters, less physician access, and emerging technologies have changed the promotional landscape, pharmaceutical manufacturers are beginning to adapt their tried-and-true strategies to the current information and mobile electronic age while still retaining their core promotional image and knowledge.

DISCUSSION QUESTIONS

1. Will the number of pharmaceutical representatives continue to decrease? What factors will determine this moving forward?
2. As the number of blockbuster medications able to reach a large consumer market declines, how will pharmaceutical manufacturers adapt their promotional strategies to fit a more specialized market?
3. Are there disadvantages to using a co-promotional or co-marketing strategy? If so, describe each in detail.

4. In the wake of the Vioxx case, what should pharmaceutical manufacturers do to avoid this problem in the future?

5. From a consumer perspective, how might the response to a disease awareness campaign differ from a brand-focused (or product-focused) promotional strategy?

6. One of the benefits of DTC promotion is that physicians can be exposed to these ads just as the intended audience of consumers is. Discuss the pros and cons of physician exposure to drug information through traditional consumer media outlets.

7. The pharmaceutical industry has received both positive and negative attention in the media. Describe the impact of nonbranded industry-sponsored media attention on the public's perception of the industry (e.g., Case in Point 6-3). Overall, what is your assessment of public perception of the pharmaceutical industry? How can this affect sales and marketing?

8. Discuss the following statement: "Although share of voice is important from a competitive perspective, the message is paramount." How might this guide a pharmaceutical marketer?

9. What strategies can pharmaceutical companies employ to reach physicians who do not wish to take time to see manufacturers' sales representatives or medical science liaisons?

10. Why might it make more sense for a pharmaceutical manufacturer to use help-seeking (or nonbranded/disease-specific) advertisements prior to launching an innovative product as compared to the launch of a "me-too" product?

REFERENCES

Bradford, D. W., & Kleit, A. N. (2006). Evaluating the welfare effects of drug advertising. *Regulation, 29*(1), 58–62.

Cutler, D. M. (2007, March 29). The demise of blockbuster. *New England Journal of Medicine, 356,* 1292–1293.

Dimasi, J. A., & Paquette, C. (2004). The economics of follow-on drug research and development: Trends in entry rates and the timing of development. *Pharmacoeconomics, 22*(Suppl. 2), 1–14.

Domanski, J. (2007, May 24). The rule of 7: How to build mindshare and prospect more effectively. EyesOnSales. Retrieved from http://www.eyesonsales.com/content/article/the_rule_of_7_how_to_build_mindshare_and_prospect_more_effectively

Ketchum. (n.d.). Novartis campaign gives overactive bladder sufferers freedom to travel. Retrieved from http://new.ketchum.com/novartis_overactive_bladder_case_study

Lazarus, D. (2008, February 6). Ads spur urge for drugs. *Los Angeles Times*, C.1.

Ledford, H. (2011, November 29). Blockbuster drug bows out. *Nature, 480*(7375), 16–17.

Lessons from Lipitor and the broken blockbuster drug model. (2011, December 10). *Lancet, 378*(9808), 1976.

Murray, E., Lo, B., Pollack, L., Donelan, K., & Lee, K. (2003). Direct-to-consumer advertising: Physicians' views of its effects on quality of care and the doctor–patient relationship. *Journal of the American Board of Family Practice, 16*(6), 513–524.

O'Reilly, K. B. (2009, March 23). Doctors increasingly close doors to drug reps, while pharma cuts ranks. American medical News. Retrieved from http://www.ama-assn.org/amednews/2009/03/23/prl10323.htm

Pharmaceutical Research and Manufacturers of America. (2005, November). *PhRMA guiding principles: Direct to consumer advertisements about prescription medicines.* Retrieved from http://www.roche.com/dtcguidingprinciples.pdf

PharmaNet. (n.d.). Retrieved from http://www.pharmanet-i3.com

Prakash, S., & Valentine, V. (2007, November 10). Timeline: The rise and fall of Vioxx. NPR. Retrieved from http://www.npr.org/templates/story/story.php?storyId=5470430

Robinson, A., Hohmann, K., Rifkin J., Topp, D., Gilroy, C., Pickard, J., & Anderson, R. (2004). Direct-to-consumer pharmaceutical advertising: Physician and public opinion and potential effects on the physician–patient relationship. *Archives of Internal Medicine, 164*(4), 427–432.

Spake, D. F., & Mathew, J. (2007). Consumer opinion and effectiveness of direct-to-consumer advertising. *Journal of Consumer Marketing, 24*(5), 283–292.

Stenberg, A. J. (2008, October 17). What is the Rule of Seven? And how will it improve your marketing? Baby Boomer Entrepreneur. Retrieved from http://thebabyboomerentrepreneur.com/258/what-is-the-rule-of-seven-and-how-will-it-improve-your-marketing/

U.S. Department of Health and Human Services, Food and Drug Administration, Center for Drug Evaluation and Research (CDER), Center for Biologics Evaluation and Research (CBER), & Center for Devices and Radiological Health (CDRH). (2004, January). *Guidance for industry: "Help-seeking" and other disease awareness communications by or on behalf of drug and device firms.* Retrieved from http://www.fda.gov/downloads/Drugs/GuidanceComplianceRegulatoryInformation/Guidances/UCM070068.pdf

U.S. Government Accountability Office. (2002, October). *Prescription drugs: FDA oversight of direct-to-consumer advertising has limitations.* Retrieved from http://www.gao.gov/new.items/d03177.pdf

U.S. Government Accountability Office. (2006, November). *Prescription drugs: Improvements needed in FDA's oversight of direct-to-consumer advertising.* Retrieved from http://www.gao.gov/new.items/d0754.pdf

Winter-Sperry, R. L. (n.d.). Medical science liaisons: Know-how or know-who? PM360 Online. Retrieved from http://www.pm360online.com/f2_1009

CHAPTER 7

Medical Affairs

Dee Fanning, PharmD, Julie Brideau, PharmD, and Timothy Poole, PharmD

LEARNING OBJECTIVES

1. Describe the evolution and role of the Medical Affairs division of a pharmaceutical manufacturer.
2. Identify and describe the guiding documents that give clear direction to the internal operation of a pharmaceutical manufacturer, specifically the Medical Affairs division.
3. Differentiate the role of a medical liaison from the role of a traditional sales representative, including the previous education, training, and compensation characteristics.
4. Define what a key opinion leader is and describe how pharmaceutical manufacturers identify and use these individuals, particularly during the various stages of a product's life cycle.
5. Differentiate between the appropriate and inappropriate use of publications, medical writers, and medical reprints.

Promotion in the pharmaceutical industry is typically associated with visual promotional pieces, such as television advertising, sponsorships, or the formerly common pens with a branded prescription name imprinted on them. The commercial operations arm of a pharmaceutical manufacturer, including, for example the Sales and Marketing departments, uses these tools with the goal of increasing awareness of the company's product and, ultimately, hopefully increasing sales.

However, from a marketing perspective, promotion takes many forms, especially in the pharmaceutical industry, because there are also nonpublic, nonvisual promotional tools used by the pharmaceutical industry to reach customers and respond to their needs.

The information age we currently live in has changed most healthcare consumers to information-seeking specialists who gather as much information as possible before making important medical decisions. Physicians are no different given that they want as much objective information as possible before diagnosing and, subsequently, deciding which medication to prescribe a patient. The pharmaceutical industry has followed suit as well because companies believe the more valid and objective information within the medical community the better, and, in the end, their product will prevail when all the evidence is taken into account. Thus, the creation and proliferation of a separate entity within most pharmaceutical manufacturers, the Medical Affairs division, that focuses not on selling a particular product, but instead on the legally compliant promotion of science and objective information.

MEDICAL AFFAIRS

In 2003, keeping with its efforts to prevent and/or reduce healthcare fraud, the federal government's **Office of Inspector General (OIG)** released a guidance titled "Compliance Program Guidance for Pharmaceutical Manufacturers" (U.S. Department of Health and Human Services, Office of Inspector General [US DHHS OIG], 2003). Although not law, compliance with OIG guidelines is an essential function of all pharmaceutical manufacturers. Transparency regarding all aspects of operations is vital to remain in compliance. This particular guidance document outlines how pharmaceutical manufacturers should internally operate to be in line with the **compliance program** and resulted in significant industry changes. Chief among the changes is the clear separation of commercial operations from a company's Research and Development (R&D) and Medical Affairs divisions, including a distinction between the roles of sales versus medical personnel from the external customer's or stakeholder's perspective. These changes have challenged pharmaceutical manufacturers and professionals working in Medical Affairs to provide objective medical information while maintaining the highest possible standards of corporate integrity and abstaining from product sales and promotion.

The Medical Affairs division is charged with being the scientific resource for both internal colleagues and external customers (healthcare providers) through dissemination of complex, scientific, fair, balanced, and nonpromotional drug information on a peer-to-peer basis. The various departments typically in this division include Medical Information, Medical Liaisons, Publications, and Medical Writing. From an organizational and regulatory perspective, firewalls typically exist to ensure that the company is not using scientific information exchange to promote sales, thus creating the need for medical governance and communication policies. In many cases, employees of a Medical Affairs department report to their own vice president, who, in turn, reports directly to the chief medical or executive officer. To comply with OIG guidelines, employee compensation, including bonuses, in this department cannot be based on sales figures, and using terms such as *return on investment* is forbidden. The goals of these departments are therefore more cognitive in nature and harder to measure as compared to sales representative goals. Given the firewall measures in place, the Food and Drug Administration (FDA) does not regulate the activities of Medical Affairs.

History of Field-Based Medical Personnel

The first **field-based medical (FBM) professionals** can be traced back to the 1960s when the Upjohn Company of Kalamazoo, Michigan, first deployed a team of technically trained healthcare professionals to "represent" its product line and respond to the traditional and unique needs of its customers (Morgan, 2000). This model was continued by Eli Lilly in Indianapolis, Indiana, through its technique of hiring only pharmacists for both traditional sales representative positions and field-based medical roles. Pharmaceutical companies employed pharmacists and/or nurses to engage prescribers and healthcare decision makers in a traditional selling model. The use of trained healthcare professionals was thought to enhance the peer-to-peer relationship in pharmaceutical product detailing. As the growth of companies' sales forces occurred and job description philosophies changed through the 1980s, most pharmaceutical companies shifted away from using healthcare professionals as their primary sales professionals.

During the era of expansion of sales opportunities, the supply of pharmacists and nurses interested in pharmaceutical industry careers could not keep up with the demand. Many companies did, however, use pharmacists, nurses, and sometimes physicians in a nontraditional, newly emerging role. The goal was to have smaller niche specialists in much fewer numbers than the numbers of traditional sales personnel. These specialists were able to gain better access to difficult-to-see healthcare decision makers, that is, pharmacists, nurses, and physicians. In the early phases, many companies' organizational charts listed these FBM personnel as reporting up through the sales and marketing leadership, with the true medical personnel predominantly based at corporate headquarters. These early FBM teams were called a variety of names, including clinical liaisons, clinical consultants, medical affairs consultants, regional clinical specialists, and scientific affairs liaisons. FBM teams were geared to enhance access for traditional field sales personnel while providing an added service with regard to product knowledge; peer working relationships with local, state, and national medical associations; and a variety of special projects. These projects often included assistance with drug use evaluation (DUE) and provision of continuing education (CE).

Over time, changes in regulatory guidelines, such as the issuance of the 2003 OIG guidance (US DHHS OIG, 2003; Winter-Sperry, 2006), required a significant modification of the reporting structure and rules of engagement for all FBM personnel. As mentioned, to be compliant with OIG guidelines companies have created firewalls to separate the activities of traditional sales personnel from their medical counterparts who also work in the field and might sometimes see the same healthcare professionals. Currently, FBM personnel report through Medical Affairs, which extends from the field up through headquarters leadership. The field-based medical colleagues still engage healthcare providers, but most often they focus on key opinion leaders (KOLs) or key decision makers (KDMs). The role of these individuals is to engage these healthcare professionals on a routine basis for the following purposes:

- Represent the company's medical interests
- Respond to unsolicited medical inquiries
- Gather market intelligence that could possibly benefit the company's overall medical strategy

THE ROLE OF THE MEDICAL LIAISON

Personnel in the Medical Affairs division typically function independently of the company's sales personnel, with the predominant field-based medical position being the medical liaison (ML). The medical liaison's role is similar throughout the industry, although this position has a multitude of titles, such as medical science liaison (MSL) and clinical science manager (CSM). It is the current industry standard that MLs have a terminal degree in a health-related field (MD, DO, PharmD, or PhD) (Winter-Sperry, 2006). This standard works to ensure that MLs can engage in a peer-to-peer exchange of scientific information with healthcare leaders and build and maintain relationships with healthcare providers who have earned notoriety and the respect of their peers based on expertise in a particular disease state. Since the mid-2000s, MLs have become more prevalent in the pharmaceutical industry, perhaps in part because of the increased reports of fraud and abuse enforcement actions against traditional sales and marketing personnel (Bylander, 2009).

The primary role of the medical liaison is to obtain advice from medical experts, often referred to as key opinion leaders (KOLs) or opinion thought leaders (OTLs), and to deliver requested medical information. The exchange of scientific information on disease states and their therapeutic management requires an in-depth, up-to-date knowledge of the medical literature. Medical liaisons rely on frequent searches of the various medical literature databases and have advanced skills on how to evaluate the published literature. Medical liaisons cannot discuss

CASE IN POINT 7-1
Neurontin and Off-Label Promotion

In May 2004, Pfizer (as the parent company to the former Parke-Davis) agreed to pay back $430 million to the federal government as a result of its illegal promotion of Neurontin (gabapentin). Dr. David Franklin, a former Parke-Davis medical liaison, initiated the lawsuit under the *qui tam* **provision** (whistleblower provision) of the federal **False Claims Act** after quitting his job when he was asked to promote Neurontin unlawfully for off-label uses.

In the course of this lawsuit, an overall company strategy to promote Neurontin for off-label uses through a variety of mechanisms, including, for example, advisory boards, continuing medical education, and key opinion leader influence, was revealed. In particular, Parke-Davis used multiple medical-oriented communications to impart promotional messages regarding Neurontin, including its use in off-label treatment for pain and migraines. Although the specific activities (e.g., advisory boards) did not create issues, especially given that most pharmaceutical manufacturers engage in the activities mentioned, the problem was created when Parke-Davis placed a promotional emphasis on activities designed to be independent from a promotional focus (Steinman, Bero, Chren, & Landefeld, 2006).

off-label information proactively. However, if a healthcare provider asks for information on an unapproved use of a drug, an ML can answer the question, stating the scientific literature as evidence. However, the ML must clarify the label in the course of the response. MLs must follow FDA guidelines on education, advertising, and promotion. Their title does not allow them any additional protection beyond that of their marketing colleagues (Bylander, 2009). Medical liaisons often plan a pivotal role in managed care because they provide health plans clinical data often requested by pharmacy and therapeutics committees, such as disease state information, pharmacoeconomics, and quality-of-life data (Winter-Sperry, 2006).

Another important role of the ML that provides multiple benefits to the company is attendance at specific medical conferences. The opportunity to see many KOLs in one spot as opposed to traveling to each of their respective offices is an effective use of the ML's time. In addition, MLs attend the clinical/plenary session presentations to stay up-to-date on disease state issues. MLs also gather competitive intelligence and new business opportunities at medical conferences. A potential venue for collecting this type of information is attendance at poster presentations. Most companies task their MLs with planning in advance which materials/information they will gather at scientific meetings and reporting their findings back to the corporate office.

Medical Liaison Compensation

As previously mentioned, an ML's performance is typically not evaluated based on product sales. Although there is not an industry standard for measuring ML outcomes, the following quantitative factors or activities are commonly used (Winter-Sperry & Mann, 2006):

- Number of presentations given
- Level of R&D project involvement
- Educational programs attended
- Level of thought leader or managed care activities participation

Metrics for measuring ML performance are also qualitative in nature, for example, assessing their ability to accomplish the following tasks:

- Maintain an expert level of scientific knowledge
- Transfer scientific knowledge to internal and external customers
- Comply with corporate and federal compliance guidelines
- Respond to inquiries from the medical community

KEY OPINION LEADER IDENTIFICATION AND DEVELOPMENT

The industry term used to describe the experts in a certain field is *key opinion leader*, or *KOL*. However, other terms are frequently used, such as opinion thought leader (OTL), healthcare leader (HCL), and key decision leader (KDL). Clinical situations and a product's life cycle are used as the primary criteria when pharmaceutical companies select KOLs. KOLs with different areas of expertise are needed for products in their preclinical and early clinical development phases as opposed to those in the later stages of development (Winter-Sperry & Mann, 2006).

KOL identification can be done in-house by the Medical Affairs department, by a consultant, or by the use of software programs. Traditional criteria used to determine if a scientist or provider is a leader in his or her field are as follows:

- A faculty appointment (associate or full professor) at a major medical/academic center
- Proven expertise in an area of interest by either multiple research grants in that area or publications on that topic in prestigious, peer-reviewed medical journals
- Being an invited speaker at national/international medical meetings
- Participation in consensus guidelines
- Leader in medical associations

Prescription data are traditionally *not* used as a determinant for top-tier KOLs. Typically, if the healthcare provider or scientist is engaged in research, publishing, and teaching, that person tends to have less time to devote to seeing patients and, therefore, does not "show up" as a high prescriber. Also, selecting KOLs on the basis of high prescribing of a product could be viewed as a kickback or reward for that prescribing.

Many departments within the pharmaceutical company use KOLs in a variety of ways. The definition of and contributions from KOLs vary among companies and even among various departments within the same company. For instance, clinical research departments can seek opinions on trial design, outcome measurements, or other needs within the medical community. Marketing and Sales departments might seek advice from experts in life cycle management, commercial advisory boards, and utilization on speaker bureaus. Medical Affairs and clinical groups use KOLs to gain advice regarding current medical trends. In addition to interdepartmental variation, the use of KOLs differs depending on the product's life cycle stage. (See **Figure 7-1.**)

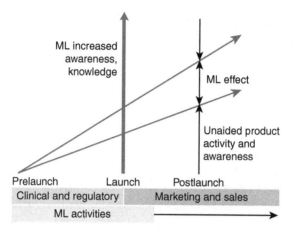

FIGURE 7-1 Medical Liaison Activities vs. Product Life Cycle

Source: Winter-Sperry, R. L. (2006, April). Leveraging the contributions of medical science liaisons in changing and challenging times. *Product Management Today,* 26–31. Retrieved from http://scientificadvantage.com/article_pmt.pdf

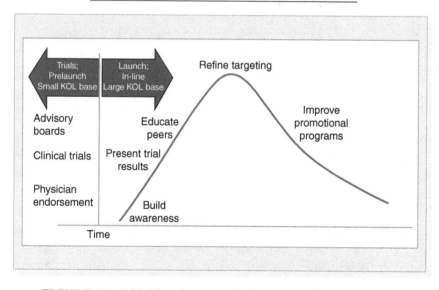

FIGURE 7-2 KOL Identification and Valuation vs. Product Life Cycle

Source: Courtesy of Cognizant Technology Solutions via marketRx®.

KOL identification typically occurs several years before a product's anticipated launch. (See **Figure 7-2.**) Pharmaceutical companies rely on a limited number of KOLs for involvement in the pivotal trials and advisory board meetings during this early stage. Just prior to launch, the involvement between the company and the KOLs begins to grow exponentially. The KOLs are involved with increasing the awareness of the disease state, therapeutic class, or actual drug through many educational venues. KOLs commonly present trial data at major medical conferences with the goal of educating their peers in the medical community. During educational activities that occur prior to the product's FDA approval, KOLs should take care to avoid drawing conclusions of safety and/or efficacy because preapproval promotion is illegal.

PUBLICATIONS

Manuscripts published in peer-reviewed biomedical journals have a significant impact on a pharmaceutical manufacturer's products, and, thus, manufacturers often develop long-term plans for publications throughout a product's life cycle. For example, manuscripts for publication might be prepared and submitted from the early stages of development prior to the drug's FDA approval to, for example, report the compound's effect in a nonclinical setting (i.e., animal studies) or in trials exploring the drug's pharmacokinetic profile. Phase III trials in which safety and efficacy data are determined and used in the submission of the drug's New Drug Application are also often published in the medical literature. Although the publications team of a pharmaceutical manufacturer is a multidisciplinary group, its core typically resides in the Medical Affairs division.

For many years, pharmaceutical manufacturers' influence on the published medical literature has come under scrutiny by the government and media. Given that the pharmaceutical industry funds many of the published randomized controlled trials that show favorable results regarding specific medications while nonfavorable results are not as frequently seen, many media members, medical associations, and physicians in general have come to question the validity of industry-backed studies. Whereas manufacturer funding of the trials necessary to gain FDA approval is expected, when manufacturers strategically fund projects aimed at providing promotional information the media pays attention.

Other complaints associated with industry involvement in the publication process include influencing study design, hiding negative results, and ghost writing. Ghost writing is when an original writer creates a work that is then credited to another author. In the pharmaceutical industry, this occurs when an outside writer drafts a medical journal publication based on data provided by the manufacturer, and then the publication is credited to another author, for example, a leading physician or researcher in the specific related field.

CASE IN POINT 7-2
Ghost Writing

The World Association of Medical Editors, a nonprofit group of medical journal editors from around the globe, has a tight policy on the issue of ghost writing. Although it accepts that medical writers "can be legitimate contributors" and their roles and affiliations should always be described in the manuscript, ghost authorship is "dishonest and unacceptable" (World Association of Medical Editors, 2005). More often than not, work is done on behalf of companies with a commercial interest in the topic, such as when a commercial company employs a professional writer to prepare an article, submits the article to a medical expert for minor revisions, and then attaches the expert's name to the article as the author. In some cases, experts are paid for their help whereas in other cases researchers hire a professional writer but present the article as their own work.

Ghost writing case descriptions have been published, in particular, the case involving AstraZeneca Pharmaceuticals in a 2005 issue of the *British Medical Journal* (Eaton, 2005). In August 2011, Linda Logdberg (2011) published a firsthand account of her life as a ghostwriter in the pharmaceutical industry. She describes drafting items such as drug monographs, journal articles, publication plans, and continuing medical education (CME) programs. She describes her lifestyle and the final straw in her career as a medical writer: For a manuscript on an attention deficit hyperactivity disorder (ADHD) medication, she wanted to consult with the primary physician author on the product, given her personal experience with the medication class. However, her attempts were unsuccessful, and eventually she was "met with the curt admonition to 'just write it'" (Logdberg, 2011).

To address these issues, in 2003 a working group of the Council of Biology Editors in Current Medical Research and Opinion published "Good Publication Practice for Pharmaceutical Companies" (Wager, Field, & Grossman, 2003). These guidelines address publication bias and the role of professional medical writers. In general, the integrity of medical literature depends on both favorable and unfavorable results being reported and, thus, becomes distorted when unfavorable findings are systematically underreported or when favorable results are published redundantly. Therefore, the Good Publication Practice guidelines call on pharmaceutical manufacturers to publish the results of all clinical trials of their marketed products. In addition, the U.S. National Institutes of Health maintains www.clinicaltrials.gov as a registry and results database of federally and privately supported clinical trials conducted in the United States and around the world. The registry supplies information about a trial's purpose, who may participate, locations, and phone numbers for more details.

As previously mentioned, the Medical Affairs division of a pharmaceutical manufacturer exists to provide as much evidenced-based information to the medical community as possible. The evidence provided must be objective and unbiased. Thus, for pharmaceutical manufacturers to avoid the negative stigma associated with this topic, it is important for companies to have a well-defined publication strategy, including justification for each planned article, abstract, and so forth. Further, it is prudent to have in place clear policy and procedures for the creation, review, and approval of publications, including how the company ensures that the International Committee of Medical Journal Editors guidelines (ICJME, 2010) are followed. These guidelines discuss the ethical requirements for the authorship, both writing and editing, of all manuscripts submitted to biomedical journals. In addition, sponsorship transparency of the manuscript must be followed.

USE OF REPRINTS

Both sales and medical affairs personnel make use of publications in their day-to-day activities. Sales representatives may disseminate certain reprints as long as they have been approved by the internal review process and fall into one of two categories: First, on-label reprints are typically reprints of the publications reporting results of the major trials that led to a product's approval, which can generally be used promotionally.

Second, the sales force sometimes disseminates "off-label" publications. These publications report results of studies of the use of approved products in unapproved indications. In January 2009, the FDA published the Guidance for Industry "Good Reprint Practices for the Distribution of Medical Journal Articles and Medical or Scientific Reference Publications on Unapproved New Uses of Approved Drugs and Approved or Cleared Medical Devices" (U.S. Department of Health and Human Services, Food and Drug Administration, Office of the Commissioner, Office of Policy, 2009). This guidance provides a **safe harbor** for the dissemination of off-label articles as long as certain conditions regarding the type of material and the method of dissemination are met.

Medical affairs personnel, such as MLs, often use publications in their communications with KOLs to aid in addressing unsolicited requests for information. In these cases, use of off-label publications does not fall under the Guidance for Industry. Companies should, however, have in place mechanisms for capturing unsolicited requests and how they are addressed, including what materials MLs provide for answers.

SUMMARY

This chapter described the services provided by the Medical Affairs division and how this area contributes to the success of a company's branded product line, even though it is not quantified in sales numbers. Key personnel in the Medical Affairs group, specifically medical information specialists and medical liaisons, are responsible for providing scientifically balanced responses to unsolicited questions and disseminating information about the company's products while complying with regulatory requirements set forth by the Food and Drug Administration.

DISCUSSION QUESTIONS

1. How might the continually declining number of sales representatives and their decreased access to physicians affect the role of the medical liaison moving forward?
2. Explain the role of scientific literature in pharmaceutical marketing and why an ML would contend that his or her job is not sales but information.
3. If a pharmaceutical company selects key opinion leaders by examining their prescribing data, in particular, their prescribing volume, might this be perceived negatively by consumers or government regulators?
4. Explain the rationale for leaving reprints with physicians. In your response, consider the selection of articles, fair balance, government regulation, company policy, and on- and off-label uses of medications.
5. At what point in the product life cycle is scientific information most useful to expand prescribers' product knowledge?
6. What are the implications of choosing a key opinion leader who is not seen as an expert by the prescribing community?
7. What are some potential implications of nonexistent or ineffective firewalls between sales and marketing and medical science divisions in a pharmaceutical company?
8. What impact has easy access to scientific information, brought about by the information age, had on pharmaceutical manufacturers?

9. What are the key differences in promotional materials and scientific materials that are distributed by a pharmaceutical manufacturer?

10. Given the increasing role of Medical Affairs, what might the FDA or legislators do from a policy perspective to decrease the oversight burden and ensure compliance of manufacturers?

REFERENCES

Bylander, J. (2009). Special medical liaisons are no back door to off-label promotion. *Gray Sheet, 35*(46), 8.

Eaton, L. (2005, April 30). Medical editors issue guidance on ghost writing. *British Medical Journal, 330*(7498), 988.

International Committee of Medical Journal Editors. (2010, April). Uniform requirements for manuscripts submitted to biomedical journals: Writing and editing for biomedical publication. Retrieved from http://www.icmje.org/urm_main.html

Logdberg, L. (2011). Being the ghost in the machine: A medical ghostwriter's personal view. *Public Library of Science, 8*(8), e1001071. Retrieved from http://www.plosmedicine.org/article/info%3Adoi%2F10.1371%2Fjournal.pmed.1001071

Morgan, D. K. (2000). History and evolution of field-based medical programs. *Drug Information Journal, 34*, 1049–1052.

Steinman, M. A., Bero, L. A., Chren, M. M., & Landefeld, S. (2006). Narrative review: The promotion of gabapentin: An analysis of internal industry documents. *Annals of Internal Medicine, 145*(4), 284–293.

U.S. Department of Health and Human Services, Food and Drug Administration, Office of the Commissioner, Office of Policy. (2009, January). Good reprint practices for the distribution of medical journal articles and medical or scientific reference publications on unapproved new uses of approved drugs and approved or cleared medical devices. Retrieved from http://www.fda.gov/regulatoryinformation/guidances/ucm125126.htm

U.S. Department of Health and Human Services, Office of Inspector General. (2003, May 5). OIG compliance program guidance for pharmaceutical manufacturers. *Federal Register, 68*(86), 23731–23743. Retrieved from http://oig.hhs.gov/authorities/docs/03/050503FRCPGPharmac.pdf

Wager, E., Field, E. A., & Grossman, L. (2003). Good publication practices for pharmaceutical companies. *Current Medical Research and Opinions, 19*(3), 149–154.

Winter-Sperry, R. L. (2006, April). Leveraging the contributions of medical science liaisons in changing and challenging times. *Product Management Today*, 26–31. Retrieved from http://scientificadvantage.com/article_pmt.pdf

Winter-Sperry, R. L., & Mann, A. (2006, July). Marketing to professionals: Deep impact. New research suggests a paradigm shift is needed to gauge MSLs' true value. *Pharmaceutical Executive*. Retrieved from http://pharmexec.findpharma.com/pharmexec/article/articleDetail.jsp?id=352795&&pageID=1

World Association of Medical Editors. (2005, June 20). Ghost writing initiated by commercial companies. Retrieved from http://www.wame.org/resources/policies#ghost

CHAPTER 8

Regulatory Affairs

Julie Brideau, PharmD, and Dee Fanning, PharmD

LEARNING OBJECTIVES

1. Identify and describe the governmental laws, regulations, events, and terms that shape prescription drug promotion oversight.
2. Define and describe the role and organization of the Office of Prescription Drug Promotion (OPDP) and how it enforces various laws and regulations.
3. Differentiate among the various OPDP industry guidance documents and describe how they influence pharmaceutical marketing.
4. Identify the organizations and structure in place for oversight of the marketing of biologic and over-the-counter (OTC) medications.
5. Define corporate compliance, integrity, and corporate integrity agreements and illustrate their significance to pharmaceutical manufacturers in the current marketing environment.
6. Describe the Office of Inspector General (OIG), its role, and the federal fraud and abuse laws' impact on pharmaceutical marketing.
7. Illustrate the role of the Pharmaceutical Research and Manufacturers of America (PhRMA) and its code on interacting with healthcare professionals.

Although general promotion of pharmaceuticals, especially to physicians, has existed for decades, promotional spending and its presence in mainstream media have grown exponentially over the past decade. Thus, given that all new pharmaceutical products and devices in the United States must be approved by the Food and Drug Administration (FDA) prior to market launch, the level of FDA and government involvement in overseeing and regulating manufacturers' marketing and promotional practices has also greatly increased. It is the FDA's responsibility, through a meticulous medical and scientific review of the safety and efficacy data presented in the New Drug Application (NDA), to ensure that a drug's benefits outweigh its risks. Once a pharmaceutical product or device is approved and available for sale, its manufacturer's marketing practices are overseen and controlled by several government agencies and industry groups. This chapter provides a brief history of the incidents that have led to the current regulation of prescription drugs and descriptions of the relevant government agencies and their jurisdiction over the marketing of prescription drugs.

BRIEF HISTORY OF GOVERNMENTAL PRESCRIPTION DRUG REGULATIONS

The federal government became involved in ensuring the safety of prescription, or "patent," drugs more than 100 years ago. Unlike over-the-counter (OTC) medications/products such as Motrin (ibuprofen) or NyQuil (acetaminophen, dextromethorphan, and doxylamine succinate), prescription medications are not considered consumer goods because their use requires a **learned intermediary** (a healthcare provider licensed to prescribe) to diagnose the condition treated by the drug, recommend the drug, and then monitor the use of the drug, including its effectiveness and adverse events. Over the years, a multitude of laws, regulations (including the **Code of Federal Regulations**), and terms have led to the current state of pharmaceutical regulation. **Table 8-1** presents a summary of these important events, regulations, and terms.

Table 8-1 Medication Regulation Events and Terms

Legislation (Year), Event, Regulation, or Term	Impact or Meaning
Pure Food and Drug Act (1906)	The first law passed regulating drugs. Came into being as a result of public outrage in response to unsafe and unsanitary conditions in the meatpacking industry, largely brought to the public's attention by Upton Sinclair's novel *The Jungle*,[a] which explained in detail the gory conditions

Legislation (Year), Event, Regulation, or Term	Impact or Meaning
	under which the nation's meat supply was processed and handled and resulted in a boycott of meat by the American public. The book pushed Congress to act on President Roosevelt's wish for a pure food bill, which he requested in December 1905.[a] The law prohibited misbranded and adulterated foods, drinks, and drugs in interstate commerce.
Food and Drug Administration (1930)	The Pure Food and Drug Act was initially enforced by the Bureau of Chemistry in the Department of Agriculture, which became the Food and Drug Administration (FDA) in 1930.[b] The FDA, an agency within the U.S. Public Health Service under the umbrella of the Department of Health and Human Services, was founded to regulate the approval of new foods and health-related products and is charged with ensuring the safety of the country's food and drug supply.
Federal Food, Drug, and Cosmetics Act (1938)	Passed by Congress after a tragedy involving an elixir used in children to treat throat infection, which contained the sweet-tasting diethylene glycol, caused kidney failure and several children died as a result.[c] The FD&C Act requires that pharmaceutical manufacturers/marketers prove their drugs are safe and mandates the submission of a New Drug Application (NDA) by the sponsor to the FDA for review and approval prior to placing the drug in commerce.
Durham-Humphrey Amendment (1951)	This amendment to the original FD&C Act defines the kinds of drugs that could not be used safely without medical supervision and, therefore, created sale by prescription only.
Kefauver-Harris Amendment (1962)	This amendment to the original FD&C Act occurred after the thalidomide scare, in which commonly used thalidomide caused numerous severe birth defects in pregnant women in Europe. The amendment required that sponsors prove their drug to be both safe and effective. In addition, this update also gave the FDA jurisdiction over prescription drug marketing, expanding the FDA's scope to products for both human and animal use, including foods, cosmetics, medicines, biologics, and medical devices.[d]
Misbranding	Under the FD&C Act, a drug is misbranded if its advertising or labeling is found to be false or misleading. For example, an advertisement for an allergy drug approved only for use in adults would be considered misbranded if it includes photos of children happily playing in a meadow, because this implies the drug is approved for use in children. See **Figure 8-1** for an example of the FDA's actions against physicians who offered misbranded Botox (botulinum toxin) injections.

(continues)

Table 8-1 Medication Regulation Events and Terms (*continued*)

Legislation (Year), Event, Regulation, or Term	Impact or Meaning
Code of Federal Regulations (CFR)	The CFR is the codification of rules and regulations by the executive departments and agencies of the U.S. federal government. The federal regulations involving advertising and promotion of prescription drugs are found in 21 CFR Part 202 and Part 314. **21 CFR Part 202** Part 202 defines the approved package insert as the official source for promotional claims and requires a fair balance of information and risk information be included. It also delineates the requirements for proprietary (brand) and established (generic) name usage, size, and placement (i.e., the established name must be at least one-half the measured size of the proprietary name) and other requirements regarding dosage forms and active and inert ingredients. Part 202 prohibits claims of safety and efficacy prior to a drug's approval (preapproval promotion) and comparison claims against a competitor's product without specific proof, usually in the form of two head-to-head studies directly comparing the drugs in the same population. This part also requires a **brief summary** of safety information to accompany all advertisements. **21 CFR Part 314** Part 314 requires that all promotional materials be submitted to FDA's Office of Prescription Drug Promotion, formerly known as the Division of Drug Marketing, Advertising and Communications (DDMAC), until late 2011, usually at time of first use. The FDA has the right to withdraw marketing approval if promotional materials are not submitted as required by Part 314. To date, however, this has not occurred.

[a] Historic Present. (2009, August 19). The FDA and government regulation of food safety. Retrieved from http://thehistoricpresent.wordpress.com/2009/08/19/the-fda-and-government-regulation-of-food-safety/

[b] Food and Drug Administration. (2009b, May 20). Food standards and the 1906 act. Retrieved from http://www.fda.gov/AboutFDA/WhatWeDo/History/ProductRegulation/ucm132666.htm

[c] Ballentine, C. (1981, June). Sulfanilamide disaster: Taste of raspberries, taste of death: The 1937 elixir sulfanilamide incident. *FDA Consumer Magazine*. Retrieved from http://www.fda.gov/AboutFDA/WhatWeDo/History/ProductRegulation/SulfanilamideDisaster/default.htm

[d] Meadows, M. (2006, January–February). Promoting safe and effective drugs for 100 years. *FDA Consumer Magazine*. Retrieved from http://www.fda.gov/AboutFDA/WhatWeDo/History/CentennialofFDA/CentennialEditionofFDAConsumer/ucm093787.htm

FDA Law Enforcers Crack Down on Illegal Botox Scammers

In November 2004, when four people became paralyzed after purportedly receiving Botox Cosmetic injections at a medical clinic in Oakland Park, Fla., the Food and Drug Administration's (FDA) Office of Criminal Investigations (OCI) was called to investigate. The four victims were hospitalized with severe botulism poisoning. The paralysis was temporary—a result of being injected with potent, unapproved botulinum toxin. The doctor who injected the toxin had passed it off as Botox Cosmetic, an FDA-approved drug to treat forehead wrinkles.

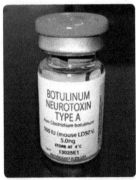

What began as one OCI investigation of a Florida medical clinic escalated into 210 investigations of health care professionals throughout the United States. As of July 2008, the work of OCI has led to 31 arrests and 29 convictions of individuals who purposely injected an unapproved, cheaper substitute toxin for FDA-approved Botox Cosmetic into nearly 1,000 unknowing patients.

Under federal law, no form of botulinum toxin may be commercially distributed for use on humans unless it has been approved by FDA. At this time, Botox Cosmetic, made by Allergan Inc. of Irvine, Calif., is the only type of botulinum toxin approved by FDA to temporarily soften the frown lines between the eyebrows. Botox Cosmetic is a sterile, purified version of the same toxin that causes botulism, a severe form of foodborne illness. In both cases, the toxin is produced by the bacterium *Clostridium botulinum*. The injectable form of sterile, purified botulinum toxin, when used in small doses, locally affects the muscles' ability to contract, smoothing out frown lines to make them invisible.

Source of the Problem

OCI agents traced the fake Botox Cosmetic used in the Florida clinic to a California laboratory that sold botulinum toxin for research purposes. The agents found more of the laboratory's research product at Toxin Research International Inc. (TRI) in Tucson, Ariz. TRI was sell-

The vials were clearly labeled, "For Research Purposes Only, Not For Human Use." Invoices and product information sheets carried the same warning.

FIGURE 8-1 Misbranding

Source: Food and Drug Administration.

For the complete Code of Federal Regulations parts involving advertising and promotion of prescription drugs, see www.accessdata.fda.gov/scripts/cdrh /cfdocs/cfcfr/CFRSearch.cfm. Enter *202* or *314* in the "Title21 *Part.Section*" search field.

OFFICE OF PRESCRIPTION DRUG PROMOTION

The hierarchy of the FDA includes multiple layers and specialty areas to cover all its various responsibilities (Food and Drug Administration [FDA], 2012f). The division responsible for drug oversight is the Center for Drug Evaluation and Research (CDER), which regulates over-the-counter and prescription drugs, including biologic and generic drugs. The CDER is then even further subdivided based on numerous specialties (FDA, 2012c). One of those subdivisions is the **Office of Prescription Drug Promotion (OPDP)**, whose mission is "to protect the public health by assuring prescription drug information is truthful, balanced and accurately communicated. This is accomplished through a comprehensive surveillance, enforcement and education program, and by fostering better communication of labeling and promotional information to both healthcare professionals and consumers," and whose responsibility is regulating prescription drug promotion (FDA, 2012a).

Reviewers within the OPDP are responsible for assessing prescription drug advertising and promotional labeling to ensure that the materials are truthful and not false or misleading. The OPDP accomplishes its goals by voluntary compliance mechanisms, such as the provision of advisory comments on draft pieces, issuance of guidance documents, educational efforts at conferences, and a comprehensive surveillance and enforcement program. All advertising and promotional pieces must, by regulation, be submitted to the OPDP at time of initial use on FDA Form 2253—Transmittal of Advertisements and Promotional Labeling for Drugs and Biologics for Human Use (**Figure 8-2**).

There is a requirement for presubmission of material for certain drugs (e.g., products receiving accelerated approval through Subpart H of the Code of Federal Regulations). Materials to be used for these products in the first 120 days after approval must be submitted before product approval. Materials to be used after the first 120 days must be submitted 30 days before time of first use (FDA, 2012a).

The OPDP performs its surveillance of the pharmaceutical industry's marketing practices through monitoring of materials submitted on FDA Form 2253 and also through attendance at medical conferences (e.g., the American Heart Association's annual meeting), where officials have been known to shut down booths where sales representatives were found to be speaking "off-label" (Mello, 2009). OPDP reviewers help companies fulfill the regulatory requirements by providing, upon request, written comments to pharmaceutical manufacturers on their

TRANSMITTAL OF ADVERTISEMENTS AND PROMOTIONAL LABELING FOR DRUGS AND BIOLOGICS FOR HUMAN USE	1. DATE SUBMITTED	3. NDA/ANDA/AADA OR BLA/PLA/PMA
		Number: Single product ☐ Multiple products ☐ For multiple products, submit completed form and specimen of advertising/promotional materials to one application of choice, and attach separate sheet addressing items 3-5 for remainder of products. Refer to No. 3 on instruction sheet.
	2. LABEL REVIEW NO. (Biologics)	

NOTE: Form 2253 is required by law. Reports are required for approved NDAs and ANDAs (21 CFR 314.81)

4. PROPRIETARY NAME	5. ESTABLISHED NAME
	Prod. Code No.
6. PACKAGE INSERT DATE and ID NO. (Latest final printed labeling)	7. MANUFACTURER NAME:
	License No. (Biologics)

FDA/CBER USE ONLY

REVIEWED BY	DATE	RETURNED BY	DATE

8.   **ADVERTISEMENT / PROMOTIONAL LABELING MATERIALS**

Please check only one: ☐ Professional   ☐ Consumer

Material Type (use FDA codes) a.	Dissemination/ Publication Date b.	Applicant's Material ID Code and/or description c.	Previous review No. if applicable / date (PLA Submissions) d.	COMMENTS
			Add Continuation Page	

9. TYPED NAME AND TITLE OF RESPONSIBLE OFFICIAL OR AGENT	10. SIGNATURE OF RESPONSIBLE OFFICIAL
11. APPLICANT'S RETURN ADDRESS	12. RESPONSIBLE OFFICIAL'S a. PHONE NO. b. FAX NO.
	13. FOR CBER PRODUCTS ONLY: (Check one) ☐ Part I/Draft ☐ Part II/Final

FIGURE 8-2 FDA Form 2253

Source: Food and Drug Administration.

proposed promotional materials to help ensure clear understanding of the laws and regulations relating to prescription drug promotion. Reviewers also compare product labeling and promotional materials of similar, or "class," products to ensure the regulatory requirements are consistently and fairly applied. Additionally, they work with other divisions at the FDA on labeling and promotional issues. A large portion of possible violations are identified through complaints received from competitors, consumers, and practitioners.

On the other hand, if promotional materials are found to be false or misleading, the OPDP is responsible for initiating enforcement actions (**Figure 8-3**). Generally speaking, every promotional item with a product name appearing is regulated. Advertisements and promotional materials must comply with the requirements laid out within the Federal Food, Drug, and Cosmetic (FD&C) Act and be consistent with the approved product labeling/package inserts (PIs). Claims must be supported by substantial evidence, and promotion must be balanced, reveal all material information, and not be false or misleading. Even for products that are the sole representative of a given category, materials or events that do not name the product can be "branded by default." A piece can be deemed as false or misleading if it contains unsubstantiated claims that a product is safer or more effective than evidence shows it to be, presents data in a misleading way (e.g., inappropriate spacing of data points on graphs), or makes comparative claims versus another product without substantial evidence.

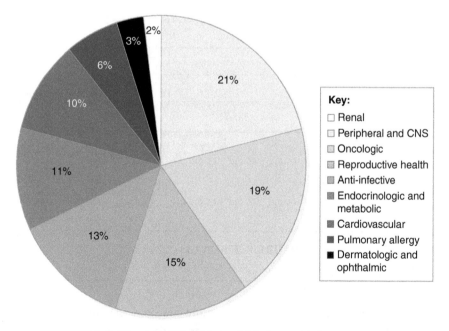

FIGURE 8-3 Trends in FDA Sales and Marketing Enforcement Actions
Source: FDA website; 2010.

CASE IN POINT 8-1
FDA's Bad Ad Program

In May 2010, the FDA launched the "Bad Ad" outreach program to increase healthcare providers' and consumers' awareness of misleading promotion. **Bad ads** are defined as ones that exclude details about a product's risks, promote unapproved uses, or overemphasize a product's effectiveness. After the first year, the FDA received more than 300 reports of potentially misleading ads, compared to 100 reports received by the agency the year prior. As a result, the FDA issued several warning letters to the pharmaceutical companies involved. The FDA plans to expand the program by reaching out to medical, nursing, and pharmacy students. A webinar intended for medical and pharmacy professionals is available on the FDA website (FDA, 2012e).

OPDP Enforcement Actions

The OPDP has several avenues available to it to enforce the advertising and promotion regulations. Enforcement actions include notice of violation (NOV) letters (also referred to as "untitled letters"), **warning letters (WLs)**, injunctions or consent decrees, and even drug seizures and criminal actions in extreme circumstances.

Notice of Violation

The most commonly seen enforcement action, **notice of violation (NOV)** letters are written to the pharmaceutical manufacturer's regulatory affairs representative responsible for the product. They provide a description of the materials found to be out of compliance, as well as the specific information (e.g., graphical representations, claims) within the piece or pieces that the OPDP has found to be noncompliant. NOVs usually contain "cease and desist" language and require the company to recall noncompliant pieces. They might also require corrective advertising or communications to repair the impression the egregious piece has made in the marketplace.

CASE IN POINT 8-2
Merck Notice of Violation Letter

In 2012, Merck and Company received a notice of violation letter from the OPDP for Saphris (asenapine) sublingual tablets for comments made by a physician speaking on behalf of Merck. The speaker stated that he "prescribes Saphris as an adjunctive treatment for major depressive disorder (MDD) just as he might prescribe Abilify, and that it works just as well." The letter states:

> The oral statement made by Dr. Favazza misleadingly suggested that Saphris is safe and effective for use as an adjunctive treatment for MDD. According to its PI [package insert], Saphris is only indicated for the treatment of patients with schizophrenia or for the acute treatment of manic or mixed episodes associated with bipolar I disorder, either as a monotherapy or adjunctive treatment with lithium or valproate. Therefore, the oral statement made by Dr. Favazza misbrands the drug by suggesting a new "intended use" for Saphris for which the PI lacks adequate directions for use.

This letter came about as a result of a complaint to the FDA's Bad Ad program by an attendee at the speaker event, and the FDA considers Merck responsible for the statements of this physician because, although not a direct employee of Merck, the physician was being paid by Merck to speak on its behalf (Food and Drug Administration, Office of Prescription Drug Promotion [FDA OPDP], 2012b).

Warning Letters

Warning letters are the next level of NOV severity. These are usually sent after a company has received one or more NOV letters but still continues the noncompliant behavior. However, sometimes the initial action is in the form of a WL if the behavior is especially egregious (e.g., could affect patient safety). Warning letters are written to the head of the manufacturer (president or CEO), often require corrective action, and are made public through posting on the OPDP website (FDA, 2012e). Continued violations can lead to further enforcement actions, including possible legal action, fines, audits, and requirements for presubmission of pieces prior to their use.

Some common issues identified in OPDP NOV and warning letters include the following:

- *Broadening of indication.* Occurs when a promotional piece directly or indirectly makes the drug appear as if it can treat indications for which it does not have approval. For example, if a drug is indicated to treat mild to moderate psoriasis only, but the wording in the header of a detail aid states only that the drug is indicated for psoriasis, thus implying it can be used for all stages of psoriasis, including severe cases, this is broadening of indication.
- *Omission of material facts.* The failure to reveal all the pertinent facts that are required to be known by prescribers or patients for proper use of the drug, resulting in misleading promotional materials. One example is if a piece fails to reveal that the product it is promoting is approved only for use by adults and pediatric patients ages 12 years and older.
- *Minimization of risk.* This occurs when a promotional item does not fully characterize the product's risk information. This is best illustrated by an advertisement that presents risk information at the bottom of the page in hard-to-read, small type, while efficacy claims are presented in large, bold headers surrounded by emphasizing white space and take up the majority of the page or spread.
- *Unsubstantiated superiority claims.* These claims occur when a promotional item touts a medication as superior to another without the clinical trial data to support the claim. An example is a promotional piece that claims that one drug lowers blood pressure more than a competitor drug based on the percentages of blood pressure lowering found in the respective package inserts as opposed to a head-to-head clinical trial comparison.
- *Overstatement of efficacy.* This involves promotional materials being viewed as misleading if they represent or suggest that a drug is more effective than has been demonstrated by the evidence or clinical experience, such as promoting that a medication reduces future cardiovascular events by 75% when trial and all other data say the number should be 55%.

OPDP Guidance for Industry Documents

The OPDP has published several Guidance for Industry documents related to advertising and promotion (FDA, 2012g). Although nonbinding and not required

CASE IN POINT 8-3
Notice of Violation Letter for Superiority Claims

In 2012, the Medicines Company received a notice of violation letter from OPDP for making unsubstantiated superiority claims about its drug Angiomax (bivalirudin) for injection in a professional booth panel. The letter indicated the panel contained the following claims (FDA OPDP, 2012a):

- "ANGIOMAX: documented *victories* across a broad spectrum of patients from stable to STEMI" (emphasis added)
- "Data-Driven ***victories***" (bolded emphasis added)
- "**Unsurpassed ischemic efficacy throughout the risk spectrum**"
- "Demonstrated unsurpassed ischemic efficacy and reduced bleeding vs heparin with or without glycoprotein (GP) IIb/IIIa inhibitor" (emphasis in original)

to be followed, guidance documents represent the FDA's current thinking on a topic. Alternative approaches can be followed if they satisfy the requirements of the applicable statutes and regulations. Per the introduction section of all FDA guidance documents, "guidances describe FDA's current thinking on a topic and should be viewed only as recommendations, unless specific regulatory or statutory requirements are cited." The use of the word *should* in agency guidances means that something is suggested or recommended, but not required. Several guidance documents are in draft form and remain so for some time. Guidances that relate to pharmaceutical marketing include the following:

- *"Industry-Supported Scientific and Educational Activities."* In 1998, the OPDP published this guidance, which explains how industry can sponsor or support events at conferences and scientific meetings in a compliant manner so that they are not regulated by the FDA.
- *"Guidance on Consumer-Directed Broadcast Advertisements."* Originally released in 1997, this guidance requires all advertisements to be accompanied by the brief summary. For broadcast ads, this is accomplished by meeting the **adequate provision** requirements outlined in 21 CFR 202. Sponsors can fulfill the requirement by providing a "major statement"

of risk information verbally in the ad, along with several mechanisms for distributing the approved package insert (including those that work for both active and passive seekers of information), such as a toll-free phone number, an Internet site, a statement to see a healthcare provider for more information, and/or instructions to see the print ad in journal *X*.

- *"Help-Seeking and Other Disease Awareness Communications by or on Behalf of Drug and Device Firms."* This draft guidance was published in 2004. These types of advertisements and communications educate consumers and/or healthcare providers about diseases or conditions, but they do not mention any drug or product name. If done correctly, these types of communications are not regulated by the FDA. This guidance provides information on how to do these types of communications in the right manner. The FDA defines these communications as those with the following characteristics:
  - Discuss a disease or health condition
  - If consumer-directed, advise the audience to "see your doctor" for possible diagnosis and/or treatment
  - If aimed at healthcare practitioners, encourage awareness of signs of the particular disease or health condition, or otherwise provide information to assist in the diagnosis of the particular disease or health condition
  - Do not mention a particular drug or device
  - Do not include any representation or suggestion relating to a particular drug or device
- *"Brief Summary: Disclosing Risk Information in Consumer-Directed Print Advertisements."* Also in 2004, the FDA published this draft guidance covering the brief summary for consumer-directed print ads. This guidance describes options available for sponsors to disclose risk information, such as use of FDA-approved patient labeling, written in language easy to understand by nonhealthcare professionals, or the "Highlights" section of the approved package insert.
- *"Presenting Risk Information in Prescription Drug and Medical Device Promotion."* Published in 2009, this much anticipated draft guidance discusses factors that are relevant to the disclosure of risk information and provides illustrative examples of the FDA's thinking on these factors. The draft guidance covers general considerations, including consistent use of language, use of signals, and the framing and hierarchy of risk information. It also covers content issues, including quantity, materiality, and comprehensiveness. Format considerations are also covered.
- *"Product Name Placement, Size, and Prominence in Advertising and Promotional Labeling."* Rules for the use, placement, and size of drug names in

advertisements are outlined in 21 CFR 202. This guidance, published in 2012, helps explain how to meet these requirements. It covers such topics as the juxtaposition of proprietary and established names, size and prominence of proprietary and established names, proprietary and established names in audiovisual and broadcast advertisements and promotional labeling, and proprietary and established names in the running text of electronic and computer-based advertisements and promotional labeling. Requirements are spelled out for both single- and multi-ingredient products.

BIOLOGICS

Whereas the OPDP is responsible for regulating the marketing of drugs approved by the CDER, products approved within the FDA's Center for Biologics Evaluation and Research (CBER) are regulated by the Advertising and Promotional Labeling Branch (APLB) within the CBER. The APLB's goal is to protect the public health by ensuring that information about a biological product's benefits and risks is adequately and accurately communicated in a nonmisleading and balanced manner. The APLB acts to ensure that biological products are marketed in a way that is compliant with the FD&C Act and the advertising and promotional labeling regulations. Advertisements and promotional materials for biologics are subject to the same rules and regulations as drug products, including the requirement to submit Form 2253 (FDA, 2010).

OVER-THE-COUNTER DRUGS

Whereas the FDA is responsible for regulating both the labeling and promotion of prescription drugs, it is responsible for the regulating only the labeling of over-the-counter (OTC) drugs and, as a general rule, dietary supplements, medical devices, and cosmetics. The Federal Trade Commission (FTC) oversees the aspects of OTC advertising, and, just like for prescription medications, advertising claims for an OTC drug must be truthful and nondeceptive. Given the health and safety issues that could arise from the inappropriate marketing of OTC products, claims made should be carefully substantiated by scientific evidence. The FTC and the FDA have a long-standing liaison agreement to allocate their efforts efficiently (Federal Trade Commission, Bureau of Consumer Protection Business Center, 2001).

CORPORATE COMPLIANCE AND CORPORATE INTEGRITY

The OPDP, the APBL, and the FTC are not the only organizations pharmaceutical manufacturers have to satisfy when planning promotional activities. The Office of Inspector General (OIG), the Department of Justice (DoJ), various federal and state laws, and even industry associations such as the Pharmaceutical Research and Manufacturers Association (PhRMA) all influence pharmaceuticals marketing and communication. A major goal of these laws, agencies, and organizations is to ensure that healthcare providers and others involved in the prescribing or purchasing of prescription drugs are not unduly and inappropriately influenced by pharmaceutical manufacturers. How does this affect the functions of sales, medical, and marketing?

When the federal government pays for items or services provided to Medicare or Medicaid beneficiaries, or other groups such as the military and the Veterans Administration (VA), the federal fraud and abuse laws can come into play. If it is discovered that a pharmaceutical manufacturer has, through illegal marketing practices, caused the federal government to overpay for prescription drugs, the result can be civil and criminal charges, which is when the OIG and DoJ become involved.

OIG Guidance for Industry Compliance Programs

The OIG is the independent oversight agency that falls under the jurisdiction of the U.S. Department of Health and Human Services and is responsible for identifying, preventing, and punishing fraud, waste, and abuse related to federal health programs. The DoJ works closely with the OIG to investigate and prosecute cases. In 2003, the OIG put out its "Compliance Program Guidance for Pharmaceutical Manufacturers" guidance (U.S. Department of Health and Human Services, Office of Inspector General [US DHHS OIG], 2003). Through this guidance, the OIG set forth "its general views on the value and fundamental principles of compliance programs for pharmaceutical manufacturers and the specific elements that pharmaceutical manufacturers should consider when developing and implementing an effective compliance program." The guidance seeks to help pharmaceutical manufacturers successfully utilize the safe harbors available to them and to aid in setting up and running a successful compliance program. It details the "seven elements" of a good compliance program, which include the following:

- Implementing written policies and procedures
- Designating a compliance officer and compliance committee

- Conducting effective training and education
- Developing effective lines of communication
- Conducting internal monitoring and auditing
- Enforcing standards through well-publicized disciplinary guidelines
- Responding promptly to detected problems and undertaking corrective action

Sales, marketing, and medical departments can help their company by cooperating and working closely with their compliance officer and department. (See www .oig.hhs.gov for the complete guidance and more information.)

Federal Fraud and Abuse Laws

Several main federal fraud and abuse laws concern pharmaceutical marketing.

False Claims Act

The False Claims Act "prohibits the submission of false or fraudulent claims to the Government." A company can be liable under the False Claims Act "if they knowingly submit false, fraudulent, or misleading information for government reimbursement." To be in compliance with this act, pharmaceutical manufacturers must report complete and accurate prices to the government. The False Claims Act makes it illegal to submit false or fraudulent claims for payment to Medicare or Medicaid or other federally funded programs. Healthcare providers would be in violation of this act if they submit claims for a service with the following characteristics:

- Not provided to the patient
- Previously reimbursed by a prior claim
- A miscoded claim
- For which proper documentation is not found in the medical record

Pharmaceutical manufacturers can be also charged with violations of this act if they engage in a scheme to report false and inflated prices for pharmaceutical products, given government agencies use these reported prices to determine payment/reimbursement rates. In addition, pharmaceutical manufacturers that engage in off-label promotion are in violation of federal laws, including the False Claims Act, because their illegal promotion could cause more prescriptions to be written and paid for by federal funds than would have been if only on-label promotion had occurred.

The False Claims Act encourages individuals to report fraudulent activity and offers statutory rewards for filing False Claims Act cases on behalf of the

CASE IN POINT 8-4
False Claims Act and Whistleblowers

A small, independent pharmacy in Florida, Ven-A-Care of the Florida Keys, has earned a unique distinction—the most successful whistleblower in United States history. The pharmacy, which participated in government insurance programs, namely, Medicaid and Medicare, realized the payments it was receiving, based on the reimbursement benchmark price known as Average Wholesale Price (AWP), were in actuality much higher than the prices generally being paid by pharmacies and were resulting in very high profits for providers who were being reimbursed based on AWP. For example, as reported in a 2005 suit filed in California, a 1-gram vial of the antibiotic vancomycin, a potent injectable antibiotic, was sold to providers for $6.29 but billed to California Medicaid (MediCal) for $58.37. The False Claims Act was implicated when pharmaceutical manufacturers reported the artificially inflated AWP prices for their products to insurers, including the government, yet sold to providers at much lower levels, causing the providers to submit false claims for reimbursement. Based on a series of cases known as the AWP litigation cases, Ven-A-Care and its counsel partnered with multiple states and the Department of Justice to recover, as of January 2011, $2.2 billion for U.S. taxpayers and itself (Zajac, 2011).

federal government under the *qui tam* provisions of the False Claims Act. *Qui tam* is Latin for "who as well." A *qui tam* action is a lawsuit under a statute that gives to the plaintiff bringing the action (also known as a whistleblower) a part of the penalty recovered and the balance to the state. The plaintiff in a *qui tam* action describes him- or herself as suing for the state as well as for him- or herself. Whistleblowers can receive up to 30% of any False Claims Act recovery. In general, the *qui tam* provisions permit any person or entity to file a False Claims Act case on behalf of the federal government (Centers for Medicare and Medicaid Services, n.d.). Since 2000, the *qui tam* pharmaceutical fraud cases settled have amounted to more than $3.5 billion and counting (Nolan & Auerbach, 2011).

Anti-Kickback Statute

Although the practice of paying for a referral is completely legitimate in some professions, it is illegal in the medical and pharmaceutical fields and a violation of the **Anti-Kickback Statute**. This statute prohibits companies from offering or receiving **remuneration** (anything of value) to induce someone to purchase, prescribe, order, or recommend any item or service that might be paid for by a federal healthcare program. It is enforced by the OIG, DoJ, and state Medicaid fraud control units (MFCUs). In other words, no quid pro quo, or I'll scratch your back if you scratch mine. Under the terms of this statute, both parties are in violation, the payer and the payee. "Kickbacks are illegal because they harm the Federal health care programs and program beneficiaries. They can lead to: overutilization of items or services, increased program costs, corruption of medical decision making, patient steering, and unfair competition" (US DHHS OIG, n.d.b).

This statute has been interpreted to relate to agreements between pharmaceutical manufacturers and prescribers, purchasers, or formulary managers. Although a number of statutory exemptions and regulatory safe harbors protect some common activities from prosecution, the exemptions and safe harbors are drawn narrowly, and practices that involve remuneration intended to induce prescribing, purchases, or recommendations can be subject to scrutiny if they do not qualify for an exemption or safe harbor. According to the online Business Dictionary, safe harbor is a provision in an agreement, law, or regulation that affords protection from liability or penalty under specified circumstances or if certain conditions are met. The consequences of violating this statute can include both civil and criminal enforcements. Civil enforcements might be: (1) $50,000 civil monetary penalty per item/ service, (2) three times the total amount of "remuneration," or (3) permissive exclusion from federal healthcare programs. Criminal enforcement might be: (1) up to 5 years in prison, (2) $250,000/$500,000 in fines (federal sentencing statute), or (3) mandatory exclusion from federal healthcare programs. The latter means that the drug can never be covered by federally funded programs (US DHHS OIG, 1999).

When investigating alleged violations of these laws and illegal marketing practices, the following might be considered:

- What is the total marketplace for the approved uses?
- Is the company making sales calls on healthcare providers who do not treat patients with the drug's approved indication?
- Does it have sales budgets for nonapproved uses?
- Are employees paid bonuses for sales for nonapproved uses?
- Did the company seek FDA approval for other uses and not get it?
- Did the company choose not to seek FDA approval and why?

CASE IN POINT 8-5
False Claims Act and the Anti-Kickback Statute

In 2004, a former sales representative and his attorneys filed a False Claims Act complaint alleging that Pfizer violated the federal Anti-Kickback Statute, 42 U.S.C. §1320a-7b(b), and the off-label marketing provision within the Federal Food, Drug, and Cosmetic Act (FD&C), 21 U.S.C. §§301-97, in its marketing practices for Bextra (valdecoxib). The company pled guilty to several civil and criminal charges and paid more than $2 billion to the government. The sales representative was awarded more than $50 million for his role as a whistleblower in the investigation. The *qui tam* provisions of the False Claims Act were triggered by the reimbursement for the drug through federal and state government programs, including Medicaid and Medicare (Harris, 2009).

- If the company is using literature to support unapproved uses, does it claim the product is safe and effective for those uses?
- Does the company use consultants to push off-label uses?
- Does it incent customers to prescribe off-label?

Congress and the OIG have created several statutory exceptions and regulatory safe harbors to protect certain arrangements that would otherwise violate the statute but that have legitimate purposes. The personal services safe harbor permits legitimate service agreements with prescribers (e.g., consulting and speaking agreements) requiring written agreement with a term of at least 1 year (may be shorter for a specific time-limited activity). The agreement must specify the services contracted for, which cannot exceed what is reasonably necessary to meet the company's needs. For services to be provided on a sporadic or part-time basis (e.g., speaking engagements), the agreement must specify the schedule, precise length, and exact charge for the intervals. Agreements must spell out the aggregate payment in advance, reflect fair market value (FMV), and not take into account the volume or value of any potential referrals of business generated (US DHHS OIG, 1999).

Corporate Integrity Agreements

False Claim Act, Anti-Kickback Statute, and Off-Label Promotion case settlements often result in **corporate integrity agreements (CIAs)**. CIAs are contractual agreements between the settling company and the OIG that are incorporated into settlements with the DoJ. These agreements create extensive obligations for the company regarding its compliance policies, procedures, and performance in specified areas of concern, usually those areas in which illegal practices caused the violations noted in the case. CIAs require the company to hire an independent review organization (IRO) to audit the company's compliance policies and procedures and the company's performance of its obligations under the CIA. If the company fails to meet its CIA obligations, it can be hit with fines and/or exclusion from federal healthcare programs (US DHHS OIG, n.d.a).

Recent CIAs have included requirements for personal certifications by the board of directors and company managers (in areas such as medical, medical information, marketing, and sales) regarding compliance within the organization, policies for the review of sales call and sampling plans, policies addressing medical science liaison (MSL) interactions with healthcare providers, policies mandating the review of all promotional and other written materials and information to be disseminated outside the company, and policies for publications, including authorship and contributorship, full disclosures, written agreements, annual publication plans, justification for publications, and monitoring/auditing requirements (US DHHS OIG, n.d.a).

PhRMA CODE ON INTERACTIONS WITH HEALTHCARE PROFESSIONALS

In addition to the various laws, regulations, and federal agencies described thus far, pharmaceutical manufacturers can choose to follow the rules outlined in the voluntary Code on Interactions with Healthcare Professionals from the Pharmaceutical Research and Manufacturers of America (PhRMA), the pharmaceutical industry's trade association, and the PhRMA "Guiding Principles: Direct to Consumer Advertisements" (PhRMA, n.d.b). The PhRMA code is a voluntary code of conduct developed initially in 2002, and then updated in 2009. The primary goal of this code is to ensure that manufacturers "reinforce our intention that our interactions with health care professionals are to benefit patients and to enhance the practice of medicine" (PhRMA, n.d.a). This code is not the law, but a well-adopted code of conduct for many of the leaders in the pharmaceutical industry.

The code describes requirements that member companies should follow in their interactions with healthcare providers (HCPs). These include rules on educational items, consultant arrangements, meals, and support of educational events such as continuing medical education (CME), speaker programs and speaker training meetings, scholarships and educational funds, interactions with HCPs on formulary committees or developers of clinical practice guidelines, use of prescriber data, training, and adherence to the code. The code prohibits entertainment and recreational events, as well as gifts and noneducational and practice-related items. Therefore, member companies are prohibited from giving away reminder items with a product name on them, such as the pens and note-pads so common in years past. This code is meant to help member companies comply with the OIG guidance and relevant laws and regulations.

Another goal of the code is to improve public perceptions of the pharmaceutical industry and its marketing and promotional practices. Although described in the document as voluntary, the OIG states in its compliance guidance:

> Although compliance with the PhRMA Code will not protect a manufac-turer as a matter of law under the anti-kickback statute, it will substantially reduce the risk of fraud and abuse and help demonstrate a good faith effort to comply with the applicable federal health care program requirements (US DHHS OIG, 2003).

Additionally, all companies that market prescription drugs should note that fol-lowing the PhRMA code is mandatory in several states, such as California as well as the District of Columbia, and even for companies that are not members of PhRMA (Snapp & Blacha, 2008).

The goal of PhRMA's voluntary guiding principles for direct-to-consumer (DTC) communications is to "express the commitment of PhRMA members to deliver DTC communications that serve as valuable contributors to public health." Revised in 2005, the principles, among other things, advise member companies to submit new television advertisements to the OPDP for comment prior to broadcast, to include disease awareness and prevention messaging in ads, and to spend an adequate amount of time educating healthcare providers about the new drug prior to beginning DTC campaigns (PhRMA, n.d.b).

RISK EVALUATION AND MITIGATION STRATEGIES

The impact of the more conservative regulatory environment is not limited to the FDA's preapproval requirements. Once approved and on the market, pharma-ceutical products now frequently are in a more controlled environment regulated by **Risk Evaluation and Mitigation Strategies (REMS)** designed to ensure the benefits of a given product outweigh its risks to patients. Many of those risk mitigation strategies include marketing restrictions and, therefore, often have an impact on the number of sales representatives required to achieve an acceptable reach as defined by the REMS.

In an effort to increase patient safety for drugs with a high-risk profile, the Food and Drug Administration Amendments Act (FDAAA) of 2007 developed Risk Evaluation and Mitigation Strategies (REMS). (REMS will eventually replace the older mechanism used by the FDA known as Risk Minimization Action Plans, or RiskMAPs.) Manufacturers submit REMS documents to the FDA, and they must include elements to assure safe use (ETASU) and evidence that the drug's benefits outweigh its risks. The most common component of a REMS program is the medication guide. This document is required to be distributed with certain prescriptions at the time of first fill and/or at subsequent refills. In addition to outpatient distribution of medication guides, some REMS require the medication guide also be distributed to hospitalized or other types of inpatients. Other possible components of REMS include criteria for specialized training for healthcare professionals to ensure the safe use of a medication and patient registries, informed consent forms from patients, restricted distribution criteria, and many others.

CASE IN POINT 8-6
Example of a REMS Program

Addiction, misuse, abuse, overdose, and death caused by long-acting or extended-release (LA/ER) opioids have resulted in a major public health crisis. The FDA and the sponsors who market the LA/ER opioids have developed and implemented a REMS program for this drug class. A major component of the REMS is required education for prescribers that focuses on the safe use of these products. These educational courses include information about proper pain management, patient selection, and ways to increase patient awareness of the potential risks. LA/ER opioids are indicated for the relief of moderate to severe pain. Following are the generic names of products that are affected by this mandated REMS program (FDA, 2011a, 2011b, 2012d):
- Hydromorphone
- Oxycodone
- Morphine

- Oxymorphone
- Methadone
- Transdermal fentanyl
- Transdermal buprenorphine
  A complete list of drugs with currently approved individual Risk Evaluation and Mitigation Strategies (REMS) can be found on the FDA's website in the Drugs tab (www.fda.gov/Drugs/DrugSafety /PostmarketDrugSafetyInformationforPatientsandProviders /ucm111350.htm). FDA's Guidance for Industry on how to prepare a REMS can be found at www.fda.gov/downloads /Drugs/GuidanceComplianceRegulatoryInformation/Guidances /UCM184128.pdf.

SUMMARY

Given the ever-increasing scope of media in the United States, in particular, social media, the FDA will continually monitor pharmaceutical promotion to ensure that claims made by pharmaceutical manufacturers are truthful and not false or misleading. This chapter outlined the structure, laws, regulations, and guidances used by the government to ensure consumer safety with regard to pharmaceuticals.

DISCUSSION QUESTIONS

1. Given the rise of Internet-based promotion and social media, how might government authorities respond to ensure patient/consumer safety?
2. If the government does not change any guidelines for the use of social media, how might pharmaceutical manufacturers adapt their marketing and promotions?
3. Are the enforcement actions by OPDP harsh enough or too harsh? Discuss the repercussions of either side.
4. Because the OPDP Guidance for Industry documents are not law, from a public relations and image perspective what is the incentive for a pharmaceutical manufacturer to comply?

5. Discuss the Brief Summary portion of various pharmaceutical advertisements from a consumer perspective. Does it make the manufacturer seem more credible or possibly induce fear in the consumer's eyes?

6. Why would manufacturers be liable under the False Claims Act for reporting prices not generally and currently paid in the marketplace?

7. Discuss the payouts received by whistleblowers in a False Claims Act suit. Discuss whether the payouts are too much or not enough and why.

8. Can a medication approved under the REMS program still be a successful product for the manufacturer? Why or why not?

9. How would the role of OPDP be expanded or contracted in response to a ban on prescription direct-to-consumer (DTC) advertising?

10. Discuss how the interaction between the FDA and FTC might work and at what point either would intervene in the other's territory.

REFERENCES

Ballentine, C. (1981, June). Sulfanilamide disaster: Taste of raspberries, taste of death: The 1937 elixir sulfanilamide incident. *FDA Consumer Magazine*. Retrieved from http://www.fda.gov/AboutFDA/WhatWeDo/History/ProductRegulation/SulfanilamideDisaster/default.htm

BusinessDictionary.com. (n.d.). Safe harbor. Retrieved from http://www.businessdictionary.com/definition/safe-harbor.html

Centers for Medicare and Medicaid Services. (n.d.). False Claims Act. Retrieved from http://downloads.cms.gov/cmsgov/archived-downloads/SMDL/downloads/smd032207att2.pdf

Federal Trade Commission, Bureau of Consumer Protection Business Center. (2001, April). *Advertising FAQ's: A guide for small business*. Retrieved from http://business.ftc.gov/documents/bus35-advertising-faqs-guide-small-business

Food and Drug Administration. (2009a, February 20). FDA law enforcers crack down on illegal Botox scammers. Retrieved from http://www.fda.gov/ForConsumers/ConsumerUpdates/ucm048377.htm

Food and Drug Administration. (2009b, May 20). Food standards and the 1906 act. Retrieved from http://www.fda.gov/AboutFDA/WhatWeDo/History/ProductRegulation/ucm132666.htm

Food and Drug Administration. (2010). Vaccines, blood and biologics: About the Advertising and Promotional Labeling Branch (APLB). Retrieved from http://www.fda.gov/BiologicsBloodVaccines/DevelopmentApprovalProcess/AdvertisingLabelingPromotionalMaterials/ucm164120.htm

Food and Drug Administration. (2011a). Drugs: Questions and answers: FDA requires a Risk Evaluation and Mitigation Strategy (REMS) for long-acting and extended-release opioids. Retrieved from http://www.fda.gov/Drugs/DrugSafety/InformationbyDrugClass/ucm251752.htm

Food and Drug Administration. (2011b, April 11). For consumers: FDA acts to reduce harm from opioid drugs. Retrieved from http://www.fda.gov/ForConsumers/ConsumerUpdates/ucm251830.htm

Food and Drug Administration. (2012a). About FDA: The Office of Prescription Drug Promotion (OPDP). Retrieved from http://www.fda.gov/AboutFDA/CentersOffices/OfficeofMedicalProductsandTobacco/CDER/ucm090142.htm

Food and Drug Administration. (2012b). About FDA: Truthful Prescription Drug Advertising and Promotion (Bad Ad Program): The prescriber's role—recognize and report. Retrieved from htttp://www.fda.gov/AboutFDA/CentersOffices/CDER/ucm090142.htm

Food and Drug Administration. (2012c, September 19). Center for Drug Evaluation and Research key officials. Retrieved from http://www.fda.gov/downloads/AboutFDA/CentersOffices/OfficeofMedicalProductsandTobacco/CDER/ContactCDER/UCM070722.pdf

Food and Drug Administration. (2012d). Drugs: Risk Evaluation and Mitigation Strategy (REMS) for extended-release and long-acting opioids. Retrieved from http://www.fda.gov/Drugs/DrugSafety/InformationbyDrugClass/ucm163647.htm

Food and Drug Administration. (2012e). Drugs: Warning letters and notice of violation letters to pharmaceutical companies. Retrieved from http://www.fda.gov/Drugs/GuidanceComplianceRegulatoryInformation/EnforcementActivitiesbyFDA/WarningLettersandNoticeofViolationLetterstoPharmaceuticalCompanies/default.htm

Food and Drug Administration. (2012f, September 14). Food and Drug Administration organizational chart. Retrieved from http://www.fda.gov/downloads/AboutFDA/CentersOffices/OrganizationCharts/UCM291886.pdf

Food and Drug Administration. (2012g). For industry: Guidances. Retrieved from http://www.fda.gov/ForIndustry/FDABasicsforIndustry/ucm234622.htm

Food and Drug Administration, Office of Prescription Drug Promotion. (2012a, April 13). Letter from James S. Dvorksy, Regulatory Review Officer (OPDP), and Karen Rulli, Team Leader (OPDP), to Ketna Patel, Manager, The Medicines Company. Retrieved from http://www.fda.gov/downloads/Drugs/GuidanceComplianceRegulatoryInformation/EnforcementActivitiesbyFDA/WarningLettersandNoticeofViolationLetterstoPharmaceuticalCompanies/UCM301931.pdf

Food and Drug Administration, Office of Prescription Drug Promotion. (2012b, February 28). Letter from Jessica N. Cleck Derenick, Regulatory Review Officer (OPDP), to Rachel Henderson, Senior Manager, Office of Promotion and Advertising Review, Merck & Co. Retrieved from http://www.fda.gov/downloads/Drugs/GuidanceComplianceRegulatoryInformation/EnforcementActivitiesbyFDA/WarningLettersandNoticeofViolationLetterstoPharmaceuticalCompanies/UCM295164.pdf

Harris, G. (2009, September 2). Pfizer pays $2.3 billion to settle marketing case. *New York Times*. Retrieved from http://www.nytimes.com/2009/09/03/business/03health.html

Historic Present. (2009, August 19). The FDA and government regulation of food safety. Retrieved from http://thehistoricpresent.wordpress.com/2009/08/19/the-fda-and-government-regulation-of-food-safety/

Meadows, M. (2006, January–February). Promoting safe and effective drugs for 100 years. *FDA Consumer Magazine*. Retrieved from http://www.fda.gov/AboutFDA/WhatWeDo/History/CentennialofFDA/CentennialEditionofFDAConsumer/ucm093787.htm

Mello, M. M., Studdert, D. M., & Brennan, T. A. (2009). Shifting terrain in the regulation of off-label promotion of pharmaceuticals. *New England Journal of Medicine, 360*(15), 1557–1566.

Nolan & Auerbach. (2011, June 27). The hefty Medicare price tag for the off-label prescriptions. Pharma 101. Retrieved from http://pharmaceutical-kickbacks.com/the-hefty-medicare-price-tag-for-the-off-label-prescriptions/

Pharmaceutical Research and Manufacturers of America. (n.d.a). Code on interactions with healthcare professionals. Retrieved from http://www.phrma.org/about/principles-guidelines/code-interactions-healthcare-professionals

Pharmaceutical Research and Manufacturers of America. (n.d.b). Direct to consumer advertising. Retrieved from http://www.phrma.org/about/principles-guidelines/direct-consumer-advertising

Snapp, E., & Blacha, M. (2008). Mandatory compliance with "voluntary" codes. Law 360. Retrieved from http://www.winston.com/siteFiles/publications/Snapp10-31-08Law360article.pdf

U.S. Department of Health and Human Services, Office of Inspector General. (n.d.a). Corporate integrity agreements. Retrieved from https://oig.hhs.gov/compliance/corporate-integrity-agreements/index.asp

U.S. Department of Health and Human Services, Office of Inspector General. (n.d.b). *Roadmap* speaker notes. Retrieved from https://oig.hhs.gov/compliance/physician-education/roadmap_speaker_notes.pdf

U.S. Department of Health and Human Services, Office of Inspector General. (1999, October). Federal Anti-Kickback Law and regulatory safe harbors [Fact Sheet]. Retrieved from https://oig.hhs.gov/fraud/docs/safeharborregulations/safefs.htm

U.S. Department of Health and Human Services, Office of Inspector General. (2003, May 5). OIG compliance program guidance for pharmaceutical manufacturers. *Federal Register, 68*(86), 23731–23743. Retrieved from http://oig.hhs.gov/authorities/docs/03/050503FRCPGPharmac.pdf

Zajac, A. (2011, January 24). Blowing the whistle on drug firms. *Los Angeles Times*. Retrieved from http://articles.latimes.com/2011/jan/24/nation/la-na-whistle-blower-20110124

CHAPTER 9

Direct-to-Consumer (DTC) Prescription Drug Advertising

Nilesh S. Bhutada, PhD

LEARNING OBJECTIVES

1. Describe the history of advertising prescription drugs directly to consumers and what has influenced its evolution and growth over time, in particular, in the different media types.
2. Describe the pros and cons of direct-to-consumer (DTC) advertising and assess how the various stakeholders view these perspectives.
3. Identify the role of DTC advertising and how it might change moving forward.
4. Discuss the implications of DTC advertising for the healthcare system in general.
5. Differentiate the strategies and uses of DTC advertising for the various stakeholders, including consumers, physicians, third-party insurers, and the pharmaceutical manufacturers themselves.
6. Describe how DTC advertising might evolve moving forward in the future and the role of government regulation in this evolution.

Traditionally, pharmaceutical manufacturers concentrated their marketing and promotional efforts on physicians—the ultimate decision makers. Physicians, the learned intermediaries, make diagnostic and prescribing decisions for their patients because consumers do not possess the technical expertise to do so and, thus, medication sales of pharmaceutical manufacturers were dependent on the number of prescriptions written by physicians. However, the physician's traditional dominance in the decision-making process has changed over time given the rapid growth of managed care organizations and the patient self-care movement. In consideration of this marketplace change, pharmaceutical marketers switched focus from their traditional promotional methods (i.e., marketing to physicians) and reached out directly to consumers. Although the final authority to prescribe still rests with the physician, the advent of direct-to-consumer (DTC) prescription drug advertising has exposed consumers/patients to a wealth of information once exclusively available only to physicians. Prescription drug DTC advertising is now ubiquitous in the mainstream media and a very well-known phenomenon among U.S. consumers. Apart from the United States, New Zealand is the only other developed country that allows advertising of prescription drugs directly to the general public. DTC advertising is defined as any promotional effort by a pharmaceutical manufacturer to present prescription drug information to the general public by using advertising media (Kessler & Pines, 1990). Even though it is only one piece of an overall marketing effort, and a novel concept from just 30 years ago, DTC advertising has dramatically changed the healthcare environment and the way prescription medications are promoted in the United States.

HISTORY OF DIRECT-TO-CONSUMER ADVERTISING

Print Media DTC

The first experiences with DTC prescription drug advertising date back to the early 1980s, when Boots Pharmaceutical launched a product-specific print advertisement for its anti-inflammatory drug Rufen (ibuprofen; Pines, 1999). Advertisements for Rufen appeared in magazines and newspapers, and it soon became a topic of radio and television talk shows. Within a short period of time, consumer awareness doubled and requests for the drug increased. In that same year, Merck Sharp & Dohme advertised its pneumonia vaccine, Pneumovax (pneumococcal vaccine; Pines, 1999); then, in 1982, Eli Lilly started a

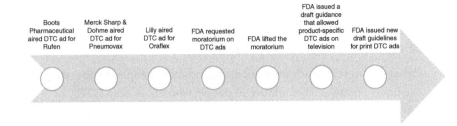

FIGURE 9-1 Evolution of Prescription Direct-To-Consumer Advertising

product-specific advertising campaign for Oraflex (benoxaprofen), which initially received very favorable publicity but was soon withdrawn from the market because the product led to adverse events and deaths (Perri & Nelson, 1987). The time line of events that have shaped the practice of DTC prescription drug advertising is highlighted in **Figure 9-1**.

In 1983, as a result of the Oraflex incident, the Food and Drug Administration (FDA) requested a voluntary industry-wide moratorium on all DTC drug advertising, wanting to conduct research on its effects (in particular its benefits and risks) and then revisit the regulatory guidelines. Two years later, after analyzing the results of numerous FDA and industry studies, the FDA lifted its moratorium and indicated that the existing regulations, intended for physicians, were sufficient for consumer protection and would be applied to all DTC prescription drug advertising.

The regulations required print DTC advertisements to include a fair balance of benefit and risk information and to provide a full disclosure of risk information in the form of a brief summary (Pines, 1997). The brief summary was also required to include the advertised drug's information about side effects, contraindications, and effectiveness. Critics have argued that the brief summary does not contribute to improving patient understanding of the disease or advertised medication.

Therefore, in February 2004, the FDA issued new draft guidance for print DTC advertisements. The new regulatory guidelines focused on manufacturers providing information about the most important and common risks in a less cluttered format and in language easier for consumers to read and understand. Recently, some manufacturers have adopted these newer and consumer-friendly formats, such as question-and-answer format, bulleted list, and facts panel, while many pharmaceutical manufacturers still use the traditional, cluttered brief summary format in their print DTC ads.

CASE IN POINT 9-1
Brief Summary in Print DTC Advertising

Results of an FDA study indicate more and more people do not read the brief summary. The number of people who saw a print DTC ad but either "did not read brief summary" or "read a little brief summary" increased from 56% in 1999 to 73% in 2002 (Berndt, 2005). Pharmaceutical manufacturers satisfy the brief summary requirements by providing a detailed product description. Most of the time, these brief summaries are a replica of the prescription drug label inserts intended for physicians—the experts. Because this information is full of technical jargon, consumers have difficulty in understanding the information. Moreover, this information is usually presented in fine print and further discourages the consumers even to attempt to read the brief summary. The FDA placed the brief summary requirement in print ads with the intention of educating consumers about their disease symptoms and available treatment options. However, if brief summaries continue to appear in their current form, DTC practices might not be meeting the objective of educating consumers and improving their overall health.

Broadcast Media DTC

DTC advertisements appearing in the broadcast media were required to include a *major statement* of risks, either in audio alone or in audio and video. Further, broadcast DTC advertisements (e.g., see www.youtube.com/watch?v=Jcn3JF9YRcw for the Cymbalta [duloxetine] advertisement) had to make *adequate provision* for viewers to have easy access to the full FDA-approved prescribing information (Pines, 1997). Because it was initially extremely difficult to include all of the information in a 30-second commercial slot, pharmaceutical marketers shunned using product-specific advertisements in the broadcast media and instead started using one of two formats in broadcast advertising: "Help-seeking" advertisements help consumers to identify signs and symptoms of a disease or condition without mentioning the drug name and urge them to consult with their physicians for treatment options. Another DTC type, "reminder" advertisements, just mentions the name of the drug without specifying an illness or condition treated by the brand.

In 1997, given the exponential growth of DTC advertising and the difficulty in informing consumers during a short broadcast commercial (Pines, 1999), the FDA issued a Draft Guidance for Industry addressing these issues and allowing product-specific DTC advertisements on television (Food and Drug Administration [FDA], 1997). This new set of regulations required the broadcast ads to provide the aforementioned fair balance of risk and benefit information, including a major statement about the most important risks associated with the drug, and to present all of the information in consumer-friendly language. Additionally, the guidance provided industry with insights on how to satisfy the adequate provision requirement without including the detailed brief summary. Broadcast DTC ads could fulfill the adequate provision requirement by referencing any of the following sources for consumers to obtain more information (FDA, 1997):

- A toll-free telephone number
- Address of the Internet website containing complete product information
- Reference to a print advertisement in circulation
- A disclosure that additional product-related information can be obtained from healthcare professionals

DTC ADVERTISING GROWTH

Since the restrictions on broadcast advertising were relaxed, the growth of spending on DTC advertising has been exponential (see **Figure 9-2**). From a relatively slow start in 1997, with spending of approximately $1 billion, pharmaceutical industry spending on DTC advertising reached $4.9 billion in 2007 (IMS Health, 2011). The DTC advertising budget of prescription drugs now competes with that of well-known consumer brands such as Coca-Cola and Pepsi, as DTC advertising spending has increased at a faster rate than expenditures for research and development.

Overall, pharmaceutical manufacturers' DTC advertising expenditures are concentrated on only a few blockbuster brands. For example, in 2008, 62% of the total DTC ad expenditure was accounted for by the top 25 advertised drugs (Gebhart, 2009). Further, the heavily advertised brands are concentrated in a few therapeutic classes, such as arthritis, asthma, allergies, depression, coronary artery disease, insomnia, and erectile dysfunction. However, as also shown in

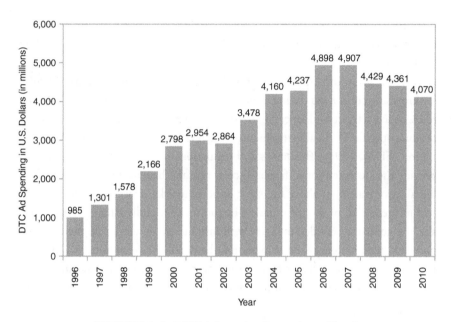

FIGURE 9-2 DTC Advertising Expenditure Trend

Adapted from: Donohue, J. M., Cevasco, M., & Rosenthal, M. B. (2007). A decade of direct-to-consumer advertising of prescription drugs. *New England Journal of Medicine, 357*(7), 673–681; IMS Health. (2011). Top-line industry data: Total U.S. promotional spend by type, 2010. Retrieved from http://www.imshealth.com/deployedfiles/imshealth /Global/Content/StaticFile/Top_Line_Data/2010_Promotional_Data.pdf

Figure 9-2, DTC advertising expenditures have declined slightly in recent years as a result of numerous factors, including the overall economic climate, fewer blockbuster medications, and increasing generic competition.

Pharmaceutical manufacturers have used diverse media in their direct-to-consumer strategy, including print, television, and the Internet. After 1997, when the FDA relaxed the regulations for broadcast media, as described earlier, there was a noticeable increase in television advertising as pharmaceutical companies started redirecting their advertising budget from print to television media. Each year, the average American television viewer is exposed to more than 30 hours of prescription drug advertisements (Brownfield, Bernhardt, Phan, Williams, & Parker, 2004). Television ad spending now accounts for the majority of DTC spending, specifically 62.5% of overall DTC spending in 2008 (Arnold, 2009). Recently, pharmaceutical companies have also increased the use of the Internet as an advertising channel. Further, because of their self-paced nature, consumers are

CASE IN POINT 9-2
Reasons for DTC Advertising Growth

The pharmaceutical industry has spent huge amounts of money on DTC advertising primarily because it is a promising return on investment. Depending on the performance of the brand, for every dollar spent on DTC advertising pharmaceutical companies generate additional sales of up to $6 (U.S. General Accounting Office [US GAO], 2006).

Promotion of prescription drugs directly to consumers is not just limited to financial gains. Consumers' brand awareness and brand name recall of the advertised drugs have increased remarkably. For instance, prescription drug brand names such as Viagra (sildenafil), Lipitor (atorvastatin), and Celebrex (celecoxib) have become just as familiar to U.S. consumers as are brands of soda and other commodity products. Increasing numbers of Americans are talking with their doctors for the first time about the health conditions they were either worried about or experiencing (e.g., this number was nearly 28 million in 2004). According to the research report from a Kaiser Family Foundation (Kaiser Family Foundation & Harvard School of Public Health, 2008) study, 91% of the sample indicated being aware of DTC advertising of prescription drugs.

more likely to get additional information from the Internet and magazines after seeing a DTC ad on television.

DTC ADVERTISING REGULATION

To ensure pharmaceutical manufacturers are disseminating truthful, balanced, and accurate information about prescription drugs, the Office of Prescription Drug Promotion (OPDP) (formerly known as the Division of Drug Marketing, Advertising and Communications, DDMAC), a division of the FDA's Center for Drug Evaluation and Research (CDER), monitors prescription drug advertising and promotional activities. Given the focused nature of this chapter, DTC advertising regulations are not discussed further.

ROLE OF DTC ADVERTISING

In the United States, the issue of DTC prescription drug advertising has been surrounded by controversy since its inception. Underlying the debate is disagreement about the perception of the role of DTC advertising. The inherent conflict of interest of pharmaceutical companies in advertising their products directly to consumers is the basis for much of the debate surrounding DTC advertising. The viewpoints of both sides are presented in **Table 9-1**.

Table 9-1 Pros and Cons of DTC Advertising

Pros	Cons
Drug Utilization	
More appropriate use of medicines, saving lives, and improving the quality of life.	Inappropriate demand for medicines and/or a demand for inappropriate medicines.
Risk information provided in the ads leads to better recognition and reporting of adverse drug reactions by patients.	Risk information in the ads might cause some patients not to take the needed medicines.
Improves compliance with the prescribed medicines.	Contributes to "off-label" drug use, beyond approved indications and the patient population group.
Doctor–Patient Relationship	
Empowers patients to take care of their own health, encourages active partnership with doctors.	Actively disrupts the therapeutic alliance between patients and doctors; encourages "doctor shopping" to obtain a wanted prescription; pressures doctors to prescribe.
Helps patients to initiate discussions, improves communication.	Doctors' time is wasted disabusing patients of misinformation.
Consumer Knowledge and Education	
Educates and informs patients about medicines.	Creates consumer demand for specific products.
Health Outcomes	
Leads to earlier symptom recognition, improving treatment outcomes.	Exaggerates disease risks and promotes anxiety.
Leads to a higher treatment rate among patients with undertreated conditions, improving outcomes.	Greater harm can result from widespread use of new drugs before their risk profile is well known.
Healthcare Service Utilization, Costs, and Public/Private Mix of Health Services	
By promoting drug use, reduces costs for surgery and other health care further down the line.	Leads to higher overall healthcare costs through the unnecessary use of new and expensive drugs when lower-cost alternatives exist.

Pros	Cons
Reduces public drug costs because drugs paid for by patients out-of-pocket tend to be heavily promoted.	Leads to higher drug prices to pay for expensive ad campaigns.
Brings patients in to doctors who can then be screened for other serious diseases; example: prostate cancer screening.	Causes distortions in care provision because of a focus on specific conditions linked to marketing needs; targets people with mild symptoms who might not need care.
TV ads are an egalitarian form of health information provision because they reach the poor.	Promotes unsustainable demand for healthcare resources, promoting division and inequality in access to health care.
Broader Social Outcomes	
Helps remove the social stigma of certain diseases.	Creates unrealistic expectations of drugs.
Helps patient groups by spreading disease awareness.	Takes advantage of extra vulnerability of the ill.
	Targets vulnerable population groups: negative potential impact on children and adolescents and on women.
	Leads to increased medicalization of healthy life stages.
Legal Issues	
Freedom of commercial communication.	Increases legal liability for manufacturers, weakening the learned intermediary defense.
Freedom of information.	Infringement of personal privacy because individual health records become valuable to marketers.

Source: Mintzes (2001): Table 4: Hypothesized Benefits and Risks of DTCA.

STAKEHOLDER PERSPECTIVES ON DTC ADVERTISING

Consumers

Historically, a paternalistic model was more prominent in the healthcare system in which there was unidirectional flow of information (i.e., from physicians to patients) and prescribing decisions were made solely by the physician. However, with the advent of DTC advertising, the current information age, and the rise of the Internet, the shared decision-making model, where information exchange is a bidirectional process (i.e., patients and physicians are both involved in the decision-making process), has increased in use. Currently, consumers are more involved and knowledgeable about their health care, actively research their medical conditions and available treatment options, and even "shop" for a physician who is willing to satisfy their wishes (even sometimes demand for a specific prescription drug).

Consumers' awareness of prescription drug advertising has continually increased. In its early days, consumer awareness of DTC ads was very low; however, recent reports indicate an increasing number of consumers (more than 95%) report that they have seen or heard at least one prescription drug advertisement. Consumers' increasing awareness of DTC advertising should be viewed in the light of significant misconceptions they have about this practice. Bell, Kravitz, and Wilkes (1999) report that nearly half of respondents believe DTC ads are approved by the FDA before they are disseminated to the general public. Further, 43% of consumers believe that only "completely safe" and 21% believe that only "extremely effective" drugs are advertised.

Not all consumers view DTC advertising equally. Younger, more educated, and regular prescription drug users exhibit more awareness of DTC ads. Further, this higher level of ad awareness is associated with more positive attitudes toward the practice. Women are more likely than men to be exposed to DTC advertising, recall the advertised prescription drugs, and talk to a doctor about the drug they have seen advertised. Additionally, consumers from higher-income households are more likely to be exposed to DTC ads and exhibit higher brand recall.

Consumers have always held relatively favorable attitudes toward DTC advertising. Even during the very early period of DTC, consumers had favorable attitudes toward DTC drug advertising, believed that the ads would benefit them, and thought they provided useful information. Further, consumers believe that DTC advertising educates them about medical conditions and treatments and provides them with the information they have a right to know. Even though consumers value both risk and benefit information present in DTC ads, their perception of risk information plays an important role in forming opinions of ad utility rather than perception of benefit information. However, consumers still perceive the quality of benefit information in DTC ads as better than that of risk information. However, recent research has suggested a shift in consumers' opinions. Consumers have become skeptical about DTC advertising and doubt its educational potential.

Following their exposure to DTC advertising, consumers try to seek additional information about the drugs from media and interpersonal resources. Consumers with positive attitudes toward DTC ads are more likely to engage in search of additional information about the disease and the advertised drug. Older consumers, motivated by DTC ads, seek additional information about the advertised prescription drug from friends and healthcare professionals. Recent data indicate that approximately 25% of American adults have looked for additional information about prescription drugs on the Internet, and, not surprisingly, consumers consult the Internet more often than they consult their physicians.

DTC advertisements have encouraged millions of consumers to talk with their doctors about medical conditions or illnesses they had never discussed before seeing advertisements about them. Consumers with generally positive perceptions of DTC advertising have a greater likelihood of using ad-conveyed information during their healthcare decision-making process. Recent reports from the Kaiser Family Foundation (Kaiser Family Foundation & Harvard School of Public Health, 2008) suggest that nearly one-third of the study population talked to their doctor about the prescription drug they saw advertised, and nearly half of these respondents even received a prescription for the drug they requested. Very few consumers believe that DTC advertising negatively affects patient–physician relationships, undermines physician authority, or has influenced them to ask for the advertised drug. On the other hand, DTC advertising is also associated with negative effects. For instance, because consumers see the advertised drug as the number one treatment choice, the number of prescriptions written for the advertised drug increase even when more appropriate alternatives are available.

Physicians

Historically, physicians, the most influential providers in the healthcare environment, have held negative attitudes toward DTC advertising. Results from earlier studies indicate physicians viewed DTC as causing problems for both themselves and their patients, such as confusing patients, increasing demand for the advertised drugs, and even leading patients to challenge physicians' authority. Most of the family physicians surveyed thought DTC ads were not a good idea, impaired the patient–physician relationship, and even discouraged the use of alternative generic drugs. Further, they said they felt pressured by their patients sometimes to prescribe a medication that was not their primary choice. Physicians also believed that DTC ads did not provide risk and benefit information about the drug in a balanced manner, and that they created unreasonable expectations among consumers.

Physicians thought DTC ads caused them to spend a considerable amount of time clarifying misconceptions of their patients regarding the advertised drug. This resulted in hampered physician productivity because the physician was forced to explain why the advertised drug was not the correct choice for the patient's condition or could have negative consequences because of drug–drug interactions. Consequently, physicians were more likely to respond negatively when a patient's request was based on DTC advertising.

However, recent research suggests a positive shift in attitudes among physicians toward DTC advertising. Physicians who see more patients, who have been practicing longer, or who are more exposed to pharmaceutical marketing are more likely to show acceptance of DTC advertising. Physicians believe that exposure to DTC advertising provides information to patients, encourages patients to seek medical care, and increases their level of confidence during counseling. Physicians think that talking about the advertised drug with their patients has a positive effect on the patient–physician relationship rather than negative. However, physicians also think patients are not good at assessing the personal relevance of the information presented in the DTC ads. Even though physicians believe that DTC advertising drives patients to request inappropriate prescriptions by confusing them about the risks and benefits of the drugs, most believe that it creates either little or no tension in the patient–physician relationship.

Both the American Medical Association (AMA) and the American College of Physicians (ACP) have expressed concerns regarding the practice of DTC advertising. The ACP is against DTC advertising because it believes that it weakens the patient–physician relationship and challenges physicians' medical judgment. On the other hand, DTC advertising is acceptable to AMA, provided that DTC advertising follows guidelines developed by AMA in consultation with the FDA.

Health Insurance Industry: Managed Care Organizations and Pharmacy Benefits Managers

The health insurance industry's opposition to DTC advertising primarily focuses on its belief that it causes increased drug spending and, therefore, results in increasing portions of premiums spent on prescription drugs. The insurance industry attributes the rapid increase in prescription drug spending to the following factors:

- Increased market introduction of newer and more expensive drugs
- Aggressive DTC advertising campaigns
- Increased volume of prescriptions used

A recent report from the Kaiser Family Foundation (Kaiser Family Foundation & Harvard School of Public Health, 2008) suggests prescription drug spending has increased sharply in the past few years and that this trend is going to continue. Managed care organizations (MCOs) believe that DTC advertising leads to excessive prescribing by physicians or prompts consumers to ask for expensive brand-name drugs rather than cheaper alternatives. The managed care industry feels pressured to include the most popular prescription drugs, which are usually expensive, in their formularies.

Using brand-name drugs instead of generic drugs has a huge impact on drug budgets because brand-name prescription drugs are usually more expensive than their generic equivalents. This is a major concern to the health insurance industry because its goal is to contain healthcare costs. Research indicates that per-member per-year utilization of the heavily advertised drugs is high (Perri, Shinde, & Banavali, 1999). Inclusion of the cost of physician's office visits to this amount could have a significant financial impact on the insurer. To control the rising costs, the health insurance industry has implemented cost-containment strategies such as higher copayments or coinsurance for all DTC-advertised drugs and formulary restrictions. However, such restrictions lead to patient dissatisfaction with the insurer. Because getting a medication approval requires extra time, physicians would also be dissatisfied with formulary restrictions.

Pharmaceutical Manufacturers

Pharmaceutical manufacturers have always been a strong supporter of DTC advertising. However, the regulatory change of broadcast DTC in 1997 was the real turning point for the pharmaceutical industry. Since then, manufacturers have embraced this practice, and it has become an important component of their marketing strategy.

Further, while consumer groups and insurers argue a direct link between overall medication prices and DTC expenditures, pharmaceutical manufacturers strongly disagree with any claims attributing the rise of prescription costs to the increase in DTC ad expenditures. Pfizer published a report indicating that no connection exists between DTC advertising budgets and prescription drug costs (Manning & Keith, 2001), and other research conducted across five major therapeutic classes indicates consumers do not pay higher prices as a result of DTC advertising (Capella, Taylor, Campbell, & Longwell, 2009). Also, supporters believe DTC advertising might even lower the price of the prescription drugs by increasing competition among manufacturers.

CASE IN POINT 9-3
Pharmaceutical Manufacturers and Politics

Just as other industries work to protect their interests, pharmaceutical manufacturers influence Congress through lobbying efforts. With more than 1,200 registered lobbyists, pharmaceutical manufacturers employ one of the largest lobbying staffs in Congress and spend generous amounts of money on lobbying and political campaigns. For instance, in 2003 alone, pharmaceutical companies spent more than $143 million on lobbying efforts and contributed more than $17 million to political campaigns (Drinkard, 2005).

CASE IN POINT 9-4
Pharmaceutical Industry Approach to Improve DTC Advertising

In 2005, in response to congressional pressures and to reinforce current FDA policies, Pharmaceutical Research and Manufacturers of America (PhRMA), the industry trade group, announced a set of new voluntary guiding principles for DTC advertising (PhRMA, 2005). The guidelines emphasize consumer education, clarity of information, balance between risk and benefit information, inclusion of a waiting period before advertising newly approved drugs, and the establishment of an office of accountability to make complaints and company actions public. Recent revisions also include guidelines for proper disclosure of paid-for endorsements by real doctors or celebrities (PhRMA, 2008). PhRMA believes the guidelines display the industry's readiness to self-monitor and hopes that it will bring the movement in Congress to impose new restrictions on DTC ads to a standstill. However, critics argue that because these guidelines are voluntary, the entire issue about their authority and influence is questionable.

In terms of benefits, pharmaceutical manufacturers believe DTC advertising improves brand recall, sales volume, and brand loyalty (Balazs, Yermolovich, & Zinkhan, 2000; Basara, 1996; US GAO, 2002) specific to their products in addition to being cost-effective and providing a positive return on investment (ROI) (Narayanan, Desiraju, & Chintagunta, 2004). Moreover, the companies argue that according to the First Amendment, they have a right to free commercial speech. Manufacturers maintain their position that DTC advertising provides consumers education about diseases, treatment availability, and encouragement to talk with their doctors and request necessary care (Calfee, 2002). Therefore, from pharmaceutical manufacturers' perspective, DTC advertising creates a win–win environment for themselves and the general public.

FUTURE OF DTC ADVERTISING

Despite the soaring debate about the benefits of DTC advertising, the practice is likely not going away, given its focus by pharmaceutical manufacturers, consumers' desire for health information access, and technological developments (e.g., the Internet and mobile technology). To maintain (or establish) their position in the market, pharmaceutical manufacturers will continue to devote DTC efforts to products that are innovative, use innovative dosing forms, have a specific niche in the marketplace, or offer other benefits desired by consumers.

Because the pharmaceutical marketplace has become extremely competitive with each passing year, pharmaceutical marketers will work hard to maintain their promotional piece of the pie. Advertising is successful when it attracts consumers' attention and keeps them engaged with the advertising message to have a positive impact on their behavior, which in the pharmaceutical industry is the future behavior of a prescription inquiry and/or request. Creative ads have the potential to make this happen, and, thus, continual creativity and personalization can be expected in future DTC ad campaigns, especially using Internet-based and mobile technologies. Pharmaceutical manufacturers have successfully applied numerous proven techniques from the marketing and advertising disciplines to DTC advertising (e.g., use of money-saving offers, celebrity endorser, attractive website design) (Bhutada, Cook, & Perri, 2009; Bhutada, Menon, Deshpande, & Perri, 2012; Sewak, Wilkin, Bentley, & Smith, 2005). Strategies like these have helped products to stand out from the clutter, get noticed by potential customers, and aid in creating a positive behavioral change (e.g., inquire about the product during a future doctor visit) among consumers.

Given the numerous lawsuits filed in recent years against pharmaceutical manufacturers (e.g., off-label marketing, pricing issues) and the subsequent negative media publicity, public favorability of the pharmaceutical industry is at an all time low. Furthermore, consumers have recently expressed skepticism and negative feelings toward DTC advertising and the imbalance of information present in these ads (Friedman & Gould, 2007; Spake & Joseph, 2007). Future effectiveness of such advertising can be hampered by this negativism. This could stir up distrust among the members of Congress, in particular, those who have questioned the value of DTC advertising, and potentially result in stricter regulations. If pharmaceutical manufacturers wish to continue the practice of DTC advertising, they will have to take actions to change these consumer perceptions through measures such as improving the clarity, user-friendliness, fair-balance, and educational potential of the information. Also, to ensure compliance, companies could develop these changes in collaboration with the FDA. Recent DTC guidelines proposed by PhRMA can be viewed as the foundation of such positive change.

Disease-education awareness, or help-seeking/nonbranded, campaigns have recently become popular among pharmaceutical marketers. These ads discuss a disease condition without mentioning the drug's brand name, are only identified by the pharmaceutical manufacturer's logo, and are used to educate consumers about their symptoms and the disease and then urge them to take the required course of actions or preventive measures. Consumers seem to respond more favorably to these ads because they induce more favorable attitudes and behavioral intentions than do product-specific ads (Mendonca, McCaffrey, Banahan, Bentley, & Yi, 2011; Rollins, King, Zinkhan, & Perri, 2010, 2011). From the manufacturers' perspective, disease-education ads provide a public health benefit through consumer education while also providing a potential fiscal benefit through market expansion.

The Internet has evolved and emerged as the primary promising medium for DTC advertising and an important source of prescription drug information for consumers. Among various types of media, Internet users perceive the Web as the most credible source of prescription drug information. From the manufacturers' perspective, the Internet is cost-effective compared to the traditional media and offers numerous unique opportunities, such as providing personalized information to customers and building relationships based on individual wants and needs. Compared to other media channels, the amount and depth of information offered by the Web to consumers is unparalleled. Further, the interactive nature of the Internet allows consumers to navigate through the information at their own pace and with functionality that cannot be matched by the current traditional mass media formats such as television and magazines. Even now, pharmaceutical marketers are just scratching the surface of the Internet's full potential. Once Internet-specific regulations or guidelines are in place, the use of social media, such as blogs and Twitter, is the next big step in Internet DTC advertising as manufacturers find ways to maximize its utilization.

Thus far, pharmaceutical manufacturers have focused their advertising efforts on drugs that treat prevalent conditions, such as allergies, arthritis, and diabetes mellitus, thus reaching a broad audience. Observers say that the industry will adopt a more targeted advertising approach in the future. Research indicates that behaviorally targeted online ads can generate 2.68 times more revenue per ad than nontargeted ads (Beales, 2010). Further, users who click on the behaviorally targeted online ads are more than twice as likely to convert into buyers compared to users who click on the nontargeted ads. Therefore, given the current economic situation, pharmaceutical companies will want to adopt this strategy to ensure the advertising budget is well spent. Additionally, implementation of such targeted approaches will curb much of the criticism attracted by DTC advertising for its spending on mass communication.

SUMMARY

Prescription drug DTC advertising, a marketing strategy once considered innovative, has now become a prevalent and common practice in the pharmaceutical industry. Medications are advertised through a wide range of channels and reach a wide-ranging audience. Over the years, industry-wide spending on DTC has increased substantially and, while it has fallen off recently, it remains a large part of manufacturers' budgets. This highlights the importance of DTC advertising to the pharmaceutical industry and the fact that it is continuously trying new promotional channels and techniques to reach a broader audience.

DTC advertising of prescription drugs plays a significant role in the U.S. pharmaceutical markets and has been pivotal in changing the dynamics of the healthcare environment and the relationship of its various stakeholders. Now more than ever before, Americans are more involved in their health care and actively seeking information from external sources about their conditions and available treatment options. In addition to several other external sources, advertising seems to help fulfill consumers' information needs.

Compared to other types of consumer advertising, however, advertising of prescription drugs to the general public is complex and challenging and surrounded by controversies and regulatory concerns. The FDA uses it authority to regulate DTC advertising properly to protect public health. It uses various processes, such as monitoring and surveillance programs, enforcement actions, advisory comments, and guidance documents to ensure that the pharmaceutical industry is providing accurate and balanced information.

Despite the amount of research conducted on DTC advertising, continual research is required to fully understand the long-term effects of DTC advertising on the health and well-being of the patients and the healthcare system. A definitive answer to the critical question "Do the benefits offered by DTC advertising outweigh the risks?" will decide its fate in this country. Pharmaceutical marketers can create a win–win situation for the public and manufacturers by creating DTC advertising that focuses on improving quality of care, educating consumers, and reducing healthcare spending.

DISCUSSION QUESTIONS

1. Given the debate surrounding DTC advertising, what do you think should be the role of DTC advertising? Justify your position.
2. What regulatory steps should be taken to clarify the role of DTC advertising?
3. Should government impose even more stringent regulations on DTC advertising? Why or why not? Justify your answer.
4. To what extent do companies comply with PhRMA guidelines? What are the consequences of noncompliance?
5. In your opinion, should the United States follow the European Union lead and ban DTC advertising? Why or why not? Justify your opinion.
6. The debate inherent to the practice of DTC advertising is about the benefits it offers and the potential risks. What side of the debate are you on? Justify your position.
7. Describe what issues need to be researched in the future to improve DTC advertising.
8. What kind of policy recommendations would you make for the FDA to better regulate DTC advertising on social media networks? Discuss this issue as a group.
9. As stakeholders, how can consumers help to minimize the negative effect of DTC advertising and help in achieving its goal?
10. What steps should the pharmaceutical industry take to ensure a secure future for the practice of DTC advertising?

REFERENCES

Arnold, M. (2009). Between screens: A shift in DTC. *Medical Marketing and Media, 44*(4), 40–47.

Balazs, A. L., Yermolovich, J., & Zinkhan, G. M. (2000). Direct-to-consumer advertising: An ad processing perspective. *Marketing in a Global Economy: Proceedings of the 2000 American Marketing Association International Marketing Conference,* 478–486.

Basara, L. R. (1996). The impact of direct-to-consumer prescription medication advertising campaign on new prescription volume. *Drug Information Journal, 30,* 715–729.

Beales, H. (2010). *The value of behavioral targeting.* Retrieved from http://www.networkadvertising.org/pdfs/Beales_NAI_Study.pdf

Bell, R. A., Kravitz, R. L., & Wilkes, M. S. (1999). Direct-to-consumer prescription drug advertising and the public. *Journal of General Internal Medicine, 14*(11), 651–657.

Berndt, E. R. (2005). To inform or persuade? Direct-to-consumer advertising of prescription drugs. *New England Journal of Medicine, 352*(4), 325–328.

Bhutada, N. S., Cook, C. L., & Perri, M., III. (2009). Consumers responses to coupons in direct-to-consumer advertising of prescription drugs. *Health Marketing Quarterly, 26*(4), 333–346.

Bhutada, N. S., Menon, A. M., Deshpande, A. D., & Perri, M., III. (2012). Impact of celebrity pitch in direct-to-consumer advertising of prescription drugs. *Health Marketing Quarterly, 29*(1), 35–48.

Brownfield, E. D., Bernhardt, J. M., Phan, J. L., Williams, M. V., & Parker, R. M. (2004). Direct-to-consumer drug advertisements on network television: An exploration of quantity, frequency, and placement. *Journal of Health Communication, 9*(6), 491–497.

Calfee, J. E. (2002). The role of marketing in pharmaceutical research and development. *PharmacoEconomics, 20*(15), 77–85.

Capella, M. L., Taylor, C. R., Campbell, R. C., & Longwell, L. S. (2009). Do pharmaceutical marketing activities raise prices? Evidence from five major therapeutic classes. *Journal of Public Policy and Marketing, 28*(2), 146–161. doi:10.1509/jppm.28.2.146

Donohue, J. M., Cevasco, M., & Rosenthal, M. B. (2007). A decade of direct-to-consumer advertising of prescription drugs. *New England Journal of Medicine, 357*(7), 673–681.

Drinkard, J. (2005, April 25). Drugmakers go furthest to sway Congress. *USA Today.*

Food and Drug Administration. (1997). Draft Guidance for Industry; consumer-directed broadcast advertisements; availability. *Federal Register, 62*(155), 43171–43173. Retrieved from http://www.gpo.gov/fdsys/pkg/FR-1997-08-12/pdf/97-21291.pdf

Friedman, M., & Gould, J. (2007). Consumer attitudes and behaviors associated with direct-to-consumer prescription drug marketing. *Journal of Consumer Marketing, 24*(2), 100–109.

Gebhart, F. (2009). DTC ad spending decreased last year. *Drug Topics.* Retrieved from http://drugtopics.modernmedicine.com/drugtopics/Chains+%26+Business/DTC-ad-spending-decreased-last-year/ArticleStandard/Article/detail/595223

IMS Health. (2011). Top-line industry data: Total U.S. promotional spend by type, 2010. Retrieved from http://www.imshealth.com/deployedfiles/imshealth/Global /Content/StaticFile/Top_Line_Data/2010_Promotional_Data.pdf

Kaiser Family Foundation & Harvard School of Public Health. (2008, March). The public on prescription drugs and pharmaceutical companies. Retrieved from http://www .kff.org/kaiserpolls/upload/7748.pdf

Kessler, D. A., & Pines, W. L. (1990). The federal regulation of prescription drug advertising and promotion. *Journal of the American Medical Association, 264*(18), 2409–2415.

Manning, R. L., & Keith, A. (2001). The economics of direct-to-consumer advertising of prescription drugs. *Economic Realities in Health Care Policy, 2*(1), 3–9. Retrieved from http://www.pfizer.com/files/policy/about_ERhealthcare.pdf

Mendonca, C. M., McCaffrey, D. J., III, Banahan, B. F., III, Bentley, J. P., & Yi, Y. (2011). Effect of direct-to-consumer drug advertising exposure on information search. *Drug Information Journal, 45*(4), 503–515.

Mintzes, B. (2001). An assessment of the health system impacts of direct-to-consumer advertising of prescription medicines. Volume 2: Literature Review. Health Policy Research Unit, University of British Columbia.

Narayanan, S., Desiraju, R., & Chintagunta, P. K. (2004). Return on investment implications for pharmaceutical promotional expenditures: The role of marketing-mix interactions. *Journal of Marketing, 68*(4), 90–105.

Perri, M., III, & Nelson, A. A., Jr. (1987). An exploratory analysis of consumer recognition of direct-to-consumer advertising of prescription medications. *Journal of Health Care Marketing, 7*(1), 9–17.

Perri, M., III, Shinde, S., & Banavali, R. (1999). The past, present, and future of direct-to-consumer prescription drug advertising. *Clinical Therapy, 21*(10), 1798–1811; discussion 1797.

Pharmaceutical Research and Manufacturers of America. (2005). PhRMA guiding principles: Direct to consumer advertisements about prescription medicines. Retrieved from http://www.roche.com/dtcguidingprinciples.pdf

Pharmaceutical Research and Manufacturers of America. (2008). PhRMA guiding principles: Direct to consumer advertisements about prescription medicines. Retrieved from http://www.phrma.org/sites/default/files/631/phrmaguidingprinciplesdec08final .pdf

Pines, W. L. (1997). Three principles that govern FDA advertising and promotion regulation. *Drug Information Journal, 31*, 137–142.

Pines, W. L. (1999). A history and perspective on direct-to-consumer promotion. *Food Drug Law J, 54*(4), 489–518.

Rollins, B. L., King, K., Zinkhan, G., & Perri, M., III. (2010). Behavioral intentions and information-seeking behavior: A comparison of nonbranded versus branded direct-to-consumer prescription advertisements. *Drug Information Journal, 44*(6), 673–683.

Rollins, B. L., King, K., Zinkhan, G., & Perri, M., III. (2011). Nonbranded or branded direct-to-consumer prescription drug advertising—which is more effective? *Health Marketing Quarterly, 28*(1), 86–98.

Sewak, S. S., Wilkin, N. E., Bentley, J. P., & Smith, M. C. (2005). Direct-to-consumer advertising via the Internet: The role of web site design. *Research in Social and Administrative Pharmacy: RSAP, 1*(2), 289–309.

Spake, D. F., & Joseph, M. (2007). Consumer opinion and effectiveness of direct-to-consumer advertising. *Journal of Consumer Marketing, 24*(5), 283–292. doi:10.1108/07363760710773102

U.S. General Accounting Office. (2002, October). *Prescription drugs: FDA oversight of direct-to-consumer advertising has limitations.* Retrieved from http://www.gao.gov /new.items/d03177.pdf

U.S. General Accounting Office. (2006, November). *Prescription drugs: Improvements needed in FDA's oversight of direct-to-consumer advertising.* Retrieved from http://www .gao.gov/new.items/d0754.pdf

10

Social Media and Pharmaceutical Marketing: Opportunities and Challenges

Kelly Dempski and Matthew Short

LEARNING OBJECTIVES

1. Define social media and describe its history.
2. Describe the benefits and potential pitfalls of social media overall and specifically within the pharmaceutical industry.
3. Describe the evolving set of logistical and legal challenges for pharmaceutical marketers using social media.
4. Apply a framework for understanding and implementing different aspects of social media to pharmaceutical marketing.

Today, the term *social media* is used frequently and loosely in both informal conversation and more formal books, articles, and the general media. A discussion of social media often describes the advantages of using social media without concretely defining what social media is or what it encompasses. Like many catch phrases, it is often defined by the goals of the speaker, rather than on its own terms. Part of the reason for this is that, at the time of this writing, the term and technologies it refers to are changing rapidly. To gain an understanding of what social media is and how it applies to the pharmaceutical industry, it is best to think of social media in relative terms and begin by comparing *social media* to our traditional forms of *media*.

EVOLUTION OF MEDIA

Historically, nearly all forms of marketing media were unidirectional and broadcast. Content was carefully crafted and distributed to a large audience with little or no direct backchannel. Short of writing a letter to an editor or switching the TV channel, the audience had no means of controlling the message they were receiving. In the mid-1990s, the growing popularity of the Internet gave more people control over what they were receiving. Instead of a relatively small number of books, magazines, and TV shows, consumers could dynamically request content from millions of different websites. However, the early versions of these sites closely resembled their traditional counterparts. Many websites looked like brochures, while e-commerce sites were merely online versions of catalogs. Amid talks of the Internet revolution and the information superhighway, few people realized just how little the content itself had changed. Later, people began referring to this period as **Web 1.0** as a way to differentiate it from changes that slowly emerged after the Internet bubble.

Web 2.0 emerged as a buzzword with the advent of user-created content such as **blogs** and **wikis**. At the same time, Internet discussion boards were also becoming more heavily used, and the use of user-generated ratings and reviews was becoming more mature and standardized. Whether it was called Web 2.0 or "the read–write Web," there was the understanding that some of the most interesting and highly consumed information on the Internet was not coming from a small number of media channels, but rather a large number of everyday users. It was at the same time that early social networks began to emerge, allowing people to connect with each other more easily. Over time, these networks matured to services like Twitter and Facebook, the latter dominating the attention of more than 1 billion users. These changes, when taken together, created an entirely new set of communication channels among ordinary people and between business and consumers. **Table 10-1** shows just a few of these channels and how they are used. The set is constantly changing and maturing, but this represents a snapshot of the channels available in the Web 2.0 era.

Table 10-1 Current Communication Channels

Channel	Definition
Online forum	Online bulletin boards and discussion threads have existed as long as the Internet has. Today they are not just hangouts for a subset of technology users. They are increasingly forums for average people to discuss issues, seek out support, and discuss topics of interest ranging from politics to favorite recipes.
Blogs	Short for "web log," blogs can be seen as a natural evolution of the home page of the early Internet. Instead of crafting and re-editing a page, people began keeping a running log of their interests and commentary. This mode of publication has had a profound impact on news reporting and even brand messaging because brands either communicate through blogs or support community-focused blogs, such as blogs by working mothers or people caring for ailing parents.
Microblog	Blogs made it very easy for people to share their thoughts without carefully crafting and publishing a standard "page." Services such as Twitter took that one step further by allowing people to easily share very short messages without the usual overhead or expectations that come with authoring a longer piece. The result is that any particular message is relatively unimportant, but, in aggregate, a set of Twitter posts can reveal the up-to-the-moment thoughts of a group of users who would not have the time or skill to write a well-crafted blog.
Social network	Before MySpace, Facebook, and other early social networks, blogs and other feeds were published on separate webpages, with limited connections. Sites such as Facebook allowed communities of friends and family to link with each other and eventually with brands. The side effect of this is that billions of people now have a defined identity on the Internet. People are no longer "visitors" to webpages. They have well-defined profiles and connections to people and companies that they care deeply about.
User-created content sites	Sites such as YouTube demonstrate the shift in content creation, away from the media companies and into the hands of everyday people using simple production tools. These channels represent powerful ways for people to share messages (factual or otherwise) and also represent new ways of reaching consumers. Pharmaceutical marketers are no longer limited to expensive television time, leading to more options for messaging through video.

Today, the term *Web 2.0* has mainly fallen out of favor, and *social media* is preferred. One reason for the shift could be the growing focus on the Internet as a network of social connections rather than a web of hyperlinked sites and pages. In any case, the present era of social media is one in which customers' online attention is focused on the actions of their friends and other social connections.

They have the ability to ask and answer questions quickly, seek out experts, and influence each other. A customer's opinion of a product is no longer shaped by a carefully honed marketing message blasted on a broadcast channel or delivered by a well-trained salesperson. Instead, it is often shaped by trusted social signals from online connections.

CASE IN POINT 10-1
The Pharmaceutical Industry and Online Message Boards

To understand the power of social media, consider the following real-world example. In certain online message boards dedicated to chronic diseases, there are superusers who post messages several times a day, every day. They are not only vocal, but also well trusted by the community. In a given day, a potential pharmaceutical customer might see one carefully crafted television commercial describing the drug and its effects. During the same time period, several superusers can engage in a deep discussion of what they believe to be the relative merits of the drug, rumors involving side effects, and reactions to pricing. Without careful planning, the brand can easily lose control over the message and the market. However, customers are not expecting the brand to "control" the message. They are expecting the brand to behave as a well-mannered member of the community. This is a challenge to traditional marketers, especially in controlled industries such as pharmaceuticals.

For example, one superuser on a diabetic discussion board posts thousands of messages a year (a current example is the Joslin Diabetic Center, affiliated with Harvard Medical School, discussion board site at forums.joslin.org). This superuser often greets new members, walks them through treatment options, and discusses many aspects of both the disease and the available treatments. For many people, this user might be more available and influential than their doctor is. This raises interesting questions. When a random, fairly anonymous user on an Internet discussion board is more trusted than the family physician, how does that change the dynamics among doctors, patients, and the makers of different treatment options?

As discussed, the exact definition of what social media is has been evolving since the first home page, blog posting, and Facebook status updates hit the Internet. Therefore, we define social media in terms of what it is not, rather than define what it is. Simply put, it is not the traditional unidirectional broadcast paradigm that most marketers are used to. To make effective use of social media, pharmaceutical manufacturers must understand how to listen to and engage with users, continually optimize and refine their message, and rapidly adapt to changing technical and legal realities. Some pharmaceutical companies have chosen to put their heads in the sand, citing the legal and ethical complexities of dealing with these new channels. However, this is not a viable approach for pharmaceutical companies and their marketing departments. Regardless of what the future holds in terms of the evolution of social media, the days of broadcast messaging through television or using the doctor as the primary trusted conduit to the consumer are gone. Pharmaceutical companies must adapt accordingly. The rest of this chapter provides a simple framework and examples for working with social media.

THREE STEPS TO EFFECTIVE SOCIAL MEDIA USE: LISTEN, ENGAGE, AND OPTIMIZE

Effective marketing is all about communication: communicating the advantages of a product, responding to queries, and refining the message to adapt to changing customer needs and competitor pressures. In traditional marketing, the focus has been on communicating with the customer through a monologue. Television commercials and print media communicate the carefully tuned marketing message and shout to the consumer during key attention-grabbing timeslots. Social media has created the opportunity for a dialogue, a conversation with the consumer where consumers can express their questions and concerns, and the brand can build a relationship. Despite the power of this, some marketers are slow to understand that metamorphosis.

Many social media gurus explain that social media is "all about the conversation," but this observation requires more explanation. The following sections describe a three-stage model of how pharmaceutical marketers should best handle social media: Listen, engage, and optimize. Each stage incorporates additional levels of interaction and analytical sophistication, so many marketers start with listening before advancing to more sophisticated stages. Each stage also creates additional levels of risk and legal oversight. These constraining factors are discussed later in the chapter.

Listen

With sites such as Twitter generating more than 200 million posts a day, there is a lot of new customer dialogue and commentary flowing over the Web. This traffic is growing not only in volume, but also in sophistication, as more brands and public figures participate in these new forums. This has created the opportunity for a radical shift in the speed in which information and news spread.

As the preceding Case in Point shows, social media listening can be viewed as a form of information gathering and a way to understand how misinformation is spreading and which communities are the carriers of that information. Within pharmaceutical marketing, there are three main classes of listening activities.

The first is listening for information about a company's own products, which is focused on listening for conversations and mentions for a given brand/product name. Typically, listening tools allow pharmaceutical brand managers to search for keywords associated with the brand and return results as they appear on different social media channels. These results allow the users to gain a better understanding of the "buzz" around a brand or product. From a technical perspective, the tools in this domain are relatively simple and straightforward. In many cases, the insights they give to the user might be of limited value, but it is beneficial (and increasingly, expected) for pharmaceutical marketers to have their "ears to the ground," listening for flare-ups of positive or negative buzz when they occur. For some, this type of listening represents a legal risk because it is possible that

---

CASE IN POINT 10-2
Information Spread

When an earthquake hit the East Coast in August 2011, Twitter followers in Washington, D.C., had 30 seconds of warning based on tweets from New York. However, this free flow of information also creates many opportunities for bad information to spread. Actress Jenny McCarthy spoke on *Oprah* about how a measles, mumps, and rubella (MMR) vaccine gave her child autism. This information came from a study that was scientifically incorrect and not agreed upon by the majority of doctors, but because of her celebrity status the information spread rapidly through message boards, Facebook, and other forms of social media. More than 4 years later, people still associate childhood vaccines with autism and choose not to inoculate their children.

the brand might hear something it is legally required to respond to. This situation is discussed in greater depth later in the chapter.

The second form of listening is listening for information and opinions about competitors and their products. This class of listening can make use of the same technical tools to scan the Internet looking for mentions of competitors and their brand/product names. However, some advanced users have taken advantage of more sophisticated tools that scan and analyze specific community sites, or even specialized databases and repositories. For instance, a scan of public patent and trademark databases could yield intelligence about future products. This type of listening might seem to go well beyond the traditional role of a pharmaceutical marketer, but it illustrates how the availability of social and other data increases the overall insight the pharmaceutical marketer has into competitors and its own company's position within the competitive landscape.

The third form of listening is listening for market intelligence. In this form, tools can be used to listen to the needs and trends within a given market or community. Instead of using a tool to scan social media channels to find a mention of a brand name, marketers can scan the buzz within, for example, a diabetic community. Through the use of automated collection tools, analytics, and human analysis, marketers can better understand how a community reacts to a class of products, what the community values, and possible product or service opportunities discussed by the members. These tools, such as websites like www.patientslikeme.com, that capture the voice of the customer provide the pharmaceutical marketer with new, highly valuable forms of insight.

Each of these three forms of listening focuses on the use of publicly available information to better understand public dialogue. Listening tools themselves do not give marketers the tools to market their products actively, but they do provide the users with valuable real-time intelligence about the target audience and their competitors. For many brands, listening is a logical first step in their social media strategy. It gives them access to information that, in the past, was either unavailable or available only through expensive and labor-intensive means such as focus groups. However, social media activities should not stop there. Armed with the insight gained from listening, marketers should seek to actively engage with the community.

Engage

One side effect of the growing popularity of social media is that more consumers expect brands to behave "socially." By the year 2000, it was expected that every brand had a website. A brand could exist without a website, but it was considered to be lagging behind the curve in terms of technology and customer engagement.

For 2010, the same could be said about Facebook pages and Twitter handles. Although Twitter or Facebook use might not be universal, brands that ignore these channels run the risk of losing opportunities to engage with customers. Worse, they create opportunities for others to engage in their name.

The two examples discussed in the following Case in Point illustrate the need for brands to accelerate the shaping and implementation of their engagement strategies. There are constraints to what a pharmaceutical brand can and cannot discuss on social media. For many brands, the subject of social media engagement must begin with a discussion of the proper procedures and approaches.

CASE IN POINT 10-3
Pharma and Facebook—Beware!

As of December 2011, a Facebook search for "Advil" yielded several results. The most popular page result (https://www.facebook .com/pages/Advil/10243329963 as of December 2011) has all the information a visitor would expect from a brand page: professional photos, active discussions, and product endorsements. The only problem is the page is not owned or controlled by the brand. A savvy user would see that Advil "likes" Pesto and Britney Spears and can determine this is not an official page. Others might not be so discerning. Pharmaceutical manufacturers often take conservative approaches to engaging their customers on social media, but as they do, others are filling the void with off-message and potentially destructive messaging.

Another example of rogue accounts can be seen with the @pfizer Twitter handle, which has 3,200 followers. When it was first created back in 2009, it was regularly reporting Pfizer-related news. However, the official Pfizer handle, @pfizer_news, has more than 22,000 followers and an active stream of relevant news articles. The rogue handle's profile is a generic blue letter *P*, but is probably intended to be confused with Pfizer's regular logo. Between 2009 and 2010, @pfizer's tweets changed from those related to the Pfizer brand to ones about sports and its need for angel investors for a startup. It is at Twitter's discretion to release accounts, and it will do so in cases of trademark infringement (Twitter, 2012).

It is crucial for pharmaceutical manufacturers to have an engagement policy in place that helps determine the right type of post. Many companies have policies defining how employees should conduct themselves on social media, both personally and professionally. Pharmaceutical manufacturers should also have guidelines for the marketing department defining the voice of the brand on social media, the strategies for engaging influencers, and the boundaries of what can and cannot be discussed. Many situations, such as patients' personal health issues, should not be discussed in a public location or by a pharmaceutical manufacturer in general. A typical practice is to mention in what way the company responds, so the policy should address how the company deals with posts that are off-label, relating to prescriptions, personal medical concerns, or other similar topics.

When people post to a brand's Facebook page or Twitter handle, the common hope or expectation is that they want to be engaged back. This can come in the form of a brief comment or like that creates the feeling that a company is connected with them. Expectations should be clearly set and described so that people understand the context of the communication. A common way to use **microblogging** services such as Twitter is to advertise press releases and other achievements. In its simplest form, this is a way to spread positive messages about the company, but to drive further engagement there should be prompts for people's opinions by asking for suggestions and commentary. For example, a post that says, "Our scientists just won the *xxxxx* award" does not drive discussion. However, "Join us in celebrating our scientists on their achievement winning the *xxxxx* award" does invite response and sharing of the message. The phrasing of the message is important to create a more personalized connection.

For pharmaceutical manufacturers, it can be critical to have a clause in the engagement policy that mentions a right to remove inappropriate posts. For some consumer brands, removal of negative posts has been seen by customers as a form of censorship. However, in the case of pharmaceutical manufacturers, reserving the right to remove posts should be used for inappropriate discussions that legally should remain private. These actions should be completed with a layer of transparency that explains why the post was removed so that users are not angered. If it is appropriate, people should be encouraged to consult the appropriate medical experts for information on their question. Generally, social media users understand there are limits to what a brand can discuss in an open forum. The users will accept moderation if it is done transparently and in a way that upholds the interests of the community, rather than the singular interests of the brand/company.

Another effective way to improve a brand's reach is by creating unique content that is approachable and helpful. The goal of any social media content should be to create **viral spread**—the spread of a message to a much wider audience through sharing and other social mechanics. This occurs when people enjoy the content enough to link and share it with their friends, who, in turn, repeat the process. There are many advantages to this, with the obvious one being that others are spreading the message on the brand's behalf. The less obvious advantage is that every shared message is actually an endorsement. When friends see a shared message, they are seeing a message that has been endorsed by a person they trust, lending credibility to the original message.

Apart from the key social media sites such as Facebook and Twitter, many smaller communities are dedicated to more specific topics. These range from communities of people who gather to talk about a disease that affects them, enabling them to discuss and share what they are experiencing, to communities of doctors who discuss medical cases. The approach for marketing to a consumer-based group versus a healthcare worker is different because the information that can be provided differs. For a patient community, a brand could create an account and begin engaging people in discussions and provide helpful insight into the pharmaceutical industry. The brand would be listening to conversations and

CASE IN POINT 10-4
Viral Marketing Campaigns

Viral campaigns have been proven very effective in creating a brand image for many companies, such as Old Spice's "The Man Your Man Could Smell Like" campaign, which used quick-witted dialogue and frequent scene changes to highlight its deodorant/antiperspirant. The idea from that campaign can be repeated for the pharmaceutical space, but pharmaceutical marketers must understand the audience base and tailor the content to them. This could include providing healthy eating tips to promote a cholesterol-lowering drug or lifestyle tips to help manage diabetes. Johnson & Johnson's Health Channel on YouTube is one example of a company creating short 1- to 5-minute videos about health issues and tips. The videos regularly get more than 5 million views and the Johnson & Johnson policy states that it moderates comments before they are viewable and that it will not approve off-topic, offensive, or promotional comments.

making sure that facts are correct and the brand is being represented correctly. This must, of course, be kept within legal regulations, and the brand representative must be trained on how to handle situations that might arise and to always ultimately refer patients to their doctors for specific medical advice.

Some communities are limited to registered medical professionals, including, for example, Sermo.com. Such sites verify each applicant to restrict the site to certified doctors and create a safe place for people to ask for advice on specific cases and share techniques. The power of a community like this for pharmaceutical marketers is that restrictions are lighter because this situation is similar to when a pharmaceutical representative talks to a doctor about prescription drugs. Sermo.com allows pharmaceutical or other industry companies to pay to engage this doctor network. The most effective way for a pharmaceutical company to utilize a community like this is to gather information on doctors' opinions in the form of surveys or sponsored discussions. These conversations work to build a sense of loyalty to and trust of the brand as well as help sales representatives engage community members offline. There are also websites controlled by pharmaceutical manufacturers, such as Fibrocenter.com, that provide a place for people suffering from a specific disease, fibromyalgia in the case of Fibrocenter.com, to share their story and encourage people to seek help. Sites moderate what is shared and are minimally branded, similar to a help-seeking advertisement.

Finally, an increasing amount of effort is being put into identifying and engaging with key influencers within a given community (e.g., researchers, doctors, or consumers). The criteria for rating influence can differ by community. For instance, academics can be identified by their publishing rates. Twitter users with high numbers of followers can be deemed influential. On disease forums, influencers can be identified through a combination of high posting rates and, in many cases, badges and scoring mechanisms that the community uses to rate their contributions. Pharmaceutical marketing campaigns that target these users can be very beneficial to a brand because each one of these influencers serves as a force multiplier in spreading messages and providing support for a larger population of customers. Independent influencers also have fewer constraints than the brand itself. However, the brand must engage with them carefully, in a way that is transparent and not overly self-serving. If a brand is seen to be bribing or strong-arming influencers, negative messages can spread very quickly through the community.

Ultimately, social media platforms provide the opportunity to build a relationship with consumers. Unlike direct-to-consumer (DTC) advertising, the message marketers are trying to send might not be a complete explanation of each new drug being created, but instead a connection to the user that promotes positive brand images. Engagement strategies should be focused on developing a rapport with users and communities to go beyond the limited unidirectional messaging of the past.

Optimize

Tools such as Facebook, Twitter, and YouTube provide great platforms to listen and engage people in discussions. This enables pharmaceutical brands/companies to interact with customers in new and very valuable ways. However, behind the scenes there is an additional and very powerful advantage to social media. Unlike traditional broadcast advertising, the reach and impact of social media can be measured throughout the engagement, allowing pharmaceutical marketers to measure the audience and, in some cases, the actual conversions that result from a campaign. Also, interactions on Facebook and other channels often are accompanied by rich and detailed user profiles. Marketers can see into the demographics, interests, and histories of individual users on those channels.

For instance, typical online marketing approaches use **cookies**, small pieces of data that make it easier to track a user's browsing history, and perhaps zip code information, to place a user in a general customer segment. As a result, online advertising uses a very coarse view of the user to try to generate tailored messages based on assumptions of the user's needs. This is further complicated if the computer is used by multiple members of a household. In contrast, a well-designed Facebook app has access to the current user's profile, which often includes age, educational and work histories, gender, interests, and more. Interactions through Facebook could be tailored differently for 30-year-old affluent runners versus 80-year-olds who are fans of fast-food brands. This level of customer understanding and targeting has not been available with traditional channels, including traditional websites.

This presents the opportunity to optimize the use of those channels with each visit and over time. When instrumented correctly, social media campaigns can be measured and improved. They can be adjusted to target different audiences or highlight effective messages. The previous discussion mentions the advantages of influencers. Sophisticated social media should use technologies to identify probable influencers, engage with that group, measure the outcomes from those engagements, and continually iterate the messaging and definition of influence to optimize the ongoing campaign. In some cases, pharmaceutical companies have identified key opinion leaders (KOLs) in the medical community, and then crafted online forums and engagement strategies to engage those KOLs and leverage their influence among their peers in the community.

CASE IN POINT 10-5
Expansion of Social Media Strategy

Eli Lilly, a top 10 pharmaceutical manufacturer based on sales volume (CNNMoney, 2011), recently developed a general healthcare and public discussion blog out of its corporate communications and government affairs group, LillyPad (lillypad.lilly.com). The blog talks "about public policy issues, corporate responsibility initiatives, and the work our employees do every day to make the world a healthier place to live" (LillyPad, 2012) and also keeps an active Twitter handle (twitter.com/LillyPad). Eli Lilly is now looking to expand this strategy company-wide and allow other areas within the company to dive into social media. The key, says the corporate communications director, is "to try and do something where they (the various departments and sites) have their own identity but are still consistent within the company" (Tyer, 2012).

The concept of optimization is not limited to the campaign itself. For instance, effective listening approaches give brands the intelligence they need to be more competitive with emerging products, redesign products to suit changing user needs, or alter their supply chains to move products into more fruitful markets. This level of optimization is still in its infancy, as marketers begin to understand the new sources of data available to them and legal teams debate the extent to which a customer can and should be analyzed. As the technical maturity of this area continues to grow, pharmaceutical marketers should look for opportunities to rethink how they measure the success of campaigns; how they instrument campaigns on rich channels, such as Facebook; and how they work within the confines of legal and industry constraints.

CONSTRAINTS

By nature, the pharmaceutical industry is strictly regulated, and, thus, typical social media interactions are far more constrained than in other industries. Although regulations such as the Health Insurance Portability and Account-ability Act (HIPAA) and administrative agencies such as the Food and Drug Administration (FDA) exist, there is already precedent set that a *fair balance* of the drug's risks and benefits can be achieved through a "one-click away" rule that has never been denied by the FDA (Mack, 2006). This rule came about because of the existing rule that states that by providing toll-free numbers in television commercials a company is sufficiently providing the information. Officially, the FDA has not created any specific guidelines for social media. In November 2009, it conducted a hearing to initially gather inputs but delayed the release of an official statement because it was afraid of it becoming outdated (Shuster, 2011). The FDA further delayed a statement in 2010 and continued to miss deadlines through June 2011, when it finally decided to remove the "Promotion of Prescription Drug Products Using Social Media Tools" from the 2011 agenda (Mack, 2011). This continued gray zone of how companies can legally proceed online has not limited them from creating their own Twitter handles and Facebook pages.

Further, pharmaceutical companies are required to report on any adverse effects associated with their medications. This process, called pharmacovigilance (PV), includes the clinical trials to certify the drug as well as any adverse effects reported by patients to databases, such as the World Health Organization Global Individual Case Safety Reports Database (WHO Global ICSR), which currently stores more than 7 million reported adverse events (Olssen, n.d.). Currently, a large fear of the pharmaceutical industry is that by participating in social media, any statement around their drugs will become subject to adverse event reporting laws. In a study conducted by Visible Technologies, over the span of 30 days 250,000+ online posts were gathered that mentioned one of 224 over-the-counter (OTC) and prescription (Rx) medications. The study was to determine how many posts were related to adverse events, and, out of those posts, how many provided sufficient detail to be recorded. Through calculation and analysis, Visible found that only 0.5% of the posts tracked, or 5 out of every 1,000 posts, contained reportable events. "For 30 days worth of data collected on 224 brands totaling over 257,000 posts, the total number of reportable [adverse events] averaged 3 per brand" (Visible Technologies, n.d.). This proves that although there is reason to be cautious when it comes to social media, the fear is out of proportion to the possible benefits of connecting to the more than 250,000 posters.

The most important thing for a pharmaceutical manufacturer to do before listening or engaging on a social media platform is to contact the legal department and make sure a strategy is in place to handle any issues that might arise. All players, from users to regulators, lawyers, and pharmaceutical manufacturers, are working to understand the boundaries that best serve the customers and their privacy. However, the measurability and visibility of social media provide brands with a basis to tune approaches based on actual data rather than perceived risks.

Generally, brands that innovate successfully and safely are the ones that craft social media strategies based on the value to the customer, and that are nimble enough to adjust their strategy rapidly as regulations or consumer reactions change.

SUMMARY

Social media channels create very powerful opportunities for pharmaceutical marketers to gain a better understanding of their customers and markets, engage with those customers, and optimize their processes based on the data the channels provide. These channels continue to evolve, but the shift from monologue to dialogue and the shift of power from the brand to the consumer are sure to hold for the long term. To take advantage of this, marketers need to transfer their focus from broadcasting to listening and engagement and take advantage of emerging tools that help them engage with customers in a new and data-driven fashion.

In all industries, social media is creating questions and risks associated with legal and compliance issues. This area is in constant flux as well, and life science marketers need to work hand in hand with the legal department to ensure that legal fully understands the new possibilities, while marketing understands the existing constraints. Although this new reality might be difficult to navigate in the near term, effective use of social media will help pharmaceutical marketers create rich relationships with their customers that yield benefits far beyond the broadcast unidirectional messaging of the past.

DISCUSSION QUESTIONS

1. Describe three areas where social media applications could create unintended consequences for pharmaceutical marketers.
2. How might social media be used to augment existing pharmaceutical promotions, such as direct-to-consumer advertising?
3. With the new drug approval process costing more and taking more time, manufacturers are always seeking ways to increase adoption and diffusion of new products. Why might social media be one avenue to accomplish this marketing goal?
4. Describe ways a pharmaceutical marketer can engage customers through the use of social media.
5. In the realm of social media, should pharmaceutical manufacturers focus on product- or disease-specific messaging? Describe the pros and cons of each strategy.

REFERENCES

CNNMoney. (2011). Fortune 500: Pharmaceuticals. Retrieved from http://money.cnn.com/magazines/fortune/fortune500/2011/industries/21/index.html

Granstra, C., & Plochman, H. (2010, November 16). More than two-thirds of U.S. consumers seek medical advice via the Internet and social media, Accenture study finds. Accenture Newsroom. Retrieved from http://newsroom.accenture.com/article_display.cfm?article_id=5096

Indvik, L. (2011, July 6). Versace deletes Facebook protest, stops 500,000 fans from posting to page. Mashable.com. Retrieved from http://mashable.com/2011/07/06/versace-facebook-protest/

LillyPad. (2012). About us. Retrieved from http://lillypad.lilly.com/about-us.html

Mack, J. (2006, November 16). The "girl from Google." Pharma Marketing Blog. Retrieved from http://pharmamkting.blogspot.com/2006/11/girl-from-google.html

Mack, J. (2011, June 1). FDA drops social media from its 2011 guidance agenda. Pharma Marketing Blog. Retrieved from http://pharmamkting.blogspot.com/2011/06/fda-drops-social-media-from-its-2011.html

Olssen, S. (n.d.). Vigibase reaches 7 million reports. Uppsala Monitoring Centre. Retrieved from http://www.who-umc.org/graphics/26114.pdf

Shuster, N. (2011, November 17). Drug companies wait for FDA guidelines on social media marketing. *Big Think*. Retrieved from http://bigthink.com/ideas/41144

Twitter. (2012, February 14). Trademark policy. Twitter Help Center. Retrieved from https://support.twitter.com/articles/18367-trademark-policy

Tyer, D. (2012, July 11). Lilly to develop company-wide social media strategy. PMLive. Retrieved from http://www.pmlive.com/digital_intelligence_blog/archive/2012/jul_2012/lilly_to_develop_company-wide_social_media_strategy

Visible Technologies. (n.d.). Adverse event reporting. Visible Technologies. Retrieved from http://www.visibletechnologies.com/resources/white-papers/adverse-events/

CHAPTER 11

The New Four Ps of Pharmaceutical Marketing

John Gardner, MBA

LEARNING OBJECTIVES

1. Identify important events in time that worked to shape the current pharmaceutical marketing landscape.
2. Describe the changing landscape and the challenges in the pharmaceutical marketing space.
3. Identify and describe the old Four Ps of pharmaceutical marketing, and then differentiate them from the new Four Ps.
4. Describe how the new Four Ps are used in practice today and how they will be used in the future.

HISTORY

Marketing in the pharmaceutical space has changed dramatically since the late 1990s. Until then, pharmaceutical product promotion focused almost exclusively on the professional audience. Marketing followed a direct sales model with high investment in product promotion and sampling aimed at physicians. The paradigm shifted when pharmaceutical manufacturers began marketing their products directly to consumers (DTC) through advertising in traditional mass channels. The following pharmaceutical marketing timeline provides an overview of this shift:

1938   Food, Drug, and Cosmetic Act passed, giving the FDA authority to require pharmaceutical manufacturers to prove product safety before allowing them to market and forming the foundation of modern pharmaceutical regulation.

1951   Durham-Humphrey Amendment to the 1938 act created two distinct categories of medications, those requiring a prescription to be dispensed under medical supervision and those that did not (over-the-counter medications).

1962   Kefauver-Harris Amendment to the 1938 act further enhanced the FDA's authority by requiring manufacturers to prove the effectiveness of their medications before marketing could occur. Also, responsibility for drug advertising oversight switched to the FDA.

1981   First U.S. DTC print ad by a pharmaceutical company, Merck, advertises Pneumovax (pneumococcal vaccine) in *Reader's Digest*.

1983   First U.S. DTC television ad by Boots Pharmaceuticals advertises ibuprofen brand Rufen.

1983   FDA issues DTC moratorium.

1985   FDA lifts DTC moratorium because of concerns over commercial free speech but still emphasizes that standards need to be met and print ads must include a brief summary of risk and other information.

1995   FDA holds public hearings on DTC advertising.

1996   Schering-Plough airs television spot for Claritin (loratadine).

1997   FDA issues guidelines titled *Guidance for Industry: Consumer-Directed Broadcast Advertisements*. This allowed product-specific DTC advertisements on television as long a fair balance of benefit and risk information was provided. These guidelines led to the exponential growth of DTC television ads.

CHANGING LANDSCAPE

In pharmaceutical marketing, the rules of the game have shifted dramatically. What used to be a straightforward process of sales representatives promoting to doctors and doctors mandating products to patients has changed. Today, multiple stakeholders are involved in the marketing and sales process. Managed care organizations (i.e., third-party payers) and pharmacists have entered the distribution channel and can influence—and even alter—the product ultimately dispensed to the patient. Pharmaceutical sales representatives do not have the direct access they enjoyed for decades and are more restricted in the promotional tools

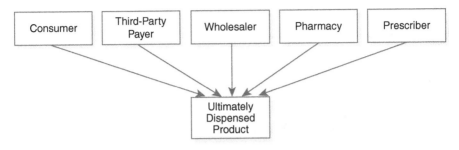

FIGURE 11-1 The Ultimately Dispensed Product—Expanded

they can utilize. Pharmaceutical firms are also constrained by legal and regulatory governance much tighter than rules for other industries. Most important, the consumer is now an active participant in the treatment process (**Figure 11-1**).

The pharmaceutical industry is miles behind traditional consumer marketing industries, such as consumer packaged goods and over-the-counter products. The industry must quickly learn to adapt marketing from a push-based distribution

CASE IN POINT 11-1
Changing Landscape in Firms' Employee Structure

In response to the changing landscape and environment described in this chapter, pharmaceutical manufacturers have drastically reshaped their sales organizations. With decreasing access to physicians and promotional tool restrictions, the number of general sales representatives has been cut dramatically with almost daily announcements that a pharmaceutical firm is cutting sales representatives. Down approximately 25% from their peak numbers, sales rep cuts are saving pharmaceutical manufacturers money while also leading to the exponential increase in the use of electronic promotions and direct access to physicians through smartphone and tablet computer applications (Spirer, 2011). In addition, companies such as GlaxoSmithKline (GSK) have restructured the incentive compensation for the sales representatives they have retained. Instead of sales-specific goals, which were typically in the form of prescriptions written, GSK reps' bonuses are determined based on three measures: selling competency, customer evaluations, and overall performance of their business unit (GlaxoSmithKline, 2011).

model to one that is now consumer-pulled. Pharmaceutical firms are adapting their focus and approach to accommodate this customer-led shift in their marketing mix. Successful firms are now effectively using the DTC marketing techniques other industries have long employed. The customer is now at the center of the marketing universe for pharmaceuticals and no longer outside the marketing continuum.

THE OLD FOUR Ps: SHIFTING PARADIGM

Since coined by E. Jerome McCarthy in 1960, the Four Ps of marketing—product, place, price, and promotion—have been a standard for organizations in developing their marketing strategies. However, the current constraints of the pharmaceutical industry, including less physician access, promotional tool restrictions, and increased pricing pressures from payers, make marketing using the classic Ps a challenge.

Product: The What

The foundation of the marketing mix—indeed, the most important element in it—is the drug itself. All medications on the market are Food and Drug Administration (FDA) indicated for a specific condition or disease, and pharmaceutical companies can market a product only for the approved indication(s). According to the most recent estimate, it costs pharmaceutical manufacturers anywhere from $800 million to $1 billion to bring a new drug to market (DiMasi, Hansen, & Grabowski, 2003; PhRMA, 2012). Because of the enormous cost and time required to bring a drug to market, companies must maximize product life cycle management. Along with this huge expense, pharmaceutical companies have a very narrow window to recoup their product investment. The development and approval processes can take 10 to 15 years, leaving only 5 to 10 years for the product marketing life cycle before patent expiration.

Price

Price is uniquely set in the pharmaceutical industry. In most other categories, the producer or manufacturer is in control of price, subject to normal market constraints. This is not the case in the pharmaceutical industry, where companies have limited time to recoup development costs, and, in most cases, the end user is not the ultimate payer. Pharmaceutical products are also constrained by managed care organizations and generic pressure. In fact, approximately 75% of all prescriptions filled are for generic equivalents of branded products (Office of the Assistant Secretary for Planning and Evaluation, Office of Science and Data Policy, U.S. Department of Health and Human Services, 2010).

Place and the Consumer

Although the distribution system of getting a medication from point A (manufactured) to point B (pharmacy/end user) has remained relatively the same over the years with the role of the wholesaler, community pharmacies, and, more recently, mail-order pharmacies, the flow of information to the ultimate end user of prescription medications, that is, the patient/consumer, has drastically changed. Largely ignored before 1997, the consumer is now a major focus of pharmaceutical promotion and information. In 1997, the industry spent $1.1 billion in DTC advertising. Twelve years later, in 2009, the pharmaceutical industry spent $4.8 billion in DTC advertising—a 291% increase (Krishnan & Yuan, 2011).

Promotion: To Whom

Although much is made of the impact of the evolution of DTC advertising, promotion in the pharmaceutical industry still used to be relatively simple. A company would hire sales representatives, train and educate them on product attributes, and arm them with product samples. These reps would then directly promote the drug to doctors. Until 2009, sales representatives enjoyed enormous freedom in promotion to professionals. In 2009, a new set of voluntary industry standards were introduced by the Pharmaceutical Research and Manufacturers of America (PhRMA), which considerably reduced the flexibility of the sales representative's independence in the promotion process. In addition to restricting gifts and promotional items, the code limited entertainment and noneducative interaction. The code states that "interactions should be focused on informing healthcare professionals about products, providing scientific and educational information, and supporting medical education" (PhRMA, 2008). These guidelines and more controlled access to doctors have reduced the direct sales impact of the pharmaceutical representative.

Another major shift in pharmaceutical promotion to professionals has been the development of **nonpersonal selling** techniques. These include educational digital asset development, e-learning, and direct marketing, including email and direct mail. Doctors are now using more external sources for information about products and bypassing the traditional representative. A 2009 study demonstrates that 33% of doctors use branded websites for product information (Google/Hall & Partners, 2009).

Since 1996, when Schering-Plough started the new era of DTC in pharmaceutical marketing with its television ad for the prescription antihistamine Claritin, many new external factors have emerged to further challenge the classic Ps. Innovation has occurred in the marketing space, largely driven by technology. In 1996, the Internet was not a commercial asset, much less the marketing force

Old Ps	New Ps
Brand-focused	Customer-focused
Capital intense	Budget conscious
Technology-enabled	Technology-powered
Longer development	Quickly deployed
Slower to modify	Highly optimized
Focus on creating the demand curve	Focus on intercepting the demand curve

FIGURE 11-2 Shifting Marketing Paradigm

it has become. Digital marketing has seen the emergence of search engines, social media, video distribution, blogging, and device ubiquity. Data collection has progressed from being defined in terms of kilobytes to terabytes. Interactive devices have evolved from an unwieldy PC to a completely mobile smartphone. All of these innovative tools have accelerated overall marketing channels beyond the classic Four Ps into a new marketing paradigm for pharmaceuticals: the new Four Ps of marketing—predictive modeling, personalization, peer-to-peer, and participation. (See **Figure 11-2**.)

THE NEW FOUR Ps

Until relatively recently, pharmaceutical marketers "owned" the relationship with the Four Ps: product, price, place, and promotion. It was straightforward: Develop a product, place it through a direct-to-physician distribution channel, set the price, and promote it with high-dollar physician events. But these Ps have shifted their nexus. Although product development might still be in the pharmaceutical company's hands, the other Ps are not. Regulatory constraints have taken placement out of the pharmaceutical marketer's control. Price is also under pressure from managed care and comparison shoppers, while promotion is no longer "directly" anywhere—it is directly everywhere.

Pharmaceutical marketers have lost control. Merely driving demand doesn't work anymore. The key to success in this new marketing landscape is a shift from a pharmaceutical-driven, push-based model toward a pull-based model, where desire for information and education drives action on the part of consumers and medical professionals. Powering this shift is a set of new Ps: predictive modeling/analysis, personalization, peer-to-peer networking, and participation.

These Ps revolve around the packaging, understanding, and commoditization of information and have to be defined in terms of controllability from a pharmaceutical company's perspective. The pharmaceutical marketer controlled the old Four Ps, whereas the marketer and consumer share control of the new Four Ps. Several pharmaceutical companies are making attempts at the new Four Ps, boldly stepping into this new paradigm with great success. Here's how pharmaceutical marketers are using them to benefit patients, physicians, and profits.

CONTROLLED

Through the use of now-standard technology, two of the new Ps of marketing are easily leveraged and implemented by pharmaceutical marketers. These "controlled" areas are predictive modeling and personalization.

Predictive Modeling

Predictive modeling is the process of data mining using statistical techniques. These techniques enable data to be utilized for forecasting probabilities and trends. Predictive modeling allows marketers to use, or optimize, variables (predictors) that are likely to influence future behavior or results. This statistical method of predicting future behavior gives pharmaceutical marketers the insight they need to know when, how, and with what message to "intercept" the patient, depending on where he or she is in the treatment cycle. **Figure 11-3** provides examples of various modeling techniques depending on the business objectives.

For example, it is understood that acne sufferers generally follow a highly predictable treatment protocol: self-treatment to OTC to OTX (a combination of both OTC and prescription treatments), and then to prescription only. Predictive modeling allows marketers to maximize patient value by understanding where the acne sufferer is in that life cycle and accelerate the time to prescription treatment. For pharmaceutical companies, the result is a compressed sales cycle, and for acne sufferers, the result is delivery of the most *relevant* information at every stage.

Personalization

Technology allows pharmaceutical marketers to intercept rather than react to consumer situations and create relevance at decision points. **Personalization** allows marketers to optimize marketing channels and investment. For pharmaceutical manufacturers, another valuable outcome of personalization is the connection of stakeholders—patients to doctors. Historically, pharmaceutical companies regarded physicians as their customers. Now, pharmaceutical companies are anxious to leverage brand communications to reach an empowered consumer audience.

Business Objectives	Modeling Techniques
Customer acquisition	Response modeling
Acquire profitable customers	Lifetime value modeling
Avoid high-risk customers	Risk or approval modeling
Customer knowledge: Attributes	Profile analysis
Customer knowledge: Markets	Cluster analysis
Increase customer's value	Up- and cross-sell modeling
Retain profitable customers	Retention modeling
Win back lost customers	Win-back modeling
Improve customer satisfaction	Market research/profiling

FIGURE 11-3 Predictive Modeling & Analysis Examples

CASE IN POINT 11-2
Predictive Modeling in Acne

One specialty dermatology company's prescription acne treatment brand uses predictive modeling to trigger communications based on a combination of behavioral and attitudinal data points: the sufferer's demographic profile, acquisition channel, predicted behavior, and place in the treatment cycle. Communication is customized to address all of these variables. For example, if the sufferer has downloaded a rebate, the company reminds and encourages the sufferer to get to the pharmacy. To encourage compliance, a rebate on a second prescription might include an even more attractive offer than the first. This program has been an enormous success to date, generating 117,000 rebates in the first 6-month measurement period. The campaign drove $2.125 million in direct sales during a 9-month measurement period, with a return on investment (ROI) of $11.30 for every acquisition dollar spent. A full 64% of rebate users were over-the-counter (OTC) users or nontreaters, important targets for the brand (Integrative Logic, 2011).

Personalized marketing communication uses specific imagery and messaging to enhance relevance. With this technique, a pharmaceutical company can provide vital information to each patient based on demographic profile and phase of treatment, using the most appropriate language and visuals. In addition to making the patient feel "recognized" by the brand, personalization helps facilitate patient–professional dialogue by prepping patients with relevant questions to ask their physicians. It helps extend postvisit care by reaching patients with relevant messages at appropriate times in the treatment cycle and managing their expectations. This, in turn, helps promote patient satisfaction.

CASE IN POINT 11-3
Personalization in Practice

A popular prescription acne treatment brand strategy involves personalized online experiences based on segment: parent, teen or adult sufferer, gender, acquisition channel, and previous treatment plan. An electronic customer relationship management (eCRM) program targeted to teens and their parents begins the cycle. Once registered on the website, they can sign up for an ongoing acne education program. Because visitors identify themselves with a segment, both the ongoing communication and a content-rich website deliver segment-appropriate talking points, FAQs, "survival guides," facts, and treatment tips. The point is to share information in a way that is most meaningful to the individual. Giving teens information and "talking points" alleviates some of the discomfort they might have in addressing this sensitive topic with their parents and physicians. The site received 850,000+ unique visits in the first 6 months. It has since built an engaged audience of users who receive ongoing acne education and has pushed a 14.2% visitor-to-rebate-registration conversion rate. The organic search channel accounted for 28% of all rebate registrations and 78% of all rebate redemptions. This indicates (among other things) that the site content compelled visitors to take the desired action—to register for the rebate, obtain a prescription, and fill it (Integrative Logic, 2011).

UNCONTROLLED

It is easy for pharmaceutical executives and marketers to buy into predictive analysis and personalization. They are proactive ideas based on proven technology. However, the next two Ps are newer to the pharmaceutical industry and more reactive in nature. They represent an area where information and technology have merged in an exciting but uncontrolled new way. For pharmaceutical marketers, they can be highly successful, but they should be approached with caution. The new Ps of marketing that are "uncontrolled" from a brand perspective are peer-to-peer and participation.

Technology has forced pharmaceutical manufacturers to play catch-up in emerging channels, especially given they are even further hampered by the lack of guidance and FDA enforcement of rules that are unclear in these uncontrolled areas. Although the FDA has strong parameters around traditional promotion, the rules for marketing through new channels remain unclear.

Peer-to-Peer (Socialization)

Given that a brand is defined by an intrauser network outside the control of the pharmaceutical company, **peer-to-peer** is the most disruptive force to brands as consumers and professionals now have amplified license to frame brands and critical information. As a result of regulatory constraints and governance, pharmaceutical companies often must remain passive in this channel. From a positive perspective, peer-to-peer initiatives allow democratization of brands and products. For pharmaceuticals, this channel should focus on simple and clear objectives:

- *Leverage key opinion leaders and influencers: **Inspire.*** A prime example of this is Bayer's "Step Up Reach Out" campaign, which asks young hemophilia patients one question: Who speaks for you and the thousands of others like you in the world? (See **Figure 11-4.**)
- *Provide value: **Inform.*** For example, Merck's Engage Health Partnership Program is a website delivering patient education, support, and specific information guidance from physicians to patients. (See **Figure 11-5.**)
- *Connect patients with one another: **Facilitate.*** Novartis Oncology's CML Earth site (www.cmlearth.com) connects people who have been diagnosed with chronic myelogenous leukemia.
- *Develop shareworthy content and assets: **Create.*** Gilead Sciences targets one underdiagnosed population, Asian Americans, with a ready-to-pass-on experience (www.asianliver.com).

Step UpReach Out

> Home   > About Us   > The Program   > Testimonials   > Apply   > Contact Us   > Links

Features   **Home**

SURO News:

- Application deadline for the 2012-13 session is June 1, 2012.
- "Step Up Reach Out - Grooming Young Leaders," Inside Minds (2010 Empowering Minds newsletter, page 4)

Are you a young person with hemophilia who wants to make a positive difference in your community? Step Up Reach Out (SURO) can help you reach that goal.

SURO is an international leadership program designed to help build tomorrow's leaders in the bleeding disorders community.

To learn more or apply, click here.

Events:

2012-13 SURO Application Process Opens April 1, 2012
Deadline: June 1, 2012

2012-13 Session: Part I
Building the Foundation of Leadership
Date: September 14-17, 2012
(includes two days of travel)
Location: San Francisco, California

2012-13 Session: Part II
Defining Your Leadership Role
Date: March 15-18, 2013
(includes two days of travel)
Location: Budapest, Hungary

FIGURE 11-4 Inspire Example

Source: Courtesy of StepUp Reach Out.

Pharmaceutical marketers have to realize that in this space, it is all about the disease. It is appropriate to facilitate and monitor peer-to-peer dialogue but not to overtake it—*nor brand it.* Once the brand appears, the consumer conversation is over. On the professional side, however, peer-to-peer has a tremendous upside

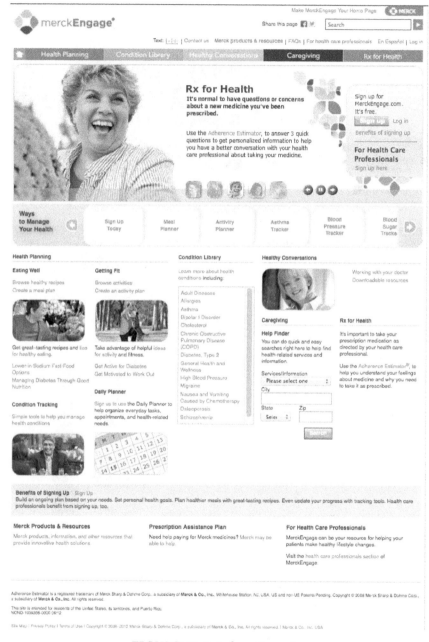

FIGURE 11-5 Inform Example

CASE IN POINT 11-4
Peer-to-Peer in Practice

A pharmaceutical manufacturer can use peer-to-peer in several ways. In the consumer realm, the company can monitor news stories, opinions, and social networking sites to keep its finger on the pulse of the market. For example, asking: What are consumers saying about our brands? In what context is a brand being discussed—positive or negative perceptions? Are there any reoccurring issues or myths that need to be addressed?

In the professional realm, for a product launch the company can leverage its association with a highly respected specialist to deliver its message. One very successful tactic could include an electronic magazine (e-zine) in which the specialist discusses the product profile and clinical data, reaching not only fellow specialists but also other frequent prescription writers in the category. Although these programs are difficult to measure, opinion monitoring is an important and beneficial way to gather consumer intelligence, and a specialist affiliation continues to add credibility to a brand.

and branding is acceptable. For example, a pharmaceutical manufacturer can align with key opinion leaders and create a peer-to-peer relationship between doctors, including specialist to generalist, to help drive understanding and education on disease states and treatments.

Participation

The final new Four P, **participation**, equates to consumers defining and driving what the brand means to them, often in public forums. Thanks to technological innovations, consumers are actively participating in most aspects of marketing, including product use, promotion, and advertising. Now an individual can discuss product attributes with a global audience instantly and inexpensively. Whereas in many industries this has positive ramifications—such as new uses for a product—participation can create risk to pharmaceuticals in terms of product indications and adverse events. For pharmaceuticals, this channel should focus on simple and clear objectives:

- *Give stakeholders what they want to make their situations better:* **Educate.** For example, Sanofi-Aventis created an iPhone application, GoMeals, which includes tools such as a restaurant finder with nutritional information; a daily food intake meter for calories, carbs, and so forth; and a searchable database to plan and save meal choices. (See **Figure 11-6.**)
- *Monitor for new insights and opportunities:* **Listen.** Through monitoring websites such as PatientsLikeMe, manufacturers can access real patients'

FIGURE 11-6 Educate Example

Source: Courtesy of GoMeals.

opinions and experiences, and then use this information to guide their own efforts. (See **Figure 11-7**.)

- *Provide connection to what stakeholders believe in: **Advocate**.* Certain companies also sponsor activities or organizations such as Your-Life.com, a website designed to bring in the voices of real people, mostly young people, who are most affected by unintended pregnancy. (See **Figure 11-8**.)
- *Develop tools and assets that allow user control: **Empower**.* For example, the Diabetes Hands Foundation runs a social network called TuDiabetes. Within the social network's website is an application, TuAnalyze, that enables the members to share and compare their diabetes data.

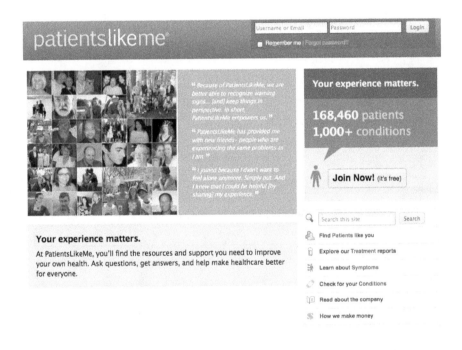

FIGURE 11-7 Listen Example

Source: Courtesy of PatientsLikeMe.

FIGURE 11-8 Advocate Example

Source: Courtesy of Your-Life.com.

Participation generally helps to define a brand. In the travel industry, for example, it is easy—share your photos taken at our resort or weigh in on your favorite day trip. In the pharmaceutical industry, however, patients don't typically want to "participate" with a disease. Patient participation is typically limited to networking and communication built around modern support groups. Through online forums, chats, and web communities, people are most interested in sharing and learning, such as on the PatientsLikeMe website. For these reasons, participation is by far the most difficult of the new Ps for pharmaceutical companies. As with peer-to-peer, the pharmaceutical manufacturer's goal with participation must be focused on the disease state, *not the brand.*

CASE IN POINT 11-5
Participation in Practice

A pharmaceutical marketer intelligently stepped into the participation waters by offering patients ways to participate in treatment "communities." The company supports disease-state awareness events, surrounding them with information and interaction opportunities. This is typically done through unbranded websites that allow visitors to consume and contribute content. For example, the sites might encourage conversation about the physical and psychosocial aspects of a disease through online treatment diaries or a FAQ. The company also launched a program that allows specialist nurses to share best practices and success stories online. It essentially extends the company's sales force into the office with blogging, roundtables, and discussion (Integrative Logic, 2011).

SUMMARY

Obviously, the traditional Four Ps are still relevant. Yet pharmaceutical marketers must understand the opportunities offered by the new Four Ps as well. They are not only effective, but also quick to deploy, cheap to implement, and they offer almost immediate results. It is an exciting time in pharmaceutical marketing. Information has indeed changed the game. But willingness to play by the new rules is what will push progressive pharmaceutical manufacturers to the next level of success.

DISCUSSION QUESTIONS

1. Compare and contrast the old Four Ps to the new Four Ps.
2. How might pharmaceutical manufacturers alter their tactics in the uncontrolled new Four Ps marketing area? Or is it best left uncontrolled?
3. What are the pros and cons of DTC advertising from the consumer's and manufacturer's perspectives?
4. For the pharmaceutical marketer (and manufacturer), how has the analytic power of the Internet benefited the industry and changed market research?

5. Given the development and expansion of various technologies addressed, what could be the next step for pharmaceutical manufacturers to reach consumers? What other tactics can pharmaceutical manufacturers glean from consumer goods marketers?

REFERENCES

DiMasi, J. A., Hansen, R. W., & Grabowski, H. G. (2003). The price of innovation: New estimates of drug development costs. *Journal of Health Economics, 22,* 151–185.

GlaxoSmithKline. (2011, July 5). GlaxoSmithKline implements next phase of new incentive compensation program for U.S. sales representatives [Press Release]. Retrieved from http://us.gsk.com/html/media-news/pressreleases/2011/2011 -pressrelease-516514.htm

Google/Hall & Partners. (2009, November). *Connecting with physicians online: Searching for answers.* Retrieved from http://www.thinkwithgoogle.com/insights/library/studies /connecting-with-physicians-online-searching-for-answers/

Integrative Logic, LLC 2011 Internal Data.

Krishnan, R., & Yuan, Y. (2011, April). *DTC investments in the pharmaceutical industry— current trends.* IMS Health. Retrieved from http://dtcnationalconference.com/delegates /DTCN2011/RameshKrishnanPresentation.pdf

Office of the Assistant Secretary for Planning and Evaluation, Office of Science and Data Policy, U.S. Department of Health and Human Services. (2010, December 1). *Expanding the use of generic drugs* [ASPE Issue Brief]. Retrieved from http://aspe.hhs .gov/sp/reports/2010/GenericDrugs/ib.pdf

Pharmaceutical Research and Manufacturers of America. (2008, July). *Code on interactions with healthcare professionals.* Retrieved from http://www.phrma.org/sites/default /files/108/phrma_marketing_code_2008.pdf

Pharmaceutical Research and Manufacturers of America. (2012, April). *Pharmaceutical industry profile 2012.* Washington, DC: Author. Retrieved from http://www.phrma .org/sites/default/files/159/phrma_industry_profile.pdf

Spirer, J. (2011, July 20). It's a new world for pharma reps. Sales Training Connection. Retrieved from http://salestrainingconnection.com/2011/07/20/its-a-new-world-for -pharma-reps/

CHAPTER 12

Prescribers, Healthcare Practitioners, and Marketing's Role in Practice

Matthew Perri, PhD, RPh, and Brent L. Rollins, PhD, RPh

LEARNING OBJECTIVES

1. Describe the concept of directed demand and characterize how this affects pharmaceutical product utilization.
2. Describe and assess the environment surrounding the prescribing process, including the influence of manufacturers, opinion leaders, and formulary decision makers.
3. Discuss how the patient–physician relationship has changed and evaluate the impact of changes in this relationship on prescribing.
4. Identify the various healthcare professionals who can influence prescribing and characterize how the pharmaceutical industry directly and indirectly communicates with them.
5. Identify and discuss the patient's role in the prescribing process, pricing perceptions, willingness to pay, and insurance.
6. Evaluate and assess how pharmaceutical marketing affects physicians, other prescribers, pharmacists, and other healthcare professionals.

The pharmaceutical industry has seen strong market growth for many decades. Total prescription utilization in the United States has grown to approximately 4 billion prescriptions annually, and, although prescription medications represent only about 10% of national healthcare spending, they are one of the fastest growing components of the healthcare system. The driving force behind this growth has been the industry's ability to attract the attention of and appeal to the prescribing physician, who has traditionally directed drug product demand. Directed demand refers to the unique aspect of pharmaceuticals: The physician or other prescriber chooses the product that will ultimately, barring a change by the pharmacist/third party, be consumed by the patient.

Over the last 50 years, pharmaceutical marketers have successfully used numerous techniques synergistically to reach prescribers. These promotional techniques and methods have included personal sales through pharmaceutical representatives, gifts, samples, meals, conference travel and trips to the "home office," company speakers, funding of continuing medical education and research projects, public relations, medical and professional journal advertising, and, in about 1980, advertising aimed directly at consumers, referred to as direct-to-consumer (DTC) advertising. Overall, it has been estimated the industry currently spends between $12 billion and $16 billion annually to reach prescribers (Blumenthal, 2004), compared to annual spending of $165 million in 1990 (Drug Topics, 1991).

Realizing that pharmaceutical promotion can have both positive and negative impacts on quality medication use, prescribers have been encouraged to be aware of the multivariate influences exerted on them by the industry. Some have taken this to the extreme point of view that physicians should avoid industry-sponsored information (Lichter, 2008). However, as a result of a combination of voluntary efforts on the part of the industry, research on the impact of marketing efforts on the cost and quality of prescribing, and regulatory scrutiny, some longstanding marketing activities are no longer employed (e.g., extravagant gifts, expensive meals, consulting fees, and honoraria for prescribers) by manufacturers (Pharmaceutical Research and Manufacturers of America [PhRMA], 2008).

With a changing promotional landscape, pharmaceutical marketers have become more focused on influencing prescribers and managed care decision makers with an emphasis on patient-level outcomes. Although there are clear benefits to the prescribing community from pharmaceutical marketing practices (such as increased information for prescribers through continuing medical education), there is some evidence that pharmaceutical marketing promotes increased prescribing, sometimes at higher cost and lower quality (Spurling et al., 2010).

Based in part on the success of the industry, it is clear that pharmaceutical marketing works: It influences the choice of a specific brand in the prescribing process. However, in addition to the evolution in the methods used to reach prescribers, the industry has also seen a change in how demand is directed for pharmaceuticals. Changes in how care is provided (the medical home model, utilization of primary care providers versus specialists, evidence-based medicine, etc.), increased influence of insurers, cost-effectiveness research, the use of supportive personnel such as nurse practitioners and physician assistants, and increasing responsibility of pharmacists and other providers have created changes in "who" directs the demand for prescription medications.

PRESCRIBERS

Given the role of the pharmaceutical marketer, namely, to generate demand for a company's products, understanding who prescribes is critical. The numbers and types of healthcare professionals who may prescribe have expanded during the last few decades (**Table 12-1**), with increases of nontraditional prescribers such as nurse practitioners, physician assistants, and, in some cases, pharmacists. Although the prescriptive role of the pharmacist is limited (e.g., under physician-approved proto-cols or limited prescribing authority for certain classes of medications), the influence of pharmacists, and to a lesser extent nurses, should not be overlooked. Pharmacists and nurses both can play a vital role in the choice of medication by prescribers. For this reason, pharmaceutical marketers have traditionally developed programs aimed at reaching these groups of health professionals in addition to just prescribers.

Table 12-1 Prescribers

Health Professional	Role in Prescribing	Marketing Issues
Physicians	With more than 750,000 U.S. physicians, frequently practicing in specialty roles, this group is the primary driver of the prescription drug market.	Reaching physicians is critical to success and requires a multifaceted approach. Busy practitioners might avoid personal sales contacts.
Dentists	According to the Kaiser Family Foundation, in 2012 there were approximately 190,000 practicing dentists in the United States. With some 750,000 physicians, it is clear dentists cannot be overlooked from a marketing perspective. The most common prescription categories for dentists are analgesics, antibiotics, anxiolytics, fluoride preparations, and topical steroids.	Because of the limited scope of products prescribed, not all pharmaceutical marketers target this group of prescribers.

(continues)

Table 12-1 Prescribers (*continued*)

Health Professional	Role in Prescribing	Marketing Issues
Podiatrists	A podiatrist is a doctor of podiatric medicine (DPM). Podiatrists diagnose and treat conditions affecting the foot, ankle, and related structures of the leg.	Although there are fewer podiatrists when compared to physicians or dentists, this segment can still be a significant driver for companies with products specific to foot care.
Pharmacists	The role of pharmacists as prescribers has been evolving for many years. Some states allow pharmacist prescribing under special circumstances, such as under the supervision of a physician or under specific clinical protocols.	Pharmaceutical marketers must be attuned to the role of the pharmacist in recommending therapy. Although the pharmacist might not write a prescription, his or her expertise is highly valued by other prescribers in drug product selection. This is especially true when therapeutic alternatives are being sought, such as when insurance requires the use of an alternate therapy or when a patient has had an adverse reaction to a medication. To this extent pharmacists serve as "opinion leaders" to physicians.
Chiropractors	This group does not prescribe medications, but many have a very loyal following.	Because chiropractic relies on physical manipulation, these health professionals might discourage the use of medications by patients.
Physician assistants	In 2010, there were more than 80,000 practicing physician assistants in the United States. PAs have the right to prescribe under the supervision of a physician.	PAs have been referred to as physician extenders and, as such, generally are busy and hard to reach through personal sales. For the majority of PAs working in primary care, the most common drugs prescribed include antibiotics, analgesics, cough and cold preparations, and drugs for hypertension or high cholesterol, diabetes, or other chronic conditions. Many PAs work in specialty areas such as dermatology or gastroenterology where their influence extends to other medications as well.

Health Professional	Role in Prescribing	Marketing Issues
Veterinarians	Veterinarians do not prescribe for human consumption.	Because some human drugs, frequently in the same packaging, are used in animals, some pharmaceutical manufacturers need to reach this segment.
Nurses and nurse practitioners	Although there are more nurses than any other group that influences prescribing, nursing assistants (NAs), licensed practical nurses (LPNs), and registered nurses (RNs) do not prescribe. However, nurse practitioners (NPs), a specialty group of nurses with advanced clinical training, have prescriptive authority when working under the supervision of a physician.	Although not all nurses prescribe, the impact of this group should not be overlooked. Nurses are the primary patient contact and are familiar with both patients and the medicines needed. So, similar to pharmacists, nurses provide important insights into patients and product choices. Additionally, in the physician's office setting, the manufacturer's representative might have access to and interaction with the nurse.

PRESCRIBING HABITS

Dating back to the 1970s, numerous empirical studies have described the impact of marketing mix decisions on physician prescribing behavior. Themes of this past work are that the physician prescribing process is multivariate (many inputs, both marketer controlled and nonmarketer controlled), pharmaceutical marketing is effective in shaping prescribing behavior, and physicians tend to be creatures of habit. Once a perception or opinion about a product is formed in the prescriber's mind, it tends to be stable. Although there is diversity among physicians in which drug is chosen for a patient, doctors tend to select their own favorite fairly consistently over time. In other words, they use what they know and what has provided positive results through trial.

The multiple information sources used by prescribers include the efforts of pharmaceutical marketers (e.g., detailing, product sampling, journal ads, continuing medical education, symposia, opinion leadership, peer influence), the physician's unique personal characteristics (including education and training), the general media (including public relations), product trial, and the individual patient characteristics (personal characteristics, expectations, health beliefs, etc.).

CASE IN POINT 12-1
Physician Use of Electronic Information

The majority of physicians (estimated at 80%) are now using many kinds of digital technology, both as consumers and in their medical practices. This includes the Internet, mobile technologies, and social media. Even though nonmedical use of this technology exceeds its use in medical practice, these resources can provide instant information on drugs and therapeutics as well as online, real-time access to patient information, including prescription formulary restrictions. Technologically advanced physicians are increasingly relying on digital and Internet-based media to communicate with patients and improve the quality of care provided. The use of electronic media must be considered in the marketing mix for reaching the modern physician (Dolan, 2011; Manhattan Research, 2011; PRWeb, 2011).

The assertion that pharmaceutical marketing efforts can shape prescribing behavior is at the heart of its criticisms, with further suggestions that it increases costs and can decrease the appropriateness of prescribing (Spurling et al., 2010). With respect to drug choice, what has emerged as the new thinking is that physicians' perceptions might be formulated early on in the product life cycle, and these perceptions can be resistant to change. The pharmaceutical marketer then needs to create a positive impression about a new drug product early on to be successful. The longer it takes to form this positive impression, the smaller the impact on the physician's ultimate loyalty to the drug. This implies that early detailing efforts are critical to a product's success and subsequent communication (sales calls, etc.) with a physician provides diminishing returns.

DIRECT FACTORS THAT AFFECT PRESCRIBING

The Physician–Patient Relationship

Unlike most other consumer goods, prescription drugs have a significant impact on public health. Although prescription medications can cure a disease or alleviate symptoms, these drugs can also result in negative consequences if they are taken incorrectly or inappropriately. Most lay consumers have difficulty understanding the information regarding prescription drugs because they do not possess the necessary technical knowledge. For this reason, physicians have traditionally made therapeutic decisions for their patients, often referred to as **paternalism**, and pharmaceutical companies primarily targeted physicians with their promotional efforts.

More recently, however, the rapid growth of managed care organizations and the patient self-care movement have displaced the traditional dominance of the physician in the decision-making process. With the rise in consumerism, patients have started taking active part in their healthcare decision-making process. Increasing numbers of patients are evaluating the health risks and benefits of the available treatment choices. Patients want their preferences to be heard and considered by their physicians while deciding the therapeutic regimen.

Therefore, it is very important for patients to possess correct and adequate knowledge about the disease and the available treatment options to become more involved in their healthcare decision-making process. In this new relationship, doctors and patients each have input into medication or other therapeutic choices. This new dynamic has affected prescribing by interjecting a new input into prescription choice: the preferences of the consumer (**Figure 12-1**).

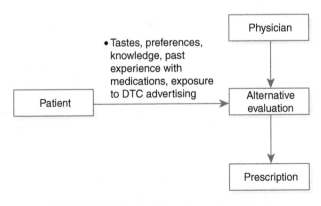

FIGURE 12-1 The New Prescribing Model

CASE IN POINT 12-2
The More Involved Patient: Drug Product Selection

Dr. Jones sees Mrs. Brown twice a year for her diabetes. Mrs. Brown is reasonably well controlled on her current medications but frequently forgets to take her diabetes medications. Recently, she has seen television commercials for a new medication that she believes will control her diabetes better than the medication she is currently taking. At her next office visit, she asks Dr. Jones about the new medication she has seen advertised. Dr. Jones has had some positive experience with the new medication. He tells Mrs. Brown that no change is indicated or necessary and advises against switching medications. However, Mrs. Brown is eager to try this new therapy. Mrs. Brown's attention to this new therapy makes him think that perhaps she will be more motivated to take her prescription if he prescribes the new drug, so he writes the new prescription.

Managed Care and Prescription Benefit Design

One of the biggest healthcare changes that affects which drugs are used has been the evolution of managed care and prescription drug insurance. Since the early 1990s, the expansion of managed care and a greater focus on controlling healthcare costs have led to a rapid expansion of formulary and preferred drug lists usage. A **prescription drug formulary** is a list of medications approved for coverage within a prescription health benefit. A **preferred drug list (PDL)** is a listing of drugs "preferred" by a health system or plan, and, generally, the use of drugs on this preferred list is encouraged and incentivized. Formulary decision makers work within a managed system of prescription insurance coverage to decide which drugs will be covered, while other decision makers focus on who will be covered, levels of cost sharing, and methods to be employed to control excess utilization (**Table 12-2**).

Table 12-2 Prescription Plan Design

Who will be covered?	Deciding who will be covered depends on the nature of the plan and program objectives, for example, for a Medicaid program covered individuals are those with significant medical needs, low ability to pay, single mothers, and dependent children. An employer-based plan would include combinations of employees, management, board of directors, and/or dependents. A Medicare plan would include coverage for those who are elderly or perhaps disabled.

What will be covered?	Choosing the drugs that the covered population needs while considering efficacy and cost. Will all medications be covered? Prescription only? Prescription and over-the-counter medications? Will there be a formulary or preferred drug list to drive utilization to preferred agents? Will there be additional prescribing rules, such as the mandatory use of generics first, clinical protocols, or prior authorization?
Will there be cost sharing?	Will the prescription plan utilize copayments, deductibles, coinsurance, or other methods to share the cost of prescription use with plan participants?
How will excess utilization be controlled?	Will there be limits on prescription use? How will this affect cost, quality, and patient outcomes? How will fraud and abuse be monitored?

The increased reliance on formularies to achieve cost-containment objectives while maintaining clinical efficacy and effectiveness has significantly affected prescribing by essentially removing some of the discretion prescribers have traditionally held. In the past, prescribers could select a medication for a patient based on knowledge of drugs acquired through education, training, and experience; various marketing efforts; and the unique needs of the patient. With a prescription drug formulary (or preferred drug list) in place, prescribers might not have the option to select certain medications for patients that are not deemed the safest and most cost-effective by formulary decision makers. The result of this has been to limit prescribing of certain agents while encouraging the use of others.

Formulary decision makers, usually following the recommendations of a panel of clinicians called the pharmacy and therapeutics committee (P&T) or the drug utilization review (DUR) committee, examine the competing alternatives. The expressed goal of this review is to determine clinical safety and efficacy, with an eye toward utilizing the most cost-effective agents. The decisions of clinicians evaluating competing therapeutic alternatives can generally be grouped into three distinct groups:

1. *Drugs the committee has determined must be available to patients.*
2. *Drugs the committee has determined must not be available to patients.* Typically, these agents have little or no benefit to patients, are considered too dangerous or unproven, or simply offer no incremental benefit to be included in the formulary.
3. *Drugs the committee has determined there is clinical evidence to use but also existing competition, thus making it the most difficult group to evaluate.*

For this group, formulary decision makers scrutinize clinical and economic data to determine which drugs best meet the prescription plan goals, namely, are the safest, most effective, and provide the most cost-effective therapeutic option.

However, physicians, in general, might not be as excited about the implementation of cost controls on prescription medications. First, prescribers do not see their role as being cost-containment enforcers. Physicians cite cumbersome and time-consuming prescribing rules such as prior-authorization requirements, mandatory use of generics, or clinical protocols and **step therapy** as factors that produce unequal access to medications and potentially less optimal health outcomes. This has led to frustration on the part of prescribers and a lack of willingness to act as their patients' advocate. Further, the increased time required by these reimbursement regulations is believed to be an ineffective use of the physician's time and contributes to lower outcomes and increased cost of care by adding unnecessary office visits and hospital care (Suggs et al., 2009).

Prior Authorization

Formularies and preferred drug lists also use a variety of other measures to drive utilization toward preferred agents. One of the most controversial of these tools is **prior authorization (PA)**. PA is a process where physicians are encouraged to prescribe "preferred medications" and discouraged from using "nonpreferred medications" by requiring advance approval from payers before a nonpreferred medication can be reimbursed. Savings are achieved by Medicare, Medicaid, and other private insurance plans when greater levels of compliance with the preferred drug list are achieved.

On the positive side, PA policies assist payers in controlling drug costs by promoting more appropriate medication use, matching patient need with appropriate indications, and achieving both the clinical and economic goals related to drug therapy. When the use of a specific medication is restricted through PA, payers can reduce costs by requiring healthcare providers to provide documentation of need with respect to the medication and, when appropriate, encourage the use of less expensive agents within a drug class. PA criteria can decrease medication-related problems when patients at high risk of adverse events (because of disease, medical conditions, and patient characteristics such as age or gender) are identified in advance.

When prior authorization policies are instituted, "grandfathering" may be allowed. **Grandfathering** allows a patient currently receiving a medication to continue receiving that medication without approval even after prior authorization is implemented. Grandfathering effectively diminishes the *initial* impact of the prior-authorization policy on the magnitude of market share shifts. On the other hand, a prior-authorization policy that attempts to drive market share toward preferred drugs without consideration of patients' current drug therapies will have a more immediate market share shift toward the preferred agent(s).

It is well understood in the industry that prior-authorization policies can shift market share to reflect a level of preferred drug list (PDL) compliance of 90% or more. Thus, regardless of the pharmaceutical marketers efforts with individual physicians, the choice of which drug will be used in a particular patient might be independent of the decision making of the prescriber. Adding to the marketing significance of decreased market share as a result of nonpreferred prior-authorization status is the potential for a spillover effect to other prescription writing. When prescribers participate in plans such as Medicaid or

CASE IN POINT 12-3
Prior Authorization in Practice

A patient who has been prescribed Zocor (simvastatin) to control his cholesterol begins to notice he is feeling tired and has some intermittent leg pain. His physician is concerned about these side effects and switches the patient to Lipitor (atorvostatin), a different statin. The patient takes his prescription to the pharmacy to be filled, but when it is submitted to the insurance plan, the claim is rejected with the notation that Lipitor requires prior authorization (PA). The patient is told that his physician must call the insurance company to have the PA approved. The patient calls his doctor's office but is told the doctor does not call insurance companies; however, the doctor's office gives the patient the information needed by the insurance company. The patient makes the call to the insurance company, and he is told he has the necessary information but that this information must come from his physician. Frustrated and angry that he cannot be granted access to a medication he needs, the patient is left without medication. The physician agrees to change this patient's prescription to a preferred formulary medication.

other large insurers, established prescribing patterns, created by strict formulary management, can be difficult to overcome. Therefore, prior-authorization policies can be a threat to manufacturers achieving market share goals.

Other utilization controls, such as varying levels of copayments, also can have an impact on prescribing but limit drug choices less than PA.

INDIRECT EFFORTS THAT AFFECT PRESCRIBERS

Pharmaceutical marketers have used numerous strategies and tactics (as mentioned earlier) over the years to communicate their messages to prescribers. These methods are aimed at creating a desired product image and generating trials with the ultimate goal of brand loyalty. When used appropriately (i.e., communicating product messages approved for dissemination by the Food and Drug Administration [FDA]), the techniques most commonly employed by pharmaceutical manufacturers are effective in generating trial. However, given the promotional nature of communicating product information in this industry, caution must be exercised by both the providers and recipients of information, with at least a recognition of the linkages between the promotional nature of marketing techniques and the sources of information.

Personal selling, directly reaching prescribers through the pharmaceutical sales representative, is one of the most effective because it utilizes *relationship building* as a means to communicate with, educate, and influence the prescriber. Further, sales personnel can provide samples, literature, and other promotional materials to prescribers during one visit. Yet, not all physicians are targeted by sales representatives. In fact, it is generally the highest-frequency prescribers or thought leaders in the field who receive the most attention from the sales force. Further, some physicians refuse to meet with drug reps because of either a perceived lack of objectivity or time constraints. Given some of the changes and constraints associated with directly communicating with prescribers, manufacturers use numerous indirect routes of advertising and promotion to influence prescriber medication choice.

Direct-to-Consumer Advertising

One of the newer strategies pharmaceutical manufacturers have employed over the years to generate trial and eventual product adoption by prescribers is direct-to-consumer (DTC) prescription drug advertising. DTC has emerged as one of the most effective routes of generating prescription demand for new agents, albeit indirectly through the voice of the consumer. Research has shown that in a majority of cases where patients request a specific medication they have seen advertised, the physician accommodates the patient request (Gonul, 2001; Koch-Laking, Park, & Tweed, 2010; Kravitz, 2005).

Educational Strategies: Continuing Medical Education

Since the early 1960s, there has been increased interest in the education of physicians and other prescribers regarding medications, largely by the pharmaceutical industry. The pharmaceutical industry has supported various educational efforts, including formal continuing medical education (CME) for physicians, which have included both promotional and nonpromotional activities. Promotional activities are supposed to be those conducted by or on behalf of a company, whereas nonpromotional activities include those supported by companies but independent of promotional influence. CME activities and events are attractive to physicians because they must earn a certain number of hours of CME each year to continue licensure.

CME is a nonpromotional activity, and standards have been established (such as the Accreditation Council for Continuing Medical Education [ACCME] Standards for Commercial Support of CME) to allow commercial support for CME. These standards were created to ensure that CME activities are independent, free of commercial bias, and not influenced by those with an economic interest in the

CASE IN POINT 12-4
Sampling

Dr. Smith is aware of the goal of the pharmaceutical marketer who bears samples: to increase prescribing of newer and typically more expensive drugs. However, although skeptical about the use of samples, Dr. Smith sees no harm in accepting samples of these new medications, which he distributes to patients without prescription insurance in an effort to help them obtain medications they might not have access to or be able to afford. However, Dr. Smith notices over time that he has begun to write prescriptions for these newer, more expensive medications for other patients as well. This spillover effect is a primary benefit of sampling new medications to physicians.

CME content. Pharmaceutical companies may employ CME to reach prescribers in exchange for the goodwill associated with the CME effort. Pharmaceutical marketers frequently utilize outside third-party vendors (e.g., Excerpta Medica or Parexel) to plan and deliver the CME programming. The use of outside vendors can be more efficient and provide a firewall between the company (sponsor) and the CME activity.

Manufacturers can assess the impact of a CME program by assessing **reach** or **hit rate**, or simply the numbers of participants attending particular programs. Other metrics have been employed to evaluate the success of CME, such as the proprietary IMS Promo.Track product (from IMS Health, Inc.). Promo.Track can assess prescription-writing practices before and after an intervention such as an educational program or scientific symposia. Through this tracking, sales or market share can be assessed before and after an educational event, allowing manufacturers to estimate the impact an event had on physicians' prescribing choices. The use of market share changes to evaluate the success of educational programming implies a marketing purpose, namely, that increases in sales are expected or desired. Care must be taken to ensure that proper procedures are followed and firewalls maintained so that scrutiny will show no commercial influence.

Opinion Leaders

Research into how prescribers choose their favorite drugs has revealed that a significant driving force behind a physician's perceptions of a drug is how the drug is perceived by his or her peers. This important marketing concept, opinion leadership, is a strong force in pharmaceutical marketing. Developing a cohort of opinion leaders, termed key opinion leaders, or KOLs, can be highly effective in creating favorable perceptions of a new drug. By engaging these KOLs, manufacturers tap into one of the routes of trial for new prescriptions, the experience of others, and the confidence this brings to the decision process.

Similar to the use of KOLs, some manufacturers have employed the use of industry advisory boards to learn more about the marketplace through the experience of practitioners. An advisory board brings together multiple opinion leaders where topics related to the product, disease, new indications, serious side effects, and so forth can be openly discussed. Through this process, a pharmaceutical manufacturer can glean significant market information, learn how its product is perceived in the medical community, and identify any competitive opportunities,

CASE IN POINT 12-5
ACCME Standards for Commercial Support of CME Activities

To limit the promotional nature of certain industry activities, the Accreditation Council for Continuing Medical Education (ACCME) developed standards to which pharmaceutical marketers must adhere to provide/sponsor CME activities. These include the following:

- *Independence:* CME providers must ensure that decisions made with respect to identification of the CME need, the educational objectives, and selection and presentation of the content and speakers as well as educational methods and evaluation are free of commercial interest.
- *Resolution of personal conflicts of interest:* All relevant financial relationships are disclosed.
- *Appropriate use of commercial support:* The CME provider must independently make the decisions about how commercial support is used for the educational activity. There should be written agreements documenting the terms of support and there should be policies in place governing honoraria and expenses for those providing CME. Further, social events or meals at CME cannot compete with the educational events. Finally, the CME provider must be able to provide written documentation for the receipt and expenditure of the commercial support.
- *Appropriate management of commercial promotion:* Commercial promotion must be kept separate from CME activities.
- *Content and format without commercial bias:* Content must be balanced and promote improvements or quality in health care and not a specific business or commercial interest.
- *Disclosures relevant to potential commercial bias:* Relevant financial relationships of those with control over the CME content and commercial support for the CME activity must be disclosed.

threats, strengths, or weaknesses. However, advisory boards are a two-way street: Key opinion leaders also hear from their colleagues in this type of meeting and this can work to support or negate existing product perceptions.

CASE IN POINT 12-6
Healthcare Reform and Physician Gifts

Dr. Smith, the principal physician at a large family medicine clinic, seldom has time to see sales representatives. Today, he has a small gap in his schedule and agrees to see a representative who has been waiting in the office. As they begin to talk, Dr. Smith comments that he really needs to slip out of the office at lunchtime to pick up a gift for his wife—a chef's knife she has been eyeing at a local restaurant supply. The representative completes the sales presentation and departs, returning shortly with the very knife the physician was to purchase at lunchtime. Dr. Smith reluctantly accepts the gift.

Previously, this situation would be commonplace among interactions with representatives and physicians. Currently, however, voluntary restrictions within the pharmaceutical industry (through the PhRMA code [PhRMA, 2008]) have severely limited these kinds of activities. Further, the recently upheld Affordable Care Act (ACA) has designated that any gifts to physicians in excess of $10 must be publicly reported beginning in September 2013 (O'Reilly, 2010). This provision of the ACA will provide an unprecedented level of transparency among physicians and the pharmaceutical industry.

Advocacy and Public Relations, Research, and Publication Support

External to the manufacturer, there are numerous non-marketer-controlled sources of product information. Pharmaceutical manufacturers support extensive research into the use of their products both before and after FDA approval. Prior to approval, these efforts focus on safety and efficacy and are conducted under strict protocols and controls, usually by the manufacturer. Post approval, research and publications can be done by outside researchers, such as those at academic institutions. Although funded by industry sources, this research can focus on topics such as postmarketing surveillance, investigation of new indications, alternative dosing schedules, routes of administration, and development of clinical protocols or cost-effectiveness. Whereas manufacturers can generally use this information to identify opportunities for product development, these scientific studies, if approved for dissemination through the FDA, are also powerful evidence that can be used by manufacturers to educate physicians about product use. Advocacy groups supporting particular diseases can affect the prescribing community just as media attention (good or bad) can catapult a drug to the top national news media headlines. Similarly, public relations must not be overlooked because of the impact that this source of information can have on prescribers. Generally, non-marketer-controlled sources of product information can be perceived as more objective, and, thus, these activities can significantly influence prescribing.

Managed Care and Reimbursement Specialists

Given the impact of prescription insurance plans limiting prescribing choices, manufacturers have developed specialists in the area of managed care or reimbursement in an attempt to influence managed care decision makers to ensure open access to their products. The goals for these professionals are to create a market environment where access to the manufacturer's medication is guaranteed, for example, by working to reduce formulary restrictions, including prior authorization. Although indirect, these industry professionals have the potential to influence prescribing even though they might not work directly with physicians.

OFF-LABEL PRESCRIBING

Recent headlines have highlighted the illegal practice of off-label marketing, or marketing medications for other than FDA-approved indications. Although this practice is certainly proscribed, the use of medications by physicians for off-label indications is not. Off-label medication use is common in outpatient care. The level of scientific support for off-label uses might or might not be well elucidated. However, most insurers pay for off-label uses as long as there is published evidence of the off-label use. For some drugs, for example, gabapentin, off-label uses constitute the largest part of utilization. For others, physicians seek benefits for patients for whom no other drugs have seemed to be effective. The sources of information for off-label use should be non-marketer dominated.

CASE IN POINT 12-7
Off-Label Marketing

Although off-label prescribing has been and continues to be an important tool for medication practitioners, off-label marketing by pharmaceutical manufacturers is prohibited by the FDA and proscribed by professional organizations. In a landmark case, the promotion of gabapentin was scrutinized. Gabapentin's promotion was carefully crafted around a multitude of promotional activities, including direct sales, advisory board meetings for key opinion leaders, consultants meetings, research and publications activities, and CME. The theme of much of the work focused on unapproved indications. Further, medical communication companies were hired to develop and publish articles about gabapentin for the medical literature—with plans to suppress unfavorable study results. Whereas many of the activities noted here (e.g., CME and publications) are traditionally independent of promotional intent, these communication channels were used to promote the use of gabapentin, resulting in a $430 million settlement and corporate integrity agreement. This was the tipping point for numerous cases, most of which have been settled prior to formal litigation.

For example, drug makers have settled numerous cases related to off-label marketing practices (Rockoff & Lublin, 2012; Staton & Palmer, 2012; U.S. Department of Justice, Office of Public Affairs, 2010), including the following:

- GlaxoSmithKline: $3 billion for Paxil (paroxetine), Wellbutrin (bupropion), and Avandia (rosiglitazone) (in addition to issues related to off-label claims, this case also involved the mitigation of safety risks and pricing and rebate issues)
- Pfizer: $1 billion for Bextra (valdecoxib), Geodon (ziprisadone), Zyvox (linezolid), and Lyrica (pregabalin)
- Johnson & Johnson: $1.6 billion to $2.2 billion primarily for Risperdal (risperidone)
- Abbott Laboratories: $1.6 billion for Depakote (valproic acid)
- Eli Lilly: $1.4 billion for Zyprexa (olanzapine)
- Merck: $950 million for Vioxx (rofecoxib)
- Purdue Pharma: $634.5 million for OxyContin (oxycodone)

SUMMARY

Regardless of the position taken surrounding the issue of reaching prescribers, it is clear that pharmaceutical manufacturers' promotional efforts aimed at generating prescriptions have been and continue to be effective. Although the landscape has changed over the last two decades, pharmaceutical marketers will continue to seek the most effective methods to appeal to, attract the attention of, and generate trial by prescribers. The roles of the consumer and health policy decision makers are expected to continue to expand related to their influence on the prescribing process. Successful pharmaceutical marketers will continue to seek the most effective means of reaching prescribers, whether through direct communication with prescribers or by reaching patients and health policy decision makers.

DISCUSSION QUESTIONS

1. Discuss the concept of directed demand. How are prescription products different from other consumer goods in this respect and how does this affect product marketing?

2. The doctor–patient relationship has evolved over time from one of physician-directed care to one of mutual participation and shared decision making by patients and prescribers. Has this change in the dynamics of the patient–physician relationship contributed to the success of prescription advertisements aimed at consumers? If so, how?

3. In your opinion, is a gift to a physician or sampling likely to be more effective in generating trial of a new pharmaceutical product?

4. What role does the pharmacist play in influencing prescribing choices? Directly? Indirectly?

5. How have prescription insurance and the role of formulary decision makers changed how pharmaceutical marketers communicate with those who direct the demand for prescription medications?

6. Discuss the positive and negative aspects of industry-sponsored continuing medical education programs. In your opinion, from a marketing perspective is industry-sponsored CME a good or bad idea? What about from an ethical perspective?

7. Contrast off-label prescribing and off-label marketing. How can pharmaceutical marketers proceed compliantly with each of these issues?

8. If DTC ads are as effective in generating requests for prescription medications as research results have indicated, why do pharmaceutical manufacturers still market their products directly to physicians? Would it be more cost-effective to simply market directly to patients?

9. Assume you are bringing a new antidepressant to market. There are currently many competing alternatives, both branded and generic. Formulary decision makers have not provided your product with a preferred status. The data on your product indicate that the product offers no unique advantages, except once–a–week dosing. How effective would creating a DTC ad campaign be if the weekly dosing schedule were the primary focus of the ads?

10. Electronic media are effective means of reaching customers, including physicians. What are the possible benefits and risks of using electronic communications such as text messaging and other social media to reach prescribers?

SUGGESTED READINGS

Chew, L. D., O'Young, T. S., Hazlet, T. K., Bradley, K. A., Maynard, C., & Lessler, D. S. (2000). A physician survey of the effect of drug sample availability on physicians' behavior. *Journal of General Internal Medicine, 15*, 478–483.

Cipher, D. J., & Hooker, R. S. (2006). Prescribing trends by nurse practitioners and physician assistants in the United States. *Journal of the American Academy of Nurse Practitioners, 18*, 291–296.

Greene, J. A. (2007). Pharmaceutical marketing research and the prescribing physician. *Annals of Internal Medicine, 146*, 742–748.

Joyce, G. F., Carrera, M. P., Goldman, D. P., & Sood, N. (2011). Physician prescribing behavior and its impact on patient-level outcomes. *American Journal of Managed Care, 17*(12), e462–e471.

Kyle, G. J., Nissen, L. M., & Tett, S. E. (2008). Pharmaceutical company influences on medication prescribing and their potential impact on quality use of medicines. *Journal of Clinical Pharmacy and Therapeutics, 33*, 553–559.

Radley, D., Finkelstein, S., & Stafford, R. (2006). Off-label prescribing among off-based physicians. *Archives of Internal Medicine, 166*, 1021–1026.

Relman, A. S. (2001). Separating continuing medical education from pharmaceutical marketing. *Journal of the American Medical Association, 285*(15), 2009–2012.

Schwartzbery, E., Rubinovich, S., Hassin, D., Haspel, J., Ben-Moshe, A., Oren, M., & Shani, S. (2006). Developing and implementing a model for changing physicians' prescribing habits—the role of clinical pharmacy in leading the change. *Journal of Clinical Pharmacy and Therapeutics, 31*, 179–185.

REFERENCES

Blumenthal, D. (2004). Doctors and drug companies. *New England Journal of Medicine, 351*(18), 1885–1890.

Dolan, P. L. (2011, September 26). Nearly all U.S. doctors are now on social media. Amednews. Retrieved from http://www.ama-assn.org/amednews/2011/09/26/bil 20926.htm

Drug Topics. (1991, January 7). Drug firms spend $165 million a year to influence prescribers. *Drug Topics,* 44–46.

Gonul, F., Carter, F., Petrova, E., & Srinivasan, K. (2001). Promotion of prescription drugs and its impact on physicians' choice behavior. *Journal of Marketing,* 65, 79–90.

Kaiser Family Foundation. (n.d.). United States: Professionally Active Dentists. Retrieved from http://www.statehealthfacts.org/profileind.jsp?ind=442&cat=8&rgn=1

Koch-Laking, A., Park, M. K., & Tweed, E. (2010). Does DTC advertising affect physician prescribing habits? *Journal of Family Practice, 50*(11), 649–650.

Kravitz R. L., Epstein R. M., Feldman M. D., Franz C. E., Azari R., Wilkes, M. S., et al. (2005). Influence of patients' requests for direct-to-consumer advertised antidepressants. *The Journal of the American Medical Association, 293*(16), 1995–2002.

Lichter, P. R. (2008). Continuing medical education, physicians and Pavlov. Can we change what happens when industry rings the bell? [Editorial]. *Archives of Ophthalmology, 126*(11), 1593–1597.

Manhattan Research. (2011, May 4). 75 percent of U.S. physicians own some form of Apple device according to new Manhattan Research study. Retrieved from http://manhattanresearch.com/News-and-Events/Press-releases/physician-iphone-ipad-adoption

O'Reilly, K. B. (2010, April 5). Health reform mandates disclosure of industry gifts. Amednews. Retrieved from http://www.ama-assn.org/amednews/2010/04/05/prsa0405.htm

Pharmaceutical Research and Manufacturers of America. (2008, July). *Code on interactions with healthcare professionals.* Retrieved from http://www.phrma.org/sites/default/files/108/phrma_marketing_code_2008.pdf

PRWeb. (2011, October 3). 80% of doctors use smartphones and medical apps in everyday medical practice. Retrieved from http://www.prweb.com/releases/2011/10/prweb8846867.htm

Rockoff, J. D., & Lublin, J. S. (2012, June 21). Johnson & Johnson close to settling off-label probes. SCHotline. Retrieved from http://schotline.us/johnson-johnson-close-to-settling/

Spurling, G., Mansfield, P. R., Montgomery, B. D., Lexchin, J., Doust, J., Othman, N., Vitry, A. I. (2010). Information from pharmaceutical companies and the quality, quantity and cost of physicians' prescribing: A systematic review. *PLOS Medicine, 7*(10), e1000352. doi:10.1371/journal.pmen.1000352

Staton, T., & Palmer, E. (2012, June 26). Pharma's top 11 marketing settlements. FiercePharma. Retrieved from http://www.fiercepharma.com/special-reports/top-10-pharma-settlements/top-10-pharma-settlements

Steinman, M. A., Bero, L. A., Chren, M. M., & Landefeld, C. S. (2006). Narrative review: The promotion of Gabapentin: An analysis of internal industry documents. *Annals of Internal Medicine, 145,* 284–293.

Suggs, S. L., Raina, P., Gafni, A., Grant, S., Skilton, K., Fan, A., & Szala-Meneok, K. (2009). Family physician attitudes about prescribing using a drug formulary. *BMC Family Practice, 10,* 69. doi:10.1186/147-2296-10-69

U.S. Department of Justice, Office of Public Affairs. (2010, September 1). Allergan agrees to plead guilty and pay $600 million to resolve allegations of off-label promotion of Botox [Press Release]. Retrieved from http://www.justice.gov/opa/pr/2010/September/10-civ-988.html

Glossary

2/10 net 30—A typical contracted pricing discount agreement with the pharmaceutical industry in which 2% of the price is discounted if the purchase order is paid within 10 days or the price is the net acquisition cost if paid within 30 days.

Abbreviated New Drug Application (ANDA)—Application generic pharmaceutical manufacturers submit to the Food and Drug Administration for drug approval that primarily focuses on proving the generic's bioequivalence to the brand-name/innovator medication.

Adequate provision—An alternate method for pharmaceutical manufacturers to provide the medication's risk information within a broadcast advertisement. The manufacturer must include the most important risk information, and then provide consumers instructions on how to access the full product prescribing information through a physician, a toll-free phone number, a current issue of a magazine in which the ad appears, or a website.

Adulterated—A corrupt, debased, or impure medication typically caused by the addition of a foreign or inferior substance or element during the manufacturing process.

Anti-Kickback Statute—A federal statute prohibiting companies from offering or receiving remuneration (anything of value) to induce someone to purchase, prescribe, order, or recommend any item or service that might be paid for by a federal healthcare program.

Average wholesale price (AWP)—Benchmark price created, controlled, and published by pharmaceutical manufacturers for third-party payers to use in reimbursement formulas. The typical formula based on AWP equals AWP minus a defined percentage plus a dispensing fee to the pharmacy.

AWP-minus pricing—Pricing system (also known as listless) in which the pharmaceutical wholesaler charges the pharmacy purchaser a price minus the average wholesale price of a product, with a built-in profit percentage included.

Bad ads—Advertisements that exclude details about a product's risk, promote unapproved uses, or overemphasize a product's effectiveness.

Bioequivalent—Two pharmaceutically equivalent products (same active ingredient, dosage form, and route of administration) whose bioavailability (rate and extent of availability) after administration is similar to such a degree that their effects, with respect to both efficacy and safety, can be expected to be essentially the same.

Black box warning—A warning designed to bring to the prescriber's attention any special problems that could lead to serious injury or death as a result of taking the drug. The black box warning must be approved by the Food and Drug Administration and is placed on any material that describes the use of the drug by healthcare providers.

Blockbuster—A medication that generates more than $1 billion in annual sales for its company.

Blog—Informal discussion website centered around any multitude of issues and topics. Typically run by an individual with allowable interaction and discussion.

Brief summary—Technical name for the detailed medication information, including, but not limited to, side effects, contraindications, and effectiveness, that appears in pharmaceutical medication advertisements.

Bundling—A promotional tactic used by sellers (pharmaceutical manufacturers) in which multiple goods (or services) are unified together and sold for a single price.

Buy-and-hold system—The early business model for the pharmaceutical wholesale industry, in which wholesalers purchased medications from pharmaceutical manufacturers in extreme bulk, and then sold the medications at a later date, counting on prices going up from the time of purchase and, thus, creating their profit margin.

Buying group—Multiple pharmacies banding together as a single unit to buy medications directly from pharmaceutical manufacturers in the hope of increasing their buying power (i.e., lowering prices) and, ultimately, improving their bottom-line profits.

Buying power—The number of goods/services that can be purchased with a unit of currency (i.e., money). For example, in the pharmaceutical industry, those with large buying power (e.g., large chain or wholesale customers) typically can negotiate lower pricing from the pharmaceutical manufacturer.

Chargeback—A reimbursement system between manufacturers and wholesalers. When the competitive contract price to the purchaser is lower than the price paid by the wholesaler (e.g., WAC-minus), manufacturers provide the wholesaler with a chargeback amount to make the wholesaler whole on the purchase.

Classes of trade—A customer's business category, such as hospitals or warehousing chain pharmacies.

Clinical hold—A stoppage on clinical trials initiated by the Food and Drug Administration. If trials under an investigational new drug (IND) application remain on clinical hold for longer than 1 year, the IND might then be placed under inactive status by the FDA.

Code of Federal Regulations—The codification of the general and permanent rules published in the *Federal Register* by the departments and agencies of the federal government.

Co-marketing—In a co-marketing agreement, the sales and marketing are performed separately and the objectives of the two companies might not be the same, which makes it different from the tactic of co-promotion, which involves joint sales and/or marketing of the same branded product, usually with the same objectives.

Compliance program—A program of a pharmaceutical manufacturer that works to ensure that the company is in compliance with all federal regulations and statutes.

Contract sales organization (CSO)—An organization that employs sales professionals who are skilled at calling on physicians and that just require training on the specific features and benefits of the hiring company's product.

Cookies—Small pieces of data from websites that make it easier to track a user's browsing history on the Internet.

Co-promotion—When small companies partner with larger, more established companies to jointly promote their products as long as no conflict of interest exists.

Corporate integrity agreement (CIA)—A contractual agreement between the settling company and the Office of the Inspector General incorporated into settlements with the Department of Justice. These agreements create extensive obligations for the company regarding its compliance policies, procedures, and performance in specified areas of concern, usually those areas in which illegal practices caused the violations noted in the case.

Couponing—A promotional tactic used to discount the original price or copayment for a prescription medication in exchange for using the product.

Demand—A want combined with the ability to pay for a given good or service.

Detailing—An educational activity by pharmaceutical manufacturer sales representatives aimed at providing details or scientific information on a product's potential uses, benefits, side/adverse effects.

Directed demand—In the pharmaceutical industry, when the prescriber, the learned intermediary and usually a physician, determines which medication(s) (i.e., directs product demand) the patient/consumer needs to treat symptoms/disease.

Disease awareness campaign—A promotional campaign used to raise awareness of a certain condition/disease state in addition to the range of treatment options.

Downstream customer—From the wholesaler's perspective, its downstream customer within the supply chain is the community/retail pharmacies. The wholesaler has the financial challenge of showing pharmacy customers how they can help them increase their own informational and financial efficiency in inventory management.

Evergreening—The process of making minor modifications to an existing product to apply for and obtain new patents as a form of product life extension.

Fair balance—An issue with prescription drug advertising in which the content and presentation of a medication's most important risks must be reasonably similar to the content and presentation of its benefits.

False Claims Act—A federal law prohibiting the submission of false or fraudulent claims to the federal government.

Federal Trade Commission (FTC)—The federal government's consumer protection agency that collects complaints about companies, business practices, identity theft, and episodes of violence in the media. In the pharmaceutical industry, the FTC is responsible for overseeing claims in over-the-counter (OTC) product advertising.

Fee-for-service (FFS) model—Payment model in which services are unbundled and paid for separately. For example, in reimbursement for physicians, the fee-for-service model reimburses the physician for every billable screening test, blood work, x-ray, and so forth provided.

Field-based medical (FBM) professional—A medical professional (PharmD, RN, etc.) working in the field for pharmaceutical manufacturers to deliver the appropriate scientific and medical product information to the medical community.

Ghost writing—The process of an original writer creating (or contributing substantially) a work that is then credited to another author.

Good manufacturing practices (GMPs)—A system for ensuring that products are consistently produced and controlled according to quality standards appropriate to their intended use and as required by the product specification.

Grandfathering—Within a prior-authorization program, this allows a patient currently receiving a medication to continue receiving that medication without approval even after prior authorization is implemented.

Group purchasing organization—Another name for a buying group, which is multiple pharmacies banding together as a single unit to buy medications directly from pharmaceutical manufacturers in the hope of increasing their buying power (i.e., lowering prices) and, ultimately, improving their bottom-line profits.

Hit rate—For a continuing medical education (CME) program, this simply refers to the numbers of participants attending particular programs.

Inelastic demand—When a change in price does not affect the quantity supplied or demanded in the marketplace. Many prescription medications exist under inelastic demand conditions, given that they can be necessary to cure a disease, alleviate a symptom, or even sustain life.

In vitro studies—Test tube-based studies frequently employed to determine a new drug's receptor-binding properties as well as to predict its pharmacologic and toxicologic actions.

Just-in-time (JIT) inventory—Demand-driven inventory system in which goods are delivered only when needed as opposed to prospectively or after the fact. Used to increase efficiency within a company's inventory management system.

Learned intermediary—A healthcare provider licensed to prescribe (e.g., physician).

Line fees—A monetary charge for each line item ordered by the pharmacy purchaser, encouraging more efficient purchasing by customers.

Mail-order pharmacy—Pharmacy benefits management–owned pharmacy that services members of the pharmacy benefit plan by relying on economies of scale created by dispensing as many prescriptions as possible to continually lower the cost of dispensing.

Market share—Percentage of a market accounted for by one item/service. For example, a certain medication in a class can have 50% market share, accounting for half of all sales within that medication class.

Market share–based bonuses/rebates—Discount incentives based on the market share created by the wholesaler/pharmacy working to lower a product's actual acquisition cost.

Marketing—The process of creating value for customers through exchange.

Marketing plan—Single document holding all the research, strategy, and forecasts for a company and its products/services. The document itself could focus specifically on one product or service or be the company's overall marketing strategy document.

Me-too product—A drug that is structurally similar to already known drugs, with only minor differences. This is popular in drug classes targeting chronic disease states as companies look to improve the safety/efficacy/side effect profile of an already successful medication.

Microblogging—Blogging in a condensed and focused manner, marked by the explosion of such social media websites as Twitter and Tumblr.

Misbranded—A medication branded or labeled misleadingly or falsely.

Needs—Those things necessary to our existence as human beings. For example, physiologic needs of food, water, and sleep in addition to safety, social, and personal needs.

New Drug Application (NDA)—The application seeking Food and Drug Administration approval for an innovative medication. The NDA presents a compilation of the data obtained from the IND as well as data from all the drug's clinical trials and a comprehensive analysis of the drug's chemistry, pharmacology, and toxicology.

Nonpersonal selling—A selling technique not involving direct person-to-person dialogue, which includes techniques such as educational digital asset development, e-learning, and direct marketing, including email and direct mail.

Nonwarehousing chain—A chain pharmacy that does not maintain its own warehouse for medication stock and delivery and, thus, depends on pharmaceutical wholesalers for inventory delivery and management.

Notice of violation (NOV)—An enforcement action used by the Food and Drug Administration against pharmaceutical manufacturers whose promotional tactics/pieces violate FDA regulations. NOVs usually contain "cease and desist" language and require the company to recall noncompliant pieces.

Office of Inspector General (OIG)—A division of the federal government's Department of Health and Human Services that protects DHHS integrity through fighting waste, fraud, and abuse in DHHS programs, including Medicare and Medicaid.

Office of Prescription Drug Promotion (OPDP)—Formerly known as the Division of Drug Marketing, Advertising, and Communications (DDMAC). This arm of the Food and Drug Administration is responsible for ensuring that prescription drug information is truthful, balanced, and accurately communicated.

Off-label prescribing—When marketed drugs are prescribed for other conditions outside of the product's Food and Drug Administration–approved indications.

Participation—Consumers defining and driving what a brand means to them, often in public forums. Thanks to technological innovations, consumers are actively participating in most aspects of marketing, including product use, promotion, and advertising. Now an individual can discuss product attributes with a global audience instantly and inexpensively.

Paternalism—An older model of the patient–physician relationship similar to a child–parent relationship in which physicians dictated the treatment without patient input.

Peer-to-peer—The most disruptive force to brands because consumers and professionals now have amplified license to frame brands and critical information. As a result of regulatory constraints and governance, pharmaceutical companies often must remain passive in this channel. From a positive perspective, peer-to-peer initiatives enable democratization of brands and products.

Personalization—Process allowing for optimization of marketing channels and investment through specific imagery and messaging to enhance relevance. With this technique, a pharmaceutical company can provide vital information to each patient based on demographic profile and phase of treatment, using the most appropriate language and visuals.

Pharmacovigilance—The discipline that looks for and assesses safety signals indicating there might be problems/adverse events with a medication's use, blending pharmacology, and epidemiology.

Pharmacy benefits manager (PBM)—Third-party administrator of prescription drug claims and benefits. Involved in this administration includes the processing of claims from pharmacies, contracting with pharmacies, overseeing a medication formulary, and negotiating with pharmaceutical manufacturers.

Pick, pack, and ship model—The core business model for the pharmaceutical wholesale industry focusing on inventory delivery and management.

Pivotal trial—The primary clinical trial (usually Phase III) designed to prove safety and efficacy as required for approval by the Food and Drug Administration.

Place—From a marketing perspective, this refers to any activity designed to create value and utility by making the product(s) available.

Product positioning—What the company wants the customer to think of its product or service, or what position the product occupies with respect to the competition. For example, in its very popular and successful "Mac vs. PC" advertising campaign, Apple famously positioned itself as the much more user-friendly computing solution compared to a personal computer running Microsoft Windows.

Predictive modeling—The process of data mining using statistical techniques, allowing data to be used for forecasting probabilities and trends. Predictive modeling enables marketers to utilize, or optimize, variables (predictors) that are likely to influence future behavior or results.

Preferred drug list (PDL)—A complete listing of medications that have been approved for use (and reimbursement) within a prescription drug plan.

Prescription drug formulary—A complete listing of medications that have been approved for use (and reimbursement) within a prescription drug plan.

Price—The amount of payment or compensation given by one party to another in exchange for a good or service.

Price elasticity—A measure of the responsiveness of the quantity of the product demanded by customers when there is a change in price; also known as price sensitivity.

Price erosion—A gradual (or swift) decline in price resulting from increasing competition within a marketplace.

Pricing (commercialization) committee—Committee within many (if not most) pharmaceutical manufacturers responsible for information gathering and strategy related to price. Typically composed of, for example, brand managers, market researchers, manufacturing, regulatory affairs, and pharmacoeconomics/outcomes researchers.

Prior authorization (PA)—Cost-containment and clinical efficacy strategy used by formulary decision makers to drive utilization of specific medications by requiring certain medications be approved for use before being covered under the plan.

Product—A tangible or intangible good or service provided or available for sale.

Promotion—The company's communication arm, transmitting to consumers the other Ps—product, price, and place—in a manner that achieves the best possible consumer attitudes and purchase interest in the company's product.

Prompt-pay discount—A discount (usually 2%) for prompt (usually within 10 days) payment of a purchase order.

Proof of concept—A stage in the clinical trial process in which the trial is designed to establish the safety of drug candidates in the target population and explore the relationship between the dose and desired activity, as either measured directly or by means of a surrogate.

Push and pull dynamic—A dynamic in which product information is pushed to physicians while patients pull those same physicians to treat their illnesses.

Qualitative research—Data that are categorical measurements expressed as a natural language description, such as gender or race.

Quantitative research—Data that are numerical measurements expressed in numbers, such as time.

***Qui tam* provision**—A *qui tam* action is a lawsuit under a statute that gives to the plaintiff bringing the action a part of the penalty recovered and the balance to the state. The plaintiff describes him- or herself as suing for the state as well as for him- or herself.

Rational drug discovery—The process of identifying a promising drug for marketing by developing an understanding of a particular disease state, hormone, or neurotransmitter and breaking the disease process into components where treatments are needed.

Reach—For a continuing medical education (CME) program, this simply refers to the numbers of participants attending particular programs.

Rebate—A specified amount returned that was a portion of the original payment for a good/service. Within the pharmaceutical industry, rebates consist of amounts negotiated by pharmacies and third-party payers in their contracts with manufacturers. Manufacturers typically pay a rebate based on volume or market share numbers.

Reference listed drug (RLD)—Another name for the medication listed on an original New Drug Application.

Reimbursement spread—The difference between the price paid for a medication (acquisition cost) and the amount reimbursed by the third-party payer for the product.

Remuneration—Compensation received in exchange for a service provided. This is prohibited based on the Anti-Kickback Statute to prevent inducing someone to purchase, prescribe, order, or recommend any item or service that might be paid for by a federal healthcare program.

Return on investment—A performance measure used to evaluate the efficiency of an investment (e.g., direct-to-consumer advertising) or to compare the efficiency of a number of different investments.

Right frequency—Refers to the number of times the message gets delivered to the physician.

Right message—Refers to the features and benefits of a product; right message implies that the information must be both factual and compelling to a prescriber.

Right reach—Used to describe the number and type of physicians targeted by the pharmaceutical company for a given brand. A company with a new treatment for diabetes, for example, might instruct a representative to achieve a reach of at least 80% of the endocrinologists in a particular sales territory each month.

Risk Evaluation and Mitigation Strategies (REMS)—Food and Drug Administration program for medications with a high-risk profile. Documents must be submitted to the FDA by the manufacturers and include elements to assure safe use (ETASU) and evidence that the drug's benefits outweigh its risks.

Rule of Seven—Often used in pharmaceutical and other types of marketing. As its name implies, this approach assumes that a customer does not fully understand a marketing message until he or she has heard it at least seven times.

Safe harbor—A provision in an agreement, law, or regulation that affords protection from liability or penalty under specified circumstances or if certain conditions are met.

Segmentation—Breaking down a mass market inclusive of all individuals into a variety of segments, or fragments, of the population who have similar characteristics. Typically, within a defined market segment, the customer group has a relatively homogenous profile of personal characteristics, common needs and wants, and, theoretically, should respond to specific marketing messages in a similar fashion.

Share of voice—The percentage of advertising each brand contributes to a particular category.

Shared decision making—Collaborative process for medical treatment decision making between the clinician and patient. Contrasted to the older style of the clinician solely making a treatment decision.

Social media—Internet-based platform for social interaction and sharing of information and resources.

Source program—A comprehensive listing of products where similar deals have been negotiated to increase wholesaler profits and to pass along part of the savings to purchasers (i.e., essentially functioning as a preferred drug list).

Stakeholder—A person, group, or organization that affects or can be affected by another's change/action/decision. Within the pharmaceutical industry, pricing decisions made by pharmaceutical manufacturers affect many stakeholders, including state Medicaid programs, Medicare, other government entities, regulators, legislators, patients, insurers, prescribers, and even advocacy organizations.

Step therapy—Cost-containment and clinical efficacy strategy used by formulary decision makers to require certain medications (often generics) be used before a patient can be approved to step up to the next tier, which typically includes branded and more expensive medications.

Targeting—Focusing marketing messages on specific segments of the population.

Upstream customer—From the wholesaler's perspective, its upstream customer in the supply chain is the pharmaceutical manufacturer. The wholesaler has the financial challenge of budgeting accordingly to take advantage of payment incentives offered by manufacturers and to be efficient in their recording for chargeback purposes.

Value—The subjective relationship between the perceived benefits and perceived costs of a product or service. Mathematically, it can be expressed in the following manner: Value = Perceived benefit(s) ÷ Perceived cost(s).

Value-added service—A complementary service option offered outside of a company's or industry's core function. For example, pharmaceutical wholesalers offer technology packages and inventory management systems as value-added services beyond their core function as a distributor of medications.

Viral spread—The spread of a message/video/post to a much wider audience through sharing and other social mechanics on the Internet.

Volume discount—A discount incentive based on the volume of product sold by the wholesaler/pharmacy that works to lower a product's actual acquisition cost.

WAC-plus pricing—Pricing system (also known as cost-plus) in which the pharmaceutical wholesaler passes on the wholesale acquisition cost to the pharmacy purchaser and charges an additional percentage markup, providing the desired profit to the wholesaler.

Wants—How individuals express their basic needs, shaped by their personalities and environments. For example, a person might *need* an automobile to get to and from work but *wants* the latest luxury sedan.

Warehousing chain—A chain pharmacy business that maintains its own warehouse for inventory delivery and management.

Warning letter (WL)—The next level of notice of violation (NOV) severity, usually sent after a company has received one or more NOV letters but has still continued the noncompliant behavior.

Web 1.0—The initial term associated with the rollout of the Internet/World Wide Web. The content was primarily focused on viewing and not reflection or discussion.

Web 2.0—The term associated with expansion of the Internet, through elements such as blogs and wikis, and the creation of a social experience centered around reflection and discussion.

Wholesale acquisition cost (WAC)—Benchmark price created, controlled, and published by pharmaceutical manufacturers for third-party payers to use in reimbursement formulas. The typical formula based on WAC equals WAC plus a defined percentage plus a dispensing fee to the pharmacy.

Wiki—A website that allows users to add, modify, or delete the website's content.

Index

CPSIA information can be obtained
at www.ICGtesting.com
Printed in the USA
BVHW070501080120
568902BV00007B/60/P